The Essence of Perfection: The Integral Existence of Jesus from the Star of Bethlehem to the Resurrection

Robert William Weber

Ste. Geneviève Press
Freeport, Illinois

First Publishing September 2017
Published by Ste. Geneviève Press
Freeport, Illinois
www.stgenepress.com

Weber, Robert William, 1966
The Essence of Perfection: The Integral Existence of Jesus from the Star of Bethlehem to the Resurrection

Includes bibliographical references and index
Copyright © 2017 Robert William Weber
All rights reserved.
ISBN-10: 0692984186
ISBN-13: 978-0692984185
Library of Congress Control Number: 2017914560
BISAC: Religion / Christian Theology / History

No part of this book may be reproduced or utilized in any form or by any means, electronic or mechanical, or by any information storage and retrieval system, without written permission from the publisher.

Scriptures taken from the Holy Bible, New International Version®, NIV®. Copyright © 1973, 1978, 1984, 2011 by Biblica, Inc.™ Used by permission of Zondervan. All rights reserved worldwide. www.zondervan.com The "NIV" and "New International Version" are trademarks registered in the United States Patent and Trademark Office by Biblica, Inc.™

Cover Design by Gisela Reguera López
Cover Photograph by Pixabay
Icons by Pixabay

From 2009 to 2016, I taught high school social studies on the Navajo Reservation in Ganado, Arizona. During that time, I learned the importance of observing God through nature while writing much of this book. This book is dedicated to my students during that important time of their lives, an equally important time in my own.

CONTENTS

Introduction   1

Part I: The Perception of Integral

    Chapter 1: The Integral Existence   12

    Chapter 2: Talmudic Rabbis and Church Fathers   53

    Chapter 3: The Jewish Calendar and Passover   103

Part II: The Passover Birth

    Chapter 4: The Nativity   125

    Chapter 5: The Magi   149

    Chapter 6: The Star of Bethlehem   175

Part III: The Passover Death

    Chapter 7: The Crucifixion   220

    Chapter 8: The Resurrection   253

    Chapter 9: Perfection in Nature   268

Epilogue   280
Appendix   283
Bibliography   292

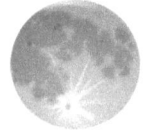

INTRODUCTION

*I*f you are reading this book, then you are curious as why such simple information as the date of the birth and death of Jesus have been lost over time. Perhaps you have also wondered why Christmas is on the same date every year, but Easter is not. I am grateful you chose to open this book, and I will do my best to inform you about a difficult topic using evidence that is so well hidden it required years of research to find. In addition to that, the topic was taken in different directions by leaders during antiquity, who at the time, were doing what they thought was best needed for Christianity.

Much of what follows draws upon existing scholarship on theology and science. I have connected these strands in hopes of creating a coherent work that is simple to comprehend. Every year around the spring equinox Christians around the world celebrate the Resurrection of Jesus by attending Easter

The Essence of Perfection

Mass, and about nine months later many of the same Christians celebrate the Nativity of Jesus during Christmas Mass. During these celebrations, some begin to question why we do not have better chronological information on both of these important holy days. This is nothing new, in fact, some of the most famous Church Fathers pondered this very question only a few years after both of these momentous events took place.

Before the Scientific Revolution, theologians were able to hypothesize about this through simple observations combined with intense knowledge of the scriptures or their own faith. This often led to much speculation. It was difficult to question or disprove the methods these theologians used because they were considered representatives of God, and so what they said was God's Law. Today, theologians face different challenges. They have far more knowledge and resources available but often find it difficult to persuade those in a post-Darwinian world in which math and science are considered much more significant factors in explaining our Universe. Johannes Kepler (1571-1630) wrote in the *Epitome,*

> I consider it a right, yes a duty, to search in cautious manner for the numbers, sizes and weights, the norms for everything He has created. For He Himself has let man take part in the knowledge of these things and thus not in a small measure has set up His image in man... For these secrets are not of the kind whose research should be forbidden; rather they are set before our eyes like a mirror so that by examining them we observe to some extent the goodness and wisdom of the Creator.[1]

---

1 Max Casper, *Kepler*, trans. C. Doris, Hellman (London; Abelard-Schuman, 1959), 381.

Introduction

Kepler believed God had a hand in everything. That was nearly 400 years ago, before the scientific revolution. Today we often forget that God is perfect. Yet, we must remember the words of, physicist Sir Nevill F. Mott (1905-1996) who stated well after the scientific revolution,

> Science can have a purifying effect on religion, freeing it from beliefs of a pre-scientific age and helping us to a truer conception of God. At the same time, I am far from believing that science will ever give us the answers to all our questions.[2]

Some wonder if it is even important to worry about such matters. My own view is that knowing with certainty the time of the birth and death of Jesus could be of great significance, and might just change how Christians think about Jesus' life and his connections to Judaism. If Christians truly want to live like Jesus, then perhaps they should worship as he did, not how later leaders believed they should based on the politics of the time. One way to better comprehend Jesus would be to understand, through the sacred scriptures, more about how unique his life was.

This is nothing new. Some early Church Fathers, in fact, devised a simple theory about the lifespan of Jesus: that he lived an integral existence, and therefore the Nativity and Passion occurred on the same date. This book revolves around that concept and submits evidence based on historical fact as well as modern dating methods. Although not the easiest task, it was accomplished through years of research and thought. There were several ways this project could have been done,

---

[2] Sir Nevill Mott, *Cosmos, Bios, Theos: Scientists Reflect on Science, God, and the Origins of the Universe, Life, and Homo Sapiens*, ed. Henry Margenau and Roy Abraham. Varghese (La Salle, IL: Open Court, 1992), 65.

and it is open to debate whether or not it could have been better thought out. To omit fine detail and counter-argument in the account of this theory would enhance the idea of an integral existence of Christ. On the other hand, it would also give an unduly favorable view of early Church theology and this thesis. The critics are sure to follow this scholarly work. Therefore, it is best to respond to their questions before they are officially submitted.

Taking a philosophical approach to the interpretation of a religious question can unlock the past and yield valuable new insights about the importance and meaning of time. A new perspective on history can be gained by approaching a chronological topic, such as the lifespan of Jesus, as a theological question, gathering as much evidence as possible, performing all of the proper research, and evaluating the findings using rational argument. By studying the ancient belief that Jesus was born and died on the same date of the calendar, that he lived an integral existence, historic and religious insights can be revealed.

The following is an attempt to arrive at deeper insight into the early Christians' attempts to resolve this question using a similar approach to interpreting history, though they were unable to advance very far due to a lack of resources and technology. In most cases, they put Christ first and then used the historical facts to prove his heavenly perfection. I will take an overly cautious approach. The majority of the work is my own, but it would also have been impossible without the painstaking work and ideas of those who came before me. I have simply connected the information that was at hand. Many of the people who pondered similar ideas were considered saints or geniuses, while some were intrigued Internet users who, like me, stumbled upon interesting facts. It is in their honor and spirit that the following was written.

Introduction

This theory is based on scripture from the Bible and Talmud and interpretations by early Christian and Jewish scholars of those texts. Those scholars were interested in finding deeper insight through what they believed was a gateway to God and Jesus. I have added to this pursuit whatever modern scientific data are available in order to confirm, deny, and decipher their work.

There will most likely be some criticism about this book over the importance of the Talmud to the integral existence theory. Some of the verses in the Talmud are offensive to Christians because of the harsh treatment of Jesus. It must be remembered that the 2nd century was a time of great turmoil for both Christians and Jews. I focus only on the verses given by God, not the 2nd century commentary of the Rabbis. Jesus said in Matt. 23:2-4, "The teachers of the law and the Pharisees sit in Moses' seat. So you must be careful to do everything they tell you. But do not do what they do, for they do not practice what they preach."

OVERVIEW

I believe this book could not have been written a hundred years ago. Much of the required ecclesiastical history existed then, but new discoveries using computer calendar programs and astronomy were still years away. Nevertheless, it is important to acknowledge a few of the many ancient sources that I drew upon. Some of these were the work of great philosophers and astronomers. Some were likeminded and others complete opposites, ideologically.

It did not take long for Christians to lose track of the chronological timeline of the life of Jesus. By the third generation, there were many assumptions about important dates like the Nativity and Crucifixion, but no valid evidence. Clement of Alexandria's *Stromata* and St. Augustine's *De Trinitate* (*On the Trinity*) become very vital and important links to Christian historiography. Although written around two hundred years apart, their conflicting dates for the Nativity demonstrate the absence of available evidence and the freedom the Church Fathers enjoyed in interpreting the scriptures. Clement's foremost student, Origen, became an effective source for this period, thanks to his honesty and frustration over the tampering with Christian writings.

Modern sources were also significant in the writing of this book, during which I required scholarly help from people with diverse backgrounds who were or are experts in their fields, having spent much of their lifetimes conducting research and thought. Some of the individuals listed in the Bibliography include experts in architecture, archeology, astrology, astronomy, chronology, computer programming, ancient history, horology, human biology, linguistics, mathematics, mythology, numismatics, philosophy, science, sociology, and theology.

This book was extremely difficult to write, especially as it is my first. It was written and researched for over a decade and remained dormant for long stretches, as I was frustrated over conflicting dates and theories. At times, this book was on the verge of being consigned to the dustbin of theology. However, what follows is a product that, I believe, presents this material in the best way. Chapter 1, "The Integral Existence," defines the idea of an integral existence. Verses found in the Talmud first suggested the concept that the Jewish Prophets were born and died during the time of the Jewish Passover, during the Jewish month of Nissan. This would include Jesus, who was considered a prophet or rabbi. Even today, the Talmud is an important part of worship for many Jews. Many non-Jews are

Introduction

also interested in the Talmud's content and read it to gain inner knowledge and peace. This chapter will also briefly explain what the Talmud is, and some of the history behind its creation.

"Chapter 2, "Talmudic Rabbis and Church Fathers," discusses the rabbis who first wrote down the integral idea from ancient oral law and provided commentary on it. It will then turn its attention to the Church Fathers, who had a similar concept. In particular, two rabbis, Hillel the Elder and Rabbi Yehoshua Ben Hananiah, and two Church Fathers, Clement of Alexandria and St. Hippolytus, are at the forefront in providing evidence for the scholarly pursuit of the integral idea. It will also attempt to explain how it was that these two similar concepts never crossed paths throughout the history of the two great religions.

In order to find appropriate years for the integral age of Jesus, the Jewish calendar needs to be properly examined. This will be the focus of Chapter 3, "The Jewish Calendar and Passover," where Jewish months, days, and years are compared with the dates of Passover. Chapter 4, "The Nativity," narrates the story of the Nativity and the alternating versions of it given in the first four books of the New Testament. In order to achieve a better understanding of the Nativity, an examination of the wise men from the East is required. This will be the subject of Chapter 5, "The Magi." Here, I examine both the existing theories and a few new ones about who the Magi were and where they came from. Looking closely at the Magi is important because they were witnesses to the infant Jesus as well as to the only solid piece of evidence from the time, the Star of Bethlehem, which guided them. Chapter 6, "The Star of Bethlehem" attempts to use the integral concept to find an acceptable date for the first Passover and a valid date for the Nativity of Jesus. "The

The Essence of Perfection

Crucifixion" and "The Resurrection" will be studied in Chapters 7 and 8, respectively. Finally, Chapter 9, "Perfection in Nature," will explore the question of whether there is a deeper meaning to the integral idea. This was in some ways the most interesting for me to write. Church Fathers like Clement and Hippolytus, men of great faith, were not afraid to suggest new concepts based partly on scripture and partly on faith. While this book is based on theory and my thoughts on God and the calendar, the final chapter, which I wrote to honor Clement and Hippolytus and their methods of theology, moves furthest into the realm of speculation. Science and theology can balance one another in harmony.

The Epilogue attempts to connect and unify the ideas presented throughout the book. The final verdict stating when, in my view, the Nativity and Resurrection occurred can be found here. The evidence will be presented and neatly summed up. Most authors have a purpose for their work. This will also be articulated here. Although intended as scholarly pursuit, this book has the potential to be used to advance many different agendas. I only hope that they are noble.

Finally, there is so much about Jesus that we do not know, and we can only contemplate how much more about him and his life is yet to be discovered. We do not know what religious sacraments he would have approved or disapproved of. For example, some Christians practice baptism. They believe that total immersion in water is considered the official conversion into the faith and that this can be performed only when the new convert is an adult or old enough to understand the complete meaning of his or her conversion. On the other hand, other Christian denominations baptize newborns using representatives for the infant known as godparents. Which is the best or correct way to baptize is a matter for others to debate. I consider myself a historian first and try not to focus

Introduction

on which theology is best.

Much of this book was written while I was an undergraduate student at Illinois State University. During that time, one Easter, I was viewing a TV documentary on the Star of Bethlehem. A man named Michael Molnar revised an old idea about a particular occultation in the sky that occurred around April 17, 6 BCE. According to him, this became the final signal to the Magi to come to worship the future king. Since this was about the time of Easter, Molnar's theory would also indicate that Jesus was born and died on the same day of the calendar. Although not completely impossible, there is a 1-in-365 chance. I was intrigued and soon discovered that this was not a new idea but had roots as early as the second century. Thus, began a quest that lasted nearly 15 years, which hopefully finds some closure with this book.

My intentions are that what I have written will be easy to comprehend. I would be pleased if the next generation of scholars became interested in the topic and conducted further research into the integral idea. When Jesus left this Earth, the details of his existence became vaguer with each new generation of Christians. We know some of his teachings and beliefs but do not have much historical information about his life. Nevertheless, time is no longer a hindrance. In fact, it is an asset. In the coming years, archeology will make new discoveries, new writings once thought to be lost will be rediscovered, and scholars will be able to piece together new information. Hopefully, the future will be kind to my research. By writing this book I have put myself, as they say, out on a limb, and I may be proven very right or wrong at some point. I only hope that likeminded individuals will take up where I have left off. The challenge is now theirs. Go with God!

PART I

THE PERCEPTION OF INTEGRAL

Chapter 1

CHAPTER I
THE INTEGRAL EXISTENCE

>During the days of Jesus' life on earth, he offered up prayers and petitions with loud cries and tears to the one who could save him from death, and he was heard because of his reverent submission. Although he was a son, he learned obedience from what he suffered and, once made perfect, he became the source of eternal salvation for all who obey him and was designated by God to be high priest in the order of Melchizedek.
>
>—Hebrews 5: 7–10

The Integral Existence

The author of Hebrews mentions the phrase "once made perfect" when describing Jesus after the Passion. This only occurred after Jesus went through more than ample amounts of suffering. When one thinks of what he endured near the conclusion of his lifetime in order to provide the world salvation, the final result becomes much more comprehensible. Jesus died with the burden of all the world's sin but was made perfect afterward because of his sacrifice. However, the question arises, what is perfect in the eyes of God, and how are people to understand its full meaning?

It may be possible that being made perfect by God is much more complex than just being free of sin or being all knowing. It might include Christ's being perfect in the number of days lived. After all, God created days and years also. Genesis is an excellent example of God's use of days and time and the importance of keeping track of such matters. This concept is nothing new; it was pondered many centuries ago by some of the most renowned Christian, Jewish, and even pagan intellectuals.

Knowledge may sometimes lead people into dark and unexplored areas, but the experience is nevertheless invaluable. The author of John provides insight into the idea that the Bible leaves out much, and that other sources should be further analyzed and evaluated in a proper method. Why stop only at a basic edification of spiritual well-being? John 21:25 states, "Jesus did many other things as well. If every one of them were written down, I suppose that even the whole world would not have room for the books that would be written."

Judaism before the time of Christ believed in the idea of the "integral age" of the great Jewish Patriarchs—that those who lived a divine life were conceived or born and died on the same date. This belief was written in the Rosh HaShanah Tractate of the Babylon Talmud. It states that the truest

Chapter 1

Jewish patriarchs were born and died during Passover, in the Jewish month of Nissan (March/April):

> R. Yehoshua, says: In Nissan the world was created, and in the same month the patriarchs were born, and in Nissan they also died; Isaac was born on the Passover; on New Year's Day Sarah, Rachel, and Hannah were visited, Joseph was released from prison, and the bondage of our fathers in Egypt ceased. In Nissan our ancestors were redeemed from Egypt, and in the same month we shall again be redeemed.[3]

Jesus has many symbolic links to Isaac. Both are perhaps the best-known "sons" from the Bible. Isaac, the son of Abraham, was spared from human sacrifice. Today he is known as the Father of the Israelites, and Jesus, the Son of God, who was not spared, is known today as the savior to the world by Christians.

The Gospels inform us that Jesus was crucified during Passover around 30 CE. It can be reasoned that Jesus, a Jewish prophet, was not only crucified and resurrected during a Passover celebration but was also born as well during a Passover celebration. Although often overlooked today, during their time the prophets were mainly held in high esteem. Henrietta Mears points to the important role they played:

> The prophets were fearless men. They denounced the sins of their day. They called people away from idols back to God. It is true that the prophets were concerned about the moral and political corruption

---

[3] Michael L. Rodkinson and Isaac M. Wise, *New Edition of the Babylonian Talmud* (Boston: Boston New Talmud Society, 1918), 917.

The Integral Existence

of the nation, but the fact that people were worshiping idols was their greatest concern... The prophets exposed the cold formalism of their religion. They constantly reminded the people that Jehovah was the only true God. They pointed men to the Law.[4]

Even though the prophets' messages were clear and precise, the Jews did not always respond to them in a timely manner—or at all. G. Campbell Morgan said that there were three elements in the prophets' messages: a message to their own age—directly from God, a message about future events (such as the failure of God's chosen people, the coming of the Messiah, and his rejection and final glory), and a living message to our own age—in the form of the eternal principles of right and wrong.[5]

The prophets were not always the most popular people. Often, they served to remind the Jews of the immoral path they were traversing and the future punishment in store for human beings if they did not change their ways. Yet, the prophets also received a lot of respect, because God had them function as his messengers. Jews believed their time on Earth was important and was measured out by God, and some Jewish rabbis debated this topic during the writing of the Talmud. This was sacred tradition for them because the Talmud was for generations handed down orally, and only later, as the Jews were exiled and dispersed, was it written down for future generations. When Christians began to look favorably upon the integral idea is not precisely known. This concept was transferred to Christianity through the early

---

4 Mears C. Henrietta, *What the Bible Is All About* (Ventura, California: Regal Books, 1999), 140.
5 Ibid.

Chapter 1

doctrines of Church leaders. located in what is today known as the Arab Republic of Egypt, which was then part of the Roman Empire.

We do know that the two religions never agreed on whether the integral idea applied to Jesus. The concept that the truest patriarchs lived a perfect life, to the point that their days were numbered and in alignment with the calendar, naturally fit with the life of Jesus. Some were particularly attracted to the idea of Jesus living an integral existence because his life was short. When that life began, however, was subject for debate. At first, a few chose a Passover date for the Nativity; later, others chose Passover for the Conception, making the Nativity on December 25. The one concept all ancient Christians believed was that Jesus was crucified during Passover. It must be remembered it was the Talmud that states that the Jewish patriarchs died during Passover.

THE TALMUD

The Talmud is second only to Torah as the most sacred and influential written work for Jews. Judaism considers studying Talmud full-time to be one of the most honorable occupations an individual can perform. Adin Steinsaltz describes the Talmud as follows:

> The Talmud has two main components: the Mishnah, a book of law written in Hebrew; and commentary on the Mishnah, known as the Talmud (or Gemarah), in the limited sense of the word, a summary of discussions and elucidations of the Mishnah written in Aramaic-Hebrew jargon . . . The Talmud is the repository of thousands of years of Jewish wisdom, and the oral law, which is as ancient

and significant as the written law (the Torah), finds expression therein.⁶

Author Morris Adler notes its complexity:

> The Talmud is *not* a code though it contains cases laws and legal decisions. It is *not* history though it abounds in historical information and is so indispensable a source-book for the period it covers that those who have written of that era without adequate knowledge of the Talmud have been invariably betrayed into error. It is *not* a biographical dictionary though sages and scholars are cited in it ... It is *not* an anthropological treatise, yet is a mine of folklore. It is *not* a theological tract though Rabbinic thought is a major element in the Jewish outlook. It does *not* present us with a philosophical system, yet perceptive students have found an organic unity underlying its rich diversity ... It is *not* a book neither of religion nor of history nor of ethic nor of philosophy, yet each of these disciplines and others are embraced by it. Indeed, the Talmud is not a book at all. It may more appropriately be described as a literature.⁷

Orthodox Jews believe that the Torah, the Five Books of Moses, was handed down from God to Moses. For Jews, the Torah is the written Law of God. The Torah is also referred to as the Pentateuch, from the Greek word, *penta-* plus *-teuch,* meaning five books. According to some sources, during the

---

6 Adin Steinsaltz, *The Essential Talmud* (New York: Basic Books, 1976), 4.
7 Adler Morris, *The World of the Talmud* (New York: Schocken Books, 1963), 16.

Chapter 1

third century BCE, a group of 72 Jewish scholars, six selected from each of the 12 tribes of Israel, translated the first part of the Hebrew Bible into Greek for the Hellenized Jews living in Egypt—a translation that was called the Septuagint. The Talmud, the other great book of Judaism, was also first spoken to Moses by God and, as I have noted, at first passed down orally.

During the second century CE the rabbis were forced into hiding during times of Roman persecution under Emperor Hadrian. The rabbis did manage to convene at Usha in 122 CE, and then reconvened at Yavneh in 158 CE. It was during these times of calm, just waiting for the next wave of Jewish persecutions by the Romans or to be forced into diaspora, that they decided to do the unprecedented and unthinkable, and to write down the oral law before its wisdom was lost.

What proceeded was the written record of rabbinic teachings that span a period of about six hundred years, beginning in the first century CE and continuing into the seventh. There are two versions of the Talmud, the Babylonian (Bavli) and Jerusalem (Yerushalmi), each from their own geographic region. The Jerusalem Talmud is shorter and has traditionally been considered the less authoritative of the two. As of late, the study of the Talmud is on the rise. *Newsweek* reports that today the Talmud is read worldwide and is currently receiving much attention in China as businessmen seek ancient secrets to gaining monetary wealth.[8] *The New Yorker* reports that in South Korea there is a school that specializes in teaching Talmud-style debates, as many South

---

8 Isaac Stone Fish, "In China, Pushing the Talmud as a Business Guide," *Newsweek*, December 30, 2010, http://www.newsweek.com/china-pushing-talmud-business-guide-69075#most-popular.

Koreans seek to learn the wisdom of a culture that has survived centuries of persecution and upheaval.[9]

THE BABYLONIAN JEWS

Grayzal Solomon notes that, "The Jews, unlike other ancient peoples, were never without a central government."[10] When the Romans tightened their rule over the Jews in Palestine, destroying the Temple in 70 CE in the process, a thriving Jewish community existed in Babylonia. As Israel was driven into war, powerlessness, and poverty by the Romans, many important scholars and citizens fled east into the traditional Jewish areas of Babylonia. The Jewish flight into Babylonia was preceded by a forced captivity. In 434 BCE, the Babylonians first marched on Israel as part of their campaign to stake claim to the former Assyrian empire. In that first foray, the Babylonians did not destroy the Temple, nor did they send the Jews into exile. However, they did succeed in taking into captivity 10,000 of the best and brightest Jews.

At first, this was devastating to Israel. Many were leaders and Torah scholars. However, upon arrival in Babylon they immediately established a Jewish infrastructure. By the time the Temple was destroyed a dozen years later, the exiled Jews had established new yeshivas, synagogues, kosher butchers, etc., all the essentials for maintaining a Jewish life. Many Jews came to regard Babylon as their home, and in fact, 70 years later, when the Babylonians fell to the Persians and the Jews were permitted to return to Judea, only a small number did so.

---

9 Ross Arbes, "How the Talmud Became a Best-Seller in South Korea," *The New Yorker*, June 23, 2015, http://www.newyorker.com/books/page-turner/how-the-talmud-became-a-best-seller-in-south-korea.
10 Grayzel, Solomon, *A History of the Jews: From the Babylonian Exile to the Present* (Philadelphia: The Jewish Publication Society of America, 1969), 221.

Chapter 1

Of what was probably a million Jews living in the Persian Empire, only 42,000 returned, meaning that the vast majority stayed in Babylonia, considering it their home, under Persian domination.

In Babylonia, some Jews became farmers, cattle herders, and winegrowers, or became involved in local commerce. Others did manual labor. Although not engaged in the most desired occupations, the Jews gainful employment allowed them to raise families and grow in large numbers, largely free from government interference. They were allowed to practice their religion and its customs in peace until 226 CE, when a civil war displaced the ruling house of the Parthians.

The new Persian kings were allied closely with the priests of the Zoroastrian religion. The priests, who at this time were extremely fanatical, began a systematic persecution of any religion different from theirs. The Jews followed. This was caused because of a number of practices that annoyed the priests, including the lighting of candles in celebration of the Sabbath and holidays, the ritual sacrifice of animals, and the burial of the dead.[11]

Another belief held by the Jews was the coming of a Messiah, later an important foundation of Christianity. The word Messiah is Hebrew for "an anointed one." The Jews in Babylonia considered themselves in captivity, waiting for the Messiah to come.[12] One of the reasons so many later denied Jesus is that, because they were living under the weight of foreign rule, they expected a warrior prophet to come who would restore the kingdom and Temple, not a teacher.

We know from the Gospels that the death of Jesus occurred during a Passover celebration. Early Christian leaders, as I've noted, went a step further, and believed that

---

11 Ibid, 221.
12 Ibid, 128.

the Conception also occurred during Passover. It is possible that the St. Hippolytus (170–ca. 235–ca CE) used similar methods when calculating the Nativity of Jesus. St. Augustine of Hippo (354–430 CE) informs us, one hundred years after Hippolytus's death, that December 25, which became the day of choice for celebrating the birth of Jesus, occurred nine months after the accepted date of the Crucifixion, which was believed to have occurred on March 25:

> Augustine states, For He is believed to have been conceived on the 25th of March, upon which day also He suffered; so the womb of the Virgin, in which He was conceived, where no one of mortals was begotten, corresponds to the new grave in which He was buried, wherein was never man laid, neither before nor since. But He was born, according to tradition, upon December the 25th.[13]

This makes the Conception of Christ the same date as what at that time was the accepted date of the Crucifixion. However, March 25 is not a possible date for the Passion; much of this will be discussed later. But while March 25 was not possible for the Crucifixion, it was very possible for the Nativity to have occurred on this same date in the Gregorian calendar, which will also be discussed later.

Perhaps Augustine had the sources to prove that March 25 was an important date but failed to realize that the Jewish and Julian calendars were different. It would be very difficult for a Nativity and Passover date on the Jewish calendar to match exactly with a Nativity and Passover date on the Julian

---

13 St. Augustine and Philip Schaff, *A Select Library of the Nicene and Post-Nicene Fathers of the Christian Church Vol. 3* (Grand Rapids, MI: Eerdmans, 1956), 74.

Chapter 1

calendar. The Jewish calendar is lunar based and the Julian is solar based (as I will also discuss later). It was one thing for Augustine to believe in the integral idea, but far more difficult to prove it. Even though the concept comes from the Talmud, and during Augustine's time the Talmud was not in favor with the Church, both Jewish and Christian scholars may have had a common influence that brought them together on this point.

The integral-age idea most likely had Greek influences. This was very evident in the writings of Clement of Alexandria (ca. 150–ca. 216 CE), a former saint in the Catholic Church. However, Clement does not acknowledge the Talmud in his dating of the Passion. One of the earliest references to the integral idea is found in Clement's account of the followers of Basilides, a Gnostic leader in Alexandria. Many early Church Fathers were concentrated in communities with Greek centers of learning and were well aware of the works of the much earlier Greek philosophers. Plato was a popular read among some of the best-known Church Fathers, who were aware of his teachings about the concepts of God and time. One of the greatest influences on Plato was Pythagoras, who must, therefore, be considered to be one of the greatest influences on Western philosophy.

THE PHILOSOPHY OF PYTHAGORAS

Philosophy is the study of the nature of knowledge, reality, and the meaning of existence. Philosophers depend on past history to explain the present; only the really great ones, however, have to ability to reshape how their world thinks. History and religion might define the meaning of existence, but philosophy explains the method of interpreting both. Pythagoras (ca. 572–ca. 497 BCE), best known for the Pythagorean theorem, was an Ionian Greek philosopher, mathe-

The Integral Existence

matician, and presumed founder of the Pythagorean movement. He may have been the earliest scientific and religious philosopher. Unfortunately, none of his own writings have survived, and they may have never existed at all, since many of his ideas were communicated verbally. Much of what we know of him comes from Plato and Aristotle. Mario Livio, in his book *Is God a Mathematician?* briefly, but neatly sums up who the Pythagoreans were:

> Pythagoras and the early Pythagoreans were neither mathematicians nor scientists in the strict sense of these terms. Rather, a metaphysical philosophy of the meaning of numbers lay at the heart of their doctrines. To the Pythagoreans, numbers were both living entities and universal principles, permeating everything from the heavens to human ethics. In other words, numbers had two distinct, complementary aspects. On one hand, they had a tangible physical existence; on the other, they were abstract prescriptions on which everything was founded.[14]

Therefore, to the Pythagoreans, numbers were the blueprint for everything, and the gods were the architects. We do not know for sure who taught Pythagoras, or if he gained knowledge during his travels, which included Egypt, Greece, and maybe India. We do not know for sure how much the Pythagoreans influenced him because they attributed most of the group's achievements to him. But the importance of numbers in all things, including God, was passed down to later generations of philosophers including Plato and Socrates. As a

---

14 Mario Livio, *Is God a Mathematician?* (New York: Simon & Schuster, 2009), 16–7.

Chapter 1

result, the role of numbers in religion became more important, and through Greece, they would influence the rest of the world.

THE PHILOSOPHY OF PLATO

Plato was a Classical Greek philosopher, mathematician, and writer of philosophical dialogs. He came from a prominent Athenian family, which allowed him the resources to study philosophy; his father Ariston, a politician, was descended from Codrus, the last king of Athens, while his mother was descended from Solon, a prominent Athenian lawmaker. His name at birth was Arisocles. Despite his family's pedigree, Arisocles embarked on a successful wrestling career, using the ring name Plato.

Plato's mentor, Socrates, and his best student, Aristotle, formed the big three of Greek philosophy, who were responsible for laying the foundation of Western philosophy and science. Plato was particularly interested in matters of religion. For him, the Creator was one who creatively took the substance or chaos of the universe and added form to it to create the material universe. A common theme in Greek mythology is the cruelty of the gods to humans, but Plato believed the gods were good, just, and not in competition with mortals. In times of despair, if prayed to in a proper manner, they could show compassion.

Ian Mueller writes in *Mathematics and the Divine* about the relationship between mathematics and theology in Plato's work. He believes that Plato had an intense admiration for mathematics, to the point that his notion of philosophical method was based in part on mathematical reasoning. He notes the following of Plato:

His frequent references to and discussions of mathematics in his dialogues played a major role in establishing the idea that mathematics is of central human importance, and his making five branches of study (*mathemata*), arithmetic, plane and solid geometry, astronomy, and harmonics, central to his notion of higher education in Book VII of the *Republic* is the source for the quadrivium, a fundamental component of later Western education.[15]

Plato's philosophy influenced most religions it came into contact with, including Judaism and Christianity. He believed that time was significant. It was the duty of humans to set about creating a refined world because that is what God intended. He wrote about the creation of the universe, believing that it was in some debatable manner the product of a supreme deity. In the *Timaeus 38d,* he wrote of the pattern behind the universe:

> Time then has come into being along with the universe, that being generated together, together they may be dissolved, should a dissolution of them ever come to pass; and it was made after the pattern of the eternal nature, that it might be as like to it as was possible. For the pattern is existent for all eternity; but the copy had been and is and shall be throughout all time continually. So, then this was the plan and the intent of God for the generation of time.[16]

---

15 Ian Mueller, "Mathematics and the Divine in Plato," in *Mathematics and the Divine* (January 1, 2005), 101, *ScienceDirect,* EBSCOhost.
16 Plato and Richard Dacre. Archer-Hind, *Platonos Timaios = The Timaeus of Plato* (London: Macmillan & Co., 1888), 123.

Chapter 1

In order to understand Plato, one must understand what he meant by forms and patterns. To him, forms, or ideas, are more real than everyday objects. Forms constitute a kind of pattern, which it is the philosopher's task to comprehend. Mueller writes: "In the *Timaeus* Plato describes the creation of our world or cosmos by a benevolent creator god ... who tries to make the world as good as possible by making it resemble the forms as much as possible."[17]

Clement often wrote about the *Timaeus* and used Plato in particular to point to the plagiarism of the Hebrew scriptures by Hellenic philosophers. Since Clement was Christian, he needed to establish a connection from Jesus to Adam, Moses, and the Book of Genesis and wished to prove that the Bible was older than Greek philosophy. This may have been one of the reasons he believed it necessary for a chronology of Christian history dating to the time of Adam; but once again, Clement was on dangerous ground. The city of Alexandria may have shown more acceptance to the Jews than elsewhere, but tensions were high between Christians and Jews in Judea.

JUDEO-CHRISTIAN CONFLICTS

One significant cause of this separation was the destruction of Herod's Temple in 70 CE by the Romans. The destruction was preceded by the rise within the city of Jerusalem of the Jewish Zealots,[18] a group composed of a new breed of elite priests fervently committed to the Temple and its cult and opposed to Rome. At one point, they barricaded themselves in the Temple while waging a campaign of blood

---

17 Mueller, "Mathematics and the Divine in Plato," 102.
18 The word fanatic originated around 16CE, because of Jewish Zealots, from the Latin word *fānāticus,* or belonging to a temple, hence, inspired by a god, frenzied, from *fānum* temple.

and fear against their enemies, those who supported Rome, throughout the city.

In 69 CE, both Rome and Jerusalem were mired in civil war. The Roman civil war became known as the "Year of the Four Emperors," which followed the suicide of emperor Nero in 68. The following year, Rome had four emperors— Galba, Otho, Vitellius, and Vespasian—who founded the Flavian dynasty. It was Vespasian's son Titus who sacked Jerusalem in 70. A year earlier, Rome's enemies took advantage of the social, military and political upheaval, and talk of revolt developed. The repercussions were soon felt outside of Rome, as revolts occurred on the border of Gaul and Germania and within Judea.

Meanwhile, in Judea, some of the factional leaders whom the Zealots had ousted from power fled Jerusalem and joined the army of Simon bar Gioras, who recaptured the city, except for the Temple where the Zealots were stationed. Upon the arrival of Titus, the opposing factions quickly united and coordinated their defenses against the Romans.

The Jewish-Christians were caught in a dilemma. According to Arnold Fruchtenbaum, "They remembered the following prophecy spoken by Jesus: But when ye see Jerusalem compassed with armies, then know that her desolation is at hand (Luke 21:20–4). It is at this time that the term *Meshumod* or *Meshumodim,* a Jewish term that connotes betrayal, began to be applied by the Jewish community to Jewish-Christians, and it is still used today.[19] The destruction of the Temple was devastating to the Jews, but to the Christians, it was in the natural order of God's plan: Jesus was to take the place of the Temple. Therefore, the Temple was no

---

19 Arnold Fruchtenbaum, *Hebrew Christianity: Its Theology, History, and Philosophy* (Washington, DC: Canon Press, 1974), 39.

longer necessary. As Christians moved away from it, the Jews rallied around the goal of rebuilding of it.

Over the next few centuries, some of the more unflattering suggestions made throughout the Talmud contributed to Christian negativity. According to James Parkes, the few references to the life of Christ mentioned included the following:

> Jesus was the illegitimate child of a soldier called Panthera. He performed His miracles by Magic, which He had learnt in Egypt. After His death, which was a legal condemnation in which He was given every chance to prove His innocence, His body was stolen by His disciples in order to invent the story of the Resurrection. He was a 'deceiver of Israel' and His teaching was evil.[20]

Before the destruction of the Temple, there still remained a small amount of civility between Christians and Jews, but that was short-lived. Their separation most likely occurred sometime after the Gospel of Matthew was written. Matthew provides evidence that Jesus desired his followers to observe the Law of Moses. In Matthew 5:17–18, Jesus said,

> "Do not think that I have come to abolish the Law or the Prophets; I have not come to abolish them but to fulfill them. I tell you the truth, until heaven and earth disappear, not the smallest letter, not the least stroke of a pen, will by any means disappear from the Law until everything is accomplished."

---

20 James Parkes, *The Conflict of the Church and the Synagogue* (Cleveland, Median Books, 1964), 109.

The Integral Existence

Most scholars place the writing of Matthew after 70 CE and as late as 110. Perhaps its selection in the New Testament occurred during a time of struggle between the two religions. Whatever the case, the Torah would remain a staple of Christianity, while the Talmud was to become a more contentious issue. It must be remembered that the Talmud was just starting to be translated from oral to written around the time of, or soon after, Matthew.

According to Parkes, it was the non-Jews who created the rift: "Had the Judeo-Christians been the only members of the new faith, the breach between them and the Jews might have been healed, for they also desired to observe the Law."[21] Therefore it was the Gentile Christians who were ignoring the Law.

This relationship became even more strained by the second century, when most of the Christian leaders were Gentiles. It was no wonder that Christians had no desire for Jesus to be connected to Judaism, as attacks against Jesus mounted in the Talmud and other Jewish writings, and Jews would not even consider Jesus a Jewish prophet. To them, his life and death were just another magician's trick, and as Messiah he failed to end Roman rule.

A DISTINCT RELIGION

Many Christians, especially the non-Jews, were attempting to distance themselves as much as possible from the Jewish religion and Greek philosophy as a predecessor in hopes of establishing an independent faith. The connection between Genesis, with its philosophy of creation and truth, and the traditional teachings of the school of Alexandria not only

---

21 Ibid, 77.

Chapter 1

paralleled each other but also bypassed the Hellenic philosophies on creation. By establishing this similarity, Clement wished to prove the insignificance of the pagan Greeks, even though he was fond of Greek philosophy and the ideal of teaching it in special schools.

Around 387 BCE, Plato had founded the first school in the Western world. Known as the Academy, it was a place where future scholars and politicians learned the teachings of Greek philosophy. Meant for the affluent of Athens, it was free of cost. The Academy remained in operation until 529 CE when Emperor Justinian, fearing competition to Christianity, seized control of it. This event has been declared the beginning of the Dark Ages by many historians.

While the end of Greek philosophy was the dawn of the age of dominance of the Church, it also hurt the advancement of science, as reasoning and critical thinking now became less important. It was not until another great philosophical movement, the Enlightenment, that there would be a return to science and reason, weakening the Church and changing the ancient political systems of Europe. However, before the closing off of Greek philosophy, Clement had the opportunity to be influenced by Plato. Through that influence, time and the chronological recording of time, took on significance in his writings.

Less than two centuries after the death of Jesus, Clement hinted about the dilemma of Christians not knowing what day Jesus died. Like Clement, scholars today seem to agree to disagree on a set date. However, when dating the two most important events in his life, modern scholars often overlook the fact that Jesus was more than just a normal person. It must be remembered that he was a Jewish prophet and Son of God. By taking into account the integral idea, and applying it to the life of Jesus, religious scholars can use ancient writings to develop theories that will lead to new and interesting discoveries about Jesus and life. Clement is an excellent link to Jewish rabbis and Greek philosophers. Therefore, his writings need further review.

BASILIDIAN CELEBRATIONS

Clement's account is quite rare among early Christian dating of the Nativity. He mentioned some of the many dates that Christians celebrated as the Passion of Christ. He leads readers to believe that as early as the second century some Christians who were followers of Basilides may have worshiped the Passion and Nativity on the same day of the year. Despite not directly stating the fact, it can be assumed when one reads his lists of days of worship for both events in Jesus' life that this is the case. Clement. stated:

> The followers of Basilides also celebrate the day of his baptism, spending the previous night in readings. They place it in the fifteenth year of Tiberius Caesar on the fifteenth (or according to others the eleventh) of the month of Tubi. Making a precise calculation, there are some who place his Passion in the sixteenth year of Tiberius Caesar on the twenty-fifth of Phamenoth; others say the twenty-fifth of Pharmuthi, and others still place the Savior's Passion on the nineteenth of Pharmuthi. Further, some of them place his nativity on the twenty-fourth or twenty-fifth of Pharmuthi.[22]

---

22 Clement. *The Stromata or Miscellanies VI*, (Whitefish, MT: Kessinger Pub., 2004), 67.

Chapter 1

Among the earliest of the Alexandrian Gnostics, Basilides flourished under the Emperors Adrian and Antoninus Pius around 120–140 CE. However, we know very little of his life or nationality, or any schools that he established. We do know that he was steeped in Hellenic culture and educated in Egyptian wisdom and Hebrew scriptures. He also had a son named Isidore, who became his successor. However, practically nothing of Basilides's writing remains, nor do we have any contemporary writings from his followers. But there is ample material from his opponents. From them we learn that Basilides invented prophets for himself named Barcabbas and Barcoph and claimed to have received verbal instructions from St. Matthias the Apostle and to be a disciple of Glaucias, who was a disciple of St. Peter.

Clement, who at times praised Basilides's virtuous lifestyle while criticizing his Gnostic teachings, also believed it essential to mention his followers' dating of important events in the lifespan of Jesus.[23] He mentions that the Basilidians observed the baptism of Jesus, thought to be on 15 of Tubi, with an intense overnight reading. He also mentioned that they were interested in the date of the Nativity, leading one to think that he was also interested in the topic. To him, it did not matter from or whom information was coming, only how he could make the best use of it. The lesson here is that it can be important to listen to those whom one disagrees with on

---

[23] Gnosticism, the idea of salvation by knowledge, comes from the Greek word gnosis, meaning knowledge. The Gnostic Christians thought of salvation as different from the conventional Christian belief that in the afterlife you will be rewarded for your deeds or behavior while on earth. The Gnostics believed that, through knowledge of the mysteries of the universe, one's soul could be saved. For Gnostics, knowledge earned them a place superior to those who remained in darkness. In this respect, their ideas were influenced by Greek philosophy, but they also appear to take beliefs from all other religions they came in contact with, from Egyptian to Babylonian.

The Integral Existence

spiritual matters, as they might still be correct on scientific or factual ones.

The precise origins of Gnosticism still remain hidden in obscurity, but it appears the Gnostics were active before Jesus. Soon after his lifetime, the Gnostics embraced his teachings and proclaimed him savior of the world, yet they still believed his knowledge was more important than his works. Before long, Orthodox Christianity was at odds with the Gnostics and their mysticism, idea of reincarnation, and questionable scriptures with problematic origins. Of course, most scriptures, including the Bible, have obscure teachings, but in the early days of Christianity, Church doctrine was still in its infancy, and the Church Fathers chose not to compete with upstarts at a fragile time in the history of Church.

By the time of the second century, the canon of the New Testament, although not yet recognized by the pope, was taking the form of what most Christians read today. Matthew, Mark, Luke, and John were, by the second century, considered valid sources, but books such as the Gospel of Thomas were suspect. In order to halt any further confusion or additional increase of Gnosticism, the Christian church banned many of their beliefs and omitted their books from the official canon. Gnosticism was practiced in the area mainly from Egypt to Persia until it was overcome, when Christianity became the official religion of the Roman Empire in the fourth century.

Most information about the Gnostics or their doctrines comes from early Christian church leaders who listed them in their writings, while leaving out much detail. But in 1945, the Nag Hammadi library was discovered near the Upper Egyptian town Nag Hammadi. The library consisted of codices comprised of 52 mostly Gnostic treatises, but it also included three works belonging to the *Corpus Hermeticum* (a syncretism of wisdom from the Greek god Hermes and the Egyptian deity

Chapter 1

Thoth), and a partial translation/alteration of Plato's *Republic*, proving the influence of Greek philosophy. It has been suggested that these codices may have belonged to a nearby Pachomian monastery and were buried after Bishop Athanasius condemned the uncritical use of non-canonical books in his Festal Letter of 367 CE. The modern translation of the codices provided insight to their beliefs and led to a resurge in Gnosticism, along with renewed controversy once again from established Christianity. Unfortunately, so far, there is no further information in the codices relating to the Basilidians' dating of important events in the lifetime of Christ, so the best and only source is the account by Clement.

Clement's absence of criticism could lead readers to think that he believed somewhat in their skills at reading and dating scriptures. This possibly could have something to do with the Basilidians' knowledge and use of Egyptian astrology or the fact that Alexandria was a great center of knowledge with ample opportunities for research and scholarly pursuits, including most likely accurate calendars and precise astrological charts. When compared to other Church Fathers, although critical of some of the Gnostic beliefs, Clement was occasionally tolerant of their existence. Perhaps he could relate to the fact that some of their ideas, like the concept of time, were heavily influenced by Greek philosophy.

Interestingly, in the Gregorian calendar the Egyptian month of Phamenoth is roughly between March and April and Pharmuthi is roughly between early April and May, which would allow both to fall sometime during Passover. Unfortunately, many modern scholars forget Clement when calculating the Nativity and Passion, overlooking the theological for proven historical connections, and disregarding the philosophical beliefs of the early Church leaders. Most scholars do not even attempt to answer or connect these two

The Integral Existence

important events. Perhaps it is time to give greater credit to those who lived closer to the time of Jesus, although they lacked today's advanced technology.

Shortly after both were lost in time, Church Fathers did debate the calendar dates for the Nativity and Passion. It is perplexing that a religion that was founded on historical events—the birth, death, Resurrection, and return of Jesus—would lose chronological track of such important dates. This became a blessing to many, as people began to acknowledge the teachings of Jesus more and focused on doing the same as him in their daily lives. Many Christians today can recite Holy Scripture from memory because of the emphases placed on the word of Jesus early in Church doctrine. Nevertheless, by 525 CE, Dionysius Exiguus's calendar, although recognized as flawed today, put the accepted date at 1 CE for the year of Jesus' birth; By this time December 25 had been established as the date of Christmas.[24]

Most Christians did not question these decisions at the time. Further complicating the matter was the fact that many early Christians were attracted to the divine rewards waiting in heaven because their earthly lives were less than desirable. Hence, they tended to be poor and uneducated, and thus unable to read or write. If they were literate, it is likely they could not afford Bibles, which were hand-copied long before the invention of the printing press. Also confusing was the fact that some Christians had three different calendar years to keep track of: the Egyptian (ancient and Alexandrian), Jewish, and Roman, and all of this was kept on extremely perishable materials.

---

24 The terms anno Domini (A.D.), Latin for year of our Lord, and before Christ (B.C) were used to label years in the Julian and Gregorian calendars. Today it is more politically correct to use the terms *Common Era* (CE) and *Before the Common Era* (BCE).

Chapter 1

It must also be remembered that besides living in a time when the average life expectancy was below 30, the hazards of being a Christian during times of great persecution had a tendency to lower even that life expectancy significantly. Therefore, it was far more important to understand Jesus' earthly teachings than it was to know what his life span was for anyone hoping to achieve the ultimate reward in heaven. By the time of the second century, the topic of the dates of the Nativity and the Passion of Jesus were debated by different groups.

We basically do not know much about Jesus. We do not have an accurate physical description of him, although many prefer the athletic fair-haired version made popular through the art of the Middle Ages. We do not have many historical sources that describe his life before his ministry. We do not know if he is pleased with the numerous and diverse forms of the Christian church that are in existence today. Because of the lack of information, early Church leaders struggled and improvised on many Church policies, including the idea of marriage for priests. Thus, they created rules and guidelines as the Church evolved. But this lack of official rules also gave them some amount of freedom when it came to Church dogma. As a result, Clement questioned matters such as time and its meaning. This influenced later leaders.

Therefore, when subsequent Church Fathers wrote about matters pertaining to the chronology of Jesus, which was rare, they also regarded not only his teaching and works as a reflection of the divine, and therefore perfect, but also the dates and duration of his time on Earth. This is something that today not discussed much. One of the early Fathers who wrote about this topic was St. Hippolytus. He left behind something that unlike most of the manuscripts of the time has survived.

The Integral Existence

THE STATUE OF ST. HIPPOLYTUS

Clement was not the only Church Father to suggest that Jesus may have been born during the celebration of Passover. Signs from the early 3rd century can be found in Italy in the form of a statue of Hippolytus [pg. 102] housed in the Lateran Museum in Rome. If evidence for an integral idea is required, then this is perhaps the best clue. The ancient statue of Hippolytus, which was likely commissioned shortly after his death, was rediscovered, although in a very highly damaged condition, in 1551. Christopher Wordsworth describes this.

> In the year 1551, some excavations were made at Rome... A marble Statue of a figure sitting in a Chair was brought to light... The right side of the Chair exhibits a Calendar, which designates the days of the months of March and April, with which the xivth of the moon coincides. This Calendar, indicating the Paschal Full-Moons, is constructed for seven cycles of xvi years each, dating from the first year of the Emperor Alexander Severus, which is proved from this Calendar to have been A.D. 222... The other side of the Chair presents a Table, indicating the Day on which Easter Festival falls each year for the same period.[25]

Alden Mosshammer adds, "There are some notes next to these weekday numerals, including one for the birth of Christ at year 2 and one for the Passion at year 32."[26] The Paschal

---

[25] Christopher Wordsworth, *St. Hippolytus and the Church of Rome* (London: Rivingtons, 1880), 29.
[26] Alden A. Mosshammer, *The Easter Computus and the Origins of the Christian Era* (New York: Oxford University Press, 2008), pp. 121–25.

[37]

Chapter 1

Table (Passover Table) has been attributed to Hippolytus. The notes, however, come from another source, and hint of Jesus being born during the Passover Moon of April 2, 2 BCE. All of these dates will be proven wrong in later chapters (Hippolytus may have believed Jesus lived 30 years based on Luke 3:23 that says Jesus began his ministry around 30 years old). Nevertheless, Hippolytus's idea of Jesus being born during Passover is in line with the integral idea, although, it is not without controversy. Johannes Quasten, in *Patrology Vol 2: The Ante-Nicene Literature After Irenaeus*, notes that a passage in Hippolytus's work *The Commentary on Daniel* provides alternative dates to Jesus' birth occurring on Passover, he states:

> In the fourth book (Ch. 23), there appears for the first time in patristic literature December 25 as the date of the birth of Christ and March 25 as that of his death. The author states that Christ was born on Wednesday, December 25, in the forty-second year of the Emperor Augustus. The passage would be very valuable for the history of the Feast of the Nativity but it seems to be an interpolation, though added very early.[27]

James Hastings seems to agree with this theory. In the *Encyclopedia of Religion and Ethics* he states the following:

> The most probable view seems to be that Hippolytus really fixed the birth of Christ on the day which 223 was the Passover, but there is reasonable room for doubt whether he intended this to be a fixed or a

---

[27] Johannes Quasten, *Patrology*, vol. 2 of *The Ante-Nicene Literature After Irenaeus* (Allen, Texas: Christian Classics, 1983), 172–3.

movable date. If the former, Apr. 2 was the date he intended; if the latter, Mar. 25. (d) Summary.—-This evidence suggests that the earliest chronology in the West [Clement seems to represent a different point of view] fixed on Mar. 25 or 28 as the date of Nativity, because of the theory that the history of the beginning is a prophecy of the end, and the Redeemer-God is in some way parallel with the Sun . . . It is also fairly plain that the transition from Mar. 25 to Dec. 25 naturally followed as soon as the conception, not the birth, of Jesus was regarded as the true beginning of the Incarnation; but there is no evidence as to the date when this change was made, and therefore this point, however probable, remains hypothetical.[28]

According to Hastings, sometime between the pontiffs of Hippolytus and Augustine, the March 25 birth of Jesus became the March 25 Conception. Moreover, Christians intended Jesus to represent not only the Son but the Sun. This was accomplished by setting important dates in the life of Jesus to a solar calendar, not a lunar one. This also further separated Christianity from Judaism, which is based on a lunar calendar. But If Jesus was a true prophet and Messiah, according to the integral age belief, either his Nativity (or Conception) and Passion occurred during Passover according to the Jewish lunar calendar. Thus, the date of choice for both the Nativity and Passion must have similar lunar qualities—for example, that both were on a Full-Moon, or the Nativity on a new Moon, with the Crucifixion on or around a Full-Moon. It

---

28 James Hastings, *Burial-Confessions,* vol. 3 of *Encyclopedia of Religion and Ethics* (Edinburgh: T. & T. Clark, 1910), 607.

Chapter 1

is known that the Crucifixion occurred near a Full-Moon because the Jewish holiday of Passover always falls near one.

Making the task of determining the life span of Jesus much more difficult is the fact that the historians who lived during the time of Jesus seldom mention a given time frame or important dates of his life; there is no mention anywhere of how old he was when he died. The most prominent historians from the time of Jesus tended to be Roman and thus were concerned mainly about matters pertaining to the Roman Empire or the emperor. Questions even abound about the accuracy of the writings of the most well-known Jewish historian of Jesus' era, Titus Flavius Josephus (37–ca. 100), including some of his passages on Jesus. Critics of Josephus have proclaimed him everything from a Roman propagandist to a Jewish apologist.

One of Josephus's earliest critics was the early Church Father Origen (ca. 185–254). It is speculated that Origen, who was a student of Clement, may have believed that some of the works of Josephus were tampered with in order to persuade readers that Josephus was a Christian. Origen does appear to have a bias toward thinking Josephus not Christian and that his work was tampered with.[29] While some writings remain questionable, it is still possible to examine the history behind some of the traditional Church holy days for clues into the integral existence theory.

THE ANNUNCIATION

The Catholic Church celebrates the Feast of the Annunciation of the Blessed Virgin Mary on March 25. If this celebration first occurred before the second century, it would

---

29 Origen, *Against Celsus*, i:47.

provide some evidence that Christians were honoring the Annunciation soon after the death of Jesus. There is some debate on when the Annunciation was first celebrated. It is not mentioned in any valid sources before the fifth century. According to the Catholic Encyclopedia, it may have been set sometime after December 25 officially became Christmas:

> The Feast of the Annunciation of the Blessed Virgin (25 March) ... probably originated shortly before or after the council of Ephesus (ca. 431). At the time of the Synod of Laodicea (372) it was not known; St. Proclus, Bishop of Constantinople (d. 446), however, seems to mention it in one of his homilies ... In the Latin Church this feast is first mentioned in the Sacramentarium of Pope Gelasius (d. 496).[30]

Christians viewed the first day of the new Sun as December 25. The new Sun follows the winter solstice, which ends the previous cycle of the Sun, before its rebirth—essentially, the sequence of life. The Sun is at its weakest, or least amount of daylight, during the winter solstice. It then grows stronger every day until the summer solstice, and then eventually weakens until the next winter solstice in perfect rhythm. This will be discussed more in Chapter 2.

Agreeing with this is Susan Roll. She states, "Yet another trait of patristic thought which lies at the foundation of the calculation hypothesis the conviction that God was constrained to act in history according to human concepts of perfection, including perfect symbolic number systems."[31]

---

30 Frederick Holweck, "The Feast of the Annunciation," in The Catholic Encyclopedia, vol. 1 (New York: Robert Appleton Company, 1907), www.newadvent.org/cathen/01542a.htm.
31 Susan K. Roll, *Toward the Origins of Christmas* (Kampen, The Netherlands:

Chapter 1

Several verses in the Bible help in this notion. Malachi 4:2 for example says, "But for you who revere my name, the sun of righteousness will rise with healing in its rays. And you will go out and frolic like well-fed calves." Some Fathers, St. Cyprian for one, were influenced by such verses. Many pagan religions had a sun god, and some of the Church Fathers, who were in charge of Church doctrine, were former pagans. According to Hugo Rahner in *Griechische Mythen in Christlicher Deutung*. By 200 CE the title 'Sun of Justice' belonged to the standard array of titles which preachers gave to Jesus.[32]

Thus, the foundation for Jesus being associated with the Sun and the winter solstice was in place before Constantine the Great (272–337) decreed December 25 as the official day celebrating the birth of Jesus. But the idea of Jesus being born around Passover was still popular. Not mentioned, but something else to consider is that in 337 most of northern Europe was still considered pagan. By the time their leaders converted to Christianity, Christmas was on December 25, and there was no reason in their minds to questions this, for these populations and their leaders had little contact with the Talmud or Greek philosophy. As time went on the integral idea was relegated to the ancient texts.

CONSTANTINE THE GREAT

In 303, the emperor Diocletian initiated the last great wave of Christian persecutions. In the first of four edicts, he demanded the destruction of the churches, along with the confiscation and burning of the sacred scriptures. But Christians refused to allow their sacred scriptures to be burned and were therefore put to death. Exactly which ones were

---

Kok Pharos, 1995), 83.
32 Ibid, 123.

The Integral Existence

burned is open to question. According to the *Encyclopedia of Early Christianity*, "Many Christians were persecuted and put to death because of their refusal to hand over their sacred books, one can assume that the churches had already identified which books were demanded. Although the churches were not in complete agreement on which books were sacred."[33] This became important later when Constantine commissioned his Bible. What Christians were allowed to read and not read would decide what direction Christianity would take. This included the future of the integral idea.

In 305, Constantine was sent by his father, Constantius, who had just become emperor of the western portion of the Roman Empire, to Britannia to campaign there. This was a time when the empire was divided and ruled by multiple emperors. When his father died a year later, he was crowned as emperor by the army at Eboracum (modern-day York, UK). Later, a series of civil wars against the other emperors, Maxentius and Licinius, started.

In October of 312, the civil war between Constantine and Maxentius began, and Constantine's army was ready to enter the city of Rome where Maxentius army was positioned. However, all the bridges into Rome over the Tiber River were cut. At the Battle of Milvian Bridge, the army encamped there was met with an unusual appearance, after which Constantine was to fight under the banner of Christ. According to Timothy Barnes, some believed that the night before the battle Constantine was commanded to place the sign of the Christ on the shield of his soldiers. Barnes states, "That belief is probably no more than an attempt to give Constantine's unexpected action a conventional religious explanation."[34]

---

33 Everett Ferguson, ed. *Encyclopedia of Early Christianity* (New York: Garland Publications, 1990), 171.
34 Timothy Barnes, *Constantine and Eusebius* (Cambridge: Harvard University

Chapter 1

Years later, Constantine, under oath, said that one afternoon on the march to Rome, both he and the whole army had seen a cross of light in the sky and the words "in this conquer." It was during the next night, in a dream, Christ appeared before him with the heavenly sign and instructed him to make standards for his army in this form. Afterward, Christians in his army explained to him that he had indeed seen Christ. Constantine then took the significant step of publicly replacing the pagan standards of his troops with the labarum, formed from the first two letters in Greek of the word *Christ*. The ensuing battle was brief; however, what occurred next was to become far more important. Constantine declared himself "God's servant," entrusted with a divine mission to convert the Roman Empire to Christianity.[35]

Constantine's declaration deeply affected the relationship between Jews and Christians. According to Barnes, "That marked a clear departure from the previous imperial policy of toleration toward the Jewish religion." The shift resulted in many restrictions toward Jews; they were allowed to set foot in Jerusalem only once a year, they could not own Christian slaves, they could not accept converts to Judaism, and if they forcibly attempted to prevent conversions from Judaism to Christianity they were burned alive.[36] Consequently, for the first time in history, a Christian state—the first one—openly persecuted Jews. Unfortunately, this was to continue throughout the Middle Ages and into the modern era.

Jews were not the only faith that Christians engaged with during the reign of Constantine. There were still many pagans practicing ancient Roman religions throughout the empire. Over time, this would change, as many converted to

---

Press, 1981), 43.
35 Ibid.
36 Ibid, 252.

The Integral Existence

Christianity. But, one pagan holiday remained steadfastly popular. It was Saturnalia, a holiday that honored Saturn, the god of agriculture. It commenced during the deepest darkest time of winter, beginning in the week leading up to the winter solstice, the longest night of the year. This was a hedonistic celebration in which the Roman social order was turned upside down for a month. During this time, slaves dressed as their masters and masters dressed as their slaves in a process known as mumming. According to Nathan Warren, the ancient Roman poets had written of a Golden Age, a time when all men were equal, when neither war, injustice, nor want were known to mankind, and that blessed time was during the rule of Saturn.

Schools and public offices were closed and all forms of business was suspended during a period of relaxation and merriment. A declaration of war during this interlude would be viewed with horror and no malefactor could be punished. There were sports and games and by law, every man was commanded to spend one-tenth of his income. The man who provided the most bountifully was declared the best citizen. Perhaps the most unbelievable aspect of Saturnalia was that slaves were free. They were allowed to wear the badge of freedom and speak ill of their masters. No slave was punished during this season of freedom.[37]

During the reign of Constantine, the Church Fathers tried to end this practice, but their efforts were in vain. The Romans would not give up their cherished games or pagan rituals. So instead they decided to create a Christian holiday that occurred around the same time. Warren states,

---

[37] Nathan Boughton Warren, *The Christmas Book: Christmas in the Olden Time, Its Customs and Their Origin: The Holly and Ivy, Sports of the Eve, Yule Log, Boar's Head, the Dinner, Mummers, Lord of Misrule, Saturnalia, Carols, Mysteries and Plays, Boxes, &c. &c* (London: James Pattie, 1859), 43–4.

Chapter 1

When the Roman and Scandinavian declared that he would keep the festival of "the new Birth of the Son," the Christian Fathers said we will show you a better reason for rejoicing—we tell of the Spiritual Son, not of the Material Sun. The people cared little which, so long as they preserved their sports, and with many sighs, at first, but at length with a desire to share their mirth, the Christian teachers gave their consent.[38]

In order to completely obliterate the practice of worshiping the birthday of the Sun, the Church Fathers needed to find a valid way to establish Jesus' supremacy over the pagan gods. After some creative math, and a similar version of the integral idea, it was decided that Jesus had not been born during Passover but instead was conceived at that time. The traditional date for the Nativity, as stated earlier, was March 25. This now became the date of the Immaculate Conception. Thus, nine months later on December 25, Jesus was born. According to Robert Grant, "By 336 Christians at Rome began observing December 25 as Christ's birthday. It is highly probable that this observance was due to the Constantinian concern for the relation between pagan and Christian celebrations."[39] This included concerns over the Christian Sunday. Constantine, who was a former Sun worshiper, wanted Sunday to replace the day some pagans worshiped. But this was not enough. Getting pagans to convert and worship on Sunday was easy when compared to asking them to give up their celebrations during the winter

---

38 Ibid, 46.
39 Robert Grant, *Augustus to Constantine: The Thrust of the Christian Movement into the Roman World* (New York: Harper & Row, 1970), 308.

The Integral Existence

solstice. What was required was a new holiday, one that replaced the old Sun gods while providing similar types of winter festivals.

Setting a date for Christmas was not the only concern Constantine had. He requested Eusebius (ca. 260–ca. 340) to produce 50 copies of scriptures to be used in the new capital city of Constantinople. It is most likely that Eusebius himself chose the scriptures to include in the canon. The choice was accepted by Constantine and probably influenced future Christians leaders' decision on the matter of producing an official canon.

Eusebius established three categories for Christian books: books that were "accepted" as scripture, those that were "questionable" or "disputed," and those that were "spurious." The first include a group of 20 of the current books of the New Testament. The second group or the "questionable" group included; James, 2 Peter, Jude, and 2 and 3 John. The spurious group consisted of the books that were rejected. Those included such scriptures as the Gospels of Peter, Thomas, and Matthias, the Acts of Andrew, Paul, and John, the Didache, and the Apocalypse of Peter. The middle group gained acceptance over time, along with Hebrews and Revelation.[40] The third group failed to win acceptance into future official canons. This became a critical factor with regard to what was preached from and what Christians were allowed to read. Over time, the scriptures of the official canon immensely affected Christians' attitudes. Constantine also set precedent, in that political leaders would have a say at times over Church leaders, even though they were still expected to obey God. Over time the power of pope increased. That is until the Protestant Revolution.

---

40 Ferguson, *Encyclopedia of Early Christianity,* 171.

Chapter 1

JUSTINIAN I

By the sixth century, the Church Fathers issued decrees that replaced the pagan religions and severally limited the practice of Judaism. Throughout his extensive reign, Emperor Justinian I (ca. 482–565) issued new changes in Roman law. These became acknowledged in Latin as *Novellae Constitutiones* ("new constitutions") and in English as *Justinian's Novels* or *Justinian's Code*. Although never made into an official manuscript, the new laws have been complied over the years by several legal and religious scholars. Significant to the integral idea was a set of new laws Justinian sent from Constantinople to Areobindas regarding new legislation concerning the Jews:

> But the Mishnah (Talmud), or as they call it the second tradition, we prohibit entirely. For it is not part of the sacred books, nor is it handed down by divine inspiration through the prophets, but the handiwork of man, speaking only of earthly things, and having nothing of the divine in it.[41]

Accordingly, anyone who was versed in the Talmud, and aware of the earlier Christian beliefs of Jesus being born during Passover, would be considered a criminal and a heretic for suggesting a connection between the two. Throughout the Middle Ages, popes became involved in the banning of the Talmud, allowing Jews to read only the Bible. Thus, the Talmud was subjected to multiple mass burnings. Many of the Roman Pontiffs condemned the Talmudic books. They include Julius III, Paul IV, Pius IV, Pius V, Gregory XIII, Clement VIII, Alexander VII, and Benedict XIV. In addition,

---

41 James Parkes, *The Conflict of the Church and the Synagogue: A Study in the Origins of Antisemitism* (New York: Meridian Books, 1964), 392.

Jews were forbidden to enter Christian churches.

Likewise, Jews also displayed some antagonism toward Christians. In the Talmud (Avadoh Zara 17b), it is ordered that Jews must distance themselves from the entrance to a house of idol worship. This would include Christian churches, because to Jews the worship of Jesus is idol worship. Fortunately, in contemporary times, the Catholic Church changed its policy on banning books. In 1966, Pope Paul VI formally abolished the *Index Librorum Prohibitorum*, a formal list of forbidden authors and writings. Further, Jews are allowed today to visit churches to admire the architecture and honor Christian friends at funerals.

CONCLUSION

The origins of the idea of an integral existence of Jesus come from diverse places (both Christian and Jewish). The Babylonian Talmud, in its oral form, dates back to the time of Moses. However, in its written form it only began to be scribed during the second century CE in Babylon.

Clement's writing describing the religious customs of the Basilidians living in Alexandria, Egypt, came from around the same time. Alexandria was a port city tolerant of diverse religions. Christians, Jews, and pagans all worshiped side-by-side there. According to Heinrich Graetz, it is possible that the Basilidians knew something of Judaism and the Talmud:

> The Talmud was the educator of the Jewish nation; and this education can by no means have been a bad one, since, in spite of the disturbing influence of isolation, degradation and systematic demoralization, it fostered in the Jewish people a degree of morality

Chapter 1

which even their enemies cannot deny them ... finally, it produced a deep intellectual life which preserved the enslaved and proscribed from stagnation, and which lit for them the torch of science.[42]

The Talmud suggest that the prophets, most importantly Isaac, were born and died during the Jewish month of Nissan, more precisely around Passover. Clement suggests that some of the Basilidians were open to debate on the matter of worshiping the birth and death of Jesus at the same time, more precisely during the Egyptian month of Pharmuthi, which falls during Passover. This makes sense since we know from the Gospels that Jesus was crucified during Passover. It is possible that the Basilidians living in the cosmopolitan city of Alexandria were influenced by the large Jewish community then living there. Clement's passage and the passage in the Talmud are somewhat similar in wording and suggest a similar theory--that persons of spiritual importance are born and die at the same time of year, in particular on Passover. The integral idea also agrees well with Jesus' promise in Matthew 5:17–18 to "fulfill them," them being the prophets. However, the two great religions would soon be at odds, and this would hamper the integral idea.

The integral idea may, in fact, be the greatest theological concept that never fully developed. Take for example St. Augustine's theory of Original Sin. Today, it is an important part of the Catholic catechism. The integral idea also started to develop at some point as Christians, including Augustine, began to believe that Jesus was conceived during Passover. Another was Hippolytus, whose statue is inscribed with Passover being the Genesis (Conception or birth) of Jesus.

---

42 Heinrich Graetz, *History of the Jews,* vol. 2 (Philadelphia: The Jewish Publication Society of America, 1956), 609.

The Integral Existence

But, the political uncertainties of the first four centuries of the Common Era made it difficult for Christians to accept Jesus as a Jewish prophet, and easier to accept him as the founder of a new faith, and so the idea never became an official part of Christian theology and was more and more overlooked. Nor did Jews ever accepted Jesus as a Jewish prophet, and the concept of an integral existence for Jesus become undesirable. Contributing to this was the banning of the Talmud. If Christians did not read it, they would never link the two religions together through the integral idea.

Therefore, as the two religions separated, the concept of Jesus being Jewish lost its popularity. This sense of an underlying unity might also have included Islam. After all, Muslims honor both the Old and New Testaments along with their most sacred book, the Koran, though for Islam, it is the Koran that has the greatest importance. Muslims also believe Moses, Abraham, Jesus, and the other prophets to be messengers of God. The irony, of course, is that at times these three major faiths have fought bitter wars and tried to destroy one another.

The concept of the integral idea, that Jesus, a Jew, was also a prophet who was born and died during Passover, became less of a possibility when December 25 became the official day of celebrating the birth of Jesus. Although it could still be said that Jesus was conceived during Passover, nine months before Christmas, a concept that may have its origins in the integral idea, Christians did not advertise the Jewish connection, given that Christianity and Judaism had separated into different religions.

Christianity and Judaism did have one thing in common. Both religions awaited the return of the Messiah. For the Jews, after several centuries of suffering at the expense of marauding invaders, new generations concluded that a Messiah would

Chapter 1

come forth in the future to rescue them from the oppression of other nations. To Christians, that event occurred over 2000 years ago, with the arrival of Jesus. His followers, through his birth, teachings, death, and Resurrection, formed a new religion, one that branched off from Judaism. But Christians, too, await the return of Jesus. Muslims can be included in this discussion as well. In the Koran, Surah 19:30–35, Muhammad speaks of the Resurrection of Jesus, stating,

> Thereupon she pointed to him. They said, "How can we talk to one who is a child in the cradle?" Jesus said, "I am a servant of ALLAH. HE has given me the Book, and has made me a Prophet; "And He had made me blessed wheresoever I may be, and had enjoyed upon me Prayer and almsgiving so long as I live; "And He has made me dutiful towards my mother, and has not made me arrogant and graceless; "And peace was on me the day I was born, and peace will be on me the day I shall die, and the day I shall be raised up to life again." That was Jesus, son of Mary. This is a statement of the truth concerning which they entertain doubt.

How can it be then, that the three great religions, who have more in common than not, are all waiting for the same important event, the return of the Messiah, which should unite them as brothers, and yet at times they have fought against one another with hate and disdain? Is this what God intended when he sent Jesus to die for the sins of mankind and make amends for the Garden of Eden?

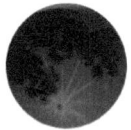

CHAPTER 2
TALMUDIC RABBIS AND CHURCH FATHERS

In order to better comprehend the idea of an integral existence as it pertains to the life of Jesus, we must understand the men who first conceived of it, the rabbis or sages who first mentioned that the prophets were born and died during the month of Nissan. Morris Adler writes:

> Many of the Rabbis gained their livelihood from worldly occupations. Serving as artisans, blacksmiths, sandal-makers, potters, grave-diggers, farmers, men of commerce, and tailors, the Rabbis were in touch with the pressures and currents alive in the community. Imbued with scholarly curiosity, their interest reached out into what would today call secular interests and studies... The Rabbis gave the

Chapter 2

community visible instruction in the good life. Their acts no less than their lectures afforded instruction in the "ways of Torah."[43]

This would also include Jesus and the apostles. It was not until later in Christianity that full-time pontiffs were required. Rabbi Shmuley Boteach writes in *Kosher Jesus* about the importance of Jesus having a daytime occupation. Jesus observed many of the traditional ways of living and working throughout his ministry. According to Rabbi Boteach,

> Jesus' occupation as a carpenter was entirely in keeping with the custom of his day. For the rabbis, teaching was a sacred duty. And they were loath to take financial support from their communities... The Talmud documents numerous examples of sages who had "blue-collar" professions so as to avoid financial dependence on their community of students... Jews disapproved of those who profited from people's desire to hear and understand God's instructions for living happily, peacefully, and prosperously.[44]

Moses was referred to as Moshe Rabbenu, Moses Our Teacher. During the period after the Second Temple, religious leaders were known as rabban, our masters, rabbi, my master, and rav master. Moses was a tough act to follow; he delivered his people from bondage in Egypt, was known as a lawgiver after receiving the Ten Commandments, and more importantly, served as God's personal spokesman to the Jews at

---

43 Morris, *The World of the Talmud*, 80-1
44 Shmuel Boteach, *Kosher Jesus* (Jerusalem: Gefen Publishing House, 2012), 23.

a pivotal time in their history. Rabbis who followed Moses had much to aspire to. Rabbi Abraham B. Witty writes:

> The title rabbi was originally used to identify; (1) those sages who had been ordained in the academies of ancient Israel, and (2) the Tana'im of the Mishnah. The title rav was applied to the Babylonian Amora'im. The most renowned scholars, of course, were those known only by their names; no title was necessary to identify them or to indicate the scope of their Torah learning.[45]

After the Talmud was completed, the title rabbi was conferred upon anyone who, by virtue of his scholarship, was qualified to decide questions of Jewish law. Therefore, rabbis were well versed in the scriptures and had to possess the common sense required to judge and lead their people. During the Talmudic period, they were unlike the modern official minister who is elected by the congregation and who is paid a salary with benefits.[46] Today, rabbis need more people skills.

HILLEL THE ELDER

Hillel the Elder (ca. 110 BCE–10 CE) was born in Babylonia about a hundred years before Jesus. His father's name has not been preserved; however, his mother was thought to hail from the family of King David. Sometime before the reign of Herod, Hillel came to Jerusalem to further his knowledge of Jewish tradition. The moved turned out to be a constructive one for him. Today, he is known as one of

---

45 Abraham Witty and Rachel Witty, *Exploring Jewish Tradition: A Transliterated Guide to Everyday Practice and Observance* (New York, Doubleday, 2001), 41.
46 Ibid.

Chapter 2

the most important figures in Judaism, is acknowledged for his role in the development of the Mishnah and Talmud, as founder of the House of Hillel school for Tannaim (sages of the Mishnah), and as founder of a long line of sages who stood at the head of Israel well into the fifth century CE.

In sum, rabbis around the time of Jesus were well versed in scripture and the interpretation of it. In reality, they most likely spent much of their time and thought on spiritual matters. In their time, true happiness was thought to originate with studying the Torah and Talmud. One was Hillel the Elder.

Currently, Hillel is considered the Father of classical Judaism. Some scholars might be tempted to also call this theology what Nahum Glatzer terms "normative Judaism." But it must be remembered that this was the time that the Talmud was being converted from the traditional oral language into a written one, something very liberal for its time. Glatzer best describes classical Judaism in his book *Hillel the Elder: The Emergence of Classical Judaism*:

> Classical Judaism, as it emerges in Hillel, stands first of all for Torah: its source is the divine revelation to Israel, but its application to the ever-changing conditions of life is in the hands of man; rational knowledge is the tool by which man may approach the law. Under the law, all aspects of life are important; there is no artificial separation between a "sacred" and a "secular realm of life. Classical Judaism emphasizes learning, which is more than an instrument for the increase of factual knowledge.[47]

---

47 Nahum N. Glatzer, Hillel the Elder: The Emergence of Classical Judaism (New York: Schocken Books, 1966), 87.

The reputation of Hillel and the school he established laid the foundation for generations of Jewish rabbis and thinkers. Many of them lived in Alexandria. This city was established to fill the void in trade left after Alexander destroyed the city of Tyre in Phoenicia. It attracted many scholars which allowed it to became an important link in the concept of the integral existence, and the rise of Jewish philosophy. This combination of Greek and Jewish philosophy later created a unique atmosphere for the Christian faith to blossom under.

PHILO OF ALEXANDRIA

The Jewish philosopher Philo of Alexandria (BCE 20–50 CE), was one of Clement's favorite sources for information from the past, and may have helped persuade him of the importance of Moses by practicing Jewish exegesis (the explanation of texts) alongside Stoic philosophy. As Philo wrote in the *De Specialibus Legibus IV*, "We look to the light by studying the Books of Moses, for they show us how God's law reflects the very intention of nature." He believed everything of importance was to be interpreted through Mosaic law. Moses was seen not only as a lawgiver but as an interpreter and judge of the law. Not only did Philo's writings influence Clement, they also influenced the students of the school of Alexandria.

Philo and Clement both used an allegorical method in interpreting scripture. They searched for higher meanings, not just the literal sense of the text. But, they did date certain events, so the human calendar must have had a certain amount of importance in their religious writings. Perhaps Clement intended his chronology of history to have some theological significance—to be more than just an attempt to establish Jewish philosophy over the Greeks. However, his historical

Chapter 2

analysis was somewhat lacking in the minds of later Church Fathers. According to Robert Grant, when Church historian Eusebius wrote of Clement's intellectual meadows, or fields ripe for harvest, that were available for theology, Eusebius was, "indicating that though it anthologized it made no use of 'historical treatment' and was, therefore, a source but not a model for the *Church History*."[48] Perhaps Eusebius believed Clement's reason for writing about historic events was solely theological and not intended for historic purposes. However, Clement's Crucifixion date, one of the intellectual meadows that Eusebius wrote of, can be used today as a historic reference. A few years after Philo, a Jewish rabbi named Yehoshua Ben Hananiah would offer another intellectual meadow for the world when he suggested in the Talmud that important Jewish leaders were born and died during Passover.

RABBI YEHOSHUA BEN HANANIAH

Rabbi Yehoshua (ca. 40–131), also called Rabbi Joshua or Johanan in some English translations, wrote in the Talmud, "In Nissan the world was created, and in the same month the patriarchs were born, and in Nissan they also died." He becomes the most important source of the integral existence theory because of his connections to both Jews and Christians and his prominent position in the Jewish community at Yavneh, Israel. He was elevated to this status following the destruction of the Temple and the city of Jerusalem by the Romans during the siege of 70 CE. This was a turbulent time for Jews. The Romans were intensifying their persecutions, and Christianity was beginning to compete with Judaism over new conversions. He complained of Jewish women marrying

---

48 Robert Grant, *Eusebius as Church Historian* (Oxford, UK: Clarendon Press, 1980), 38.

non-Jews and having children. In the Babylonian Talmud Yebamoth 46, he states:

> With reference to the children, R. Johanan expressed the same opinion elsewhere, saying that one is not considered a proselyte (convert) unless he is both circumcised and legally bathed (ritual cleansing), hence the above are still considered heathens; and Rabbi b. 'Hana said in the name of R. Johanan: When a heathen or a slave seduces a Jewish girl, the offspring is regarded as a bastard.[49]

The issue was that Christians were beginning to allow new converts to forego circumcision, but Jews would not budge on the issue. While Yehoshua lived at a time when the Roman Empire was at its pinnacle, he was still a man of great integrity when it came to his faith, leading his people, and keeping the peace. In the outside world, Barbarians in Germany and Parthians in the east were all waiting for the best time to free the world from Roman tyranny. For Rome a revolt could occur at any time or any place.

Although a Jew, Yehoshua was also a competent Greek scholar. He understood the Roman world and knew that his people were more than enthusiastic to revolt. Nevertheless, he still believed that peace was the answer. Much of this had to do with his own background as a student.

Yehoshua belonged to the school founded by Hillel, which taught that the public good must be considered in terms of the misery or happiness of individuals. This included the pursuit of peace during difficult times. According to Pordo, "The Hillelite motto was, "Seek peace and pursue it (Psalm

---

[49] Rodkinson, *New Edition of the Babylonian Talmud*, 2613-4.

24:14)." He was an enemy of foolish piety, of hypocrisy, and of visionary fanatics who tried to negate the values of this world by harping on the next. He opposed the imposition of additional ceremonial and legal burdens because the people might find them hard to bear."[50]

Yehoshua's death, at age 90, proved to be a critical setback to the impermanent peace between the Jews and Romans. Shortly afterward, Jews were in rebellion in what became known as the Bar-Kokhba revolt. Lead by Shimon Bar-Kokhba (ca. 15–135) Jews were able to gain an independent Jewish state with an army of over 300,000 men. Rabbi Akiva even ascribed to Bar-Kokhba the famous messianic verse: "A star will shoot forth from Jabob" (*Num* 24:17). Afterward, Bar-Kokhba was known as "Kochba." Rabbi Akiva was so respected among Jews that they considered Bar-Kokhba to be on the same level spiritually as the Messiah. However, while this gave Bar-Kokba support from the Jews, it also deterred Christians from aiding the rebellion, because two Messiahs were more than they required for salvation.

The rebellion became so successful that the Romans were quickly pressured to transport troops from throughout the empire to end the uprising. In the end, it was not the Jewish resistance at the important city of Beitar that faltered, but the betrayal from insiders who revealed Beitar's secret fortifications and entrances. Nevertheless, Bar-Kokhba made a critical error when he blamed the rabbis for betraying him, executing Rabbi Elazar as a spy. Soon afterward, he lost the support of the rabbis completely. They began calling him "Bar

---

[50] Joshua Podro et al., "A 1st-Century Jewish Sage: The Life and Teachings of Rabbi Joshua ben Hananiah," Commentary Magazine, March 14, 2017, www.commentarymagazine.com/articles/a-1st-century-jewish-sagethe-life-and-teachings-of-rabbi-joshua-ben-hananiah.

Koziba," meaning false Messiah. Roman legions were eventually able to defeat Bar-Kokhba, and he was killed in battle. According to historian Dio Cassius in *History of Rome, LXIX*, 580,000 men were killed in the various skirmishes and battles and there is no knowing how many died through famine, disease, and fire.[51]

THE EARLY CHURCH FATHERS

During the second century, as rabbis were transferring the Talmud into written form, Christian leaders were issuing commentary on the books of the New Testament and designing the hierarchy of the Church. Father Oscar Lukefahr, C.M., wrote about this hierarchy in *The Catholic Catechism Handbook*:

> A hierarchy is a governing body of individuals organized into orders, each subordinate to the one above. Catholics believe that Christ instituted the Church with its authority, mission, orientation, and goal. The hierarchy (order of ministers) in the Church, therefore, comes from Christ, who alone can authorize people to preach and baptize in his name. Grace comes, not from ourselves, but from God through those whom God sends (Romans 10:14–15.) Christ empowers ministers to do and give by God's grace what they could not do and give on their own.[52]

The Early Church Fathers, also called Christian Fathers or

---

51 Lavinia and Dan Cohn-Sherbok, *A Short Reader of Judaism* (Oxford: Oneword, 1997), 64–5.
52 Oscar Lukefahr, C.M., *The Catholic Catechism Handbook* (Perryville, Missouri: Wehmeyer Printing Co., 1996), 40.

Chapter 2

Fathers of the Church were the ancient leaders of the Church. Their influences affected Christian theology and later Western civilization. Most are considered eminent teachers, some were important bishops, some are saints today, others were saints at one time but are no longer, and others could have been saints, except that their views were later deemed heretical. Western churches tend to regard only early teachers of Christianity as Fathers. However, the Orthodox Church honors as "Fathers" many saints far beyond the early centuries of Church history. It is even possible to be considered a Father of the Church in the modern era. Harry Wolfson addresses this issue in *The Philosophy of the Church Fathers: Volume I*:

> To the rabbis of the time of the Fathers, the Oral Law was that which was handed down to them by the Pharisees and it was they, as the successors of the Pharisees, who were entrusted with its further development. To the Fathers, the Oral Law was that which was handed down to them by Jesus and it was they, as the successors of Jesus, who were entrusted with its further development.[53]

Therefore, the Church Fathers believed that they were entrusted to take Christianity in the direction they best saw fit according to their interpretations of the word of Jesus. Problems arose when the different apostles saw things differently. Perhaps of all the apostles, the one who knew Jesus best was his own brother, James, although it is uncertain if he was a spiritual or actual brother. After the death of Jesus, the Christian community at Jerusalem was led by Peter, and to a lesser extent, John, but James role soon increased.

---

53 Harry A. Wolfson, *The Philosophy of the Church Fathers,* vol. 1 (Cambridge: Harvard University Press, 1970), 94.

JAMES, THE LORD'S BROTHER

At first, the Jerusalem congregation was filled with what Walker calls "Messianic hope, it would seem at first in a cruder and less spiritual form than Jesus had taught."[54] They were devoted to Jesus, who they believed would surely return within their own lifetimes. But, this did not halt attacks by the Pharisaic Jews. One result of this was the death of the first Christian martyr, Stephen, by stoning at the hands of an angry mob. Stephen's death was a harsh blow to the fragile community and resulted in many Christians dispersing throughout Judaea and Samaria and into Damascus, Antioch, and the island of Cyprus.

Tensions between Christians and Jews were present at the beginning, but with Stephen as leader of the church in Jerusalem, the opposing sides might have coexisted much more easily. He was a member of the synagogue of the Libertines, made up of Jews from Cyrene, Alexandria, Cilicia, and Asia. Acts 6: 3–11 informs that he was "full of the Spirit and wisdom" and "a man full of faith and the Holy Spirit." Nevertheless, Jews from his own synagogue argued with him, "but they could not stand up against his wisdom or the Spirit he spoke." In response, they secretly persuaded some men to say, "We have heard Stephen speak words of blasphemy against Moses and against God." What resulted next was something unprecedented. Stephen was stoned to death by an angry mob. Elizabeth McNamer and Bargil Pixner note, "One can imagine the dread that descended on his friends. According to Eusebius, a panic situation prevailed, and many Greek-speakers left Jerusalem."[55]

---

54 Walker, *A History of the Christian Church*, 22.
55 Elizabeth Mary McNamer and Bargil Pixner, *Jesus and First-Century Christianity in Jerusalem (New York: Paulist Press, 2008)*, 26.

Chapter 2

For a short time after the death of Stephen, a period of peace followed. But, in 44 CE, the king of Judea, Herod Agrippa I, the grandson of Herod the Great, initiated a severe round of persecutions. Peter was imprisoned but managed to escape death, and the apostle James was beheaded. Tradition holds that the apostles left Jerusalem 12 years after the Crucifixion. Whatever the timing, Peter now spent less time in Jerusalem. After this, James, the brother of Jesus, acquired a greater role in leading the Christian community thereafter.

In 42 CE, James became the foremost leader of the Church in Jerusalem. James made an excellent choice. The Church was made up almost entirely of Aramaic-speaking Jewish-Christians after the mass exodus of Greek-speaking Christians. Together, McNamer and Pixner inform us that "perhaps it was his outstanding piety, adherence to Jewish customs and laws, and constant attendance at the Temple that put him beyond the suspicion of Agrippa."[56] Shortly later, in 44 CE Agrippa died, and the Herod dynasty was temporally halted when Agrippa's son, only 17, was deemed too young to rule, hence terminating the agreement with Rome. As a result, Judea once again became a Roman province.

James quickly became the Megaqqer, or superintendent, of the Jewish believers. Under his leadership, the congregation attended the synagogue, read the Torah, and still honored the prophets on the Sabbath. They fasted on Wednesday and Friday and celebrated the Resurrection of Jesus on Sunday. Passover, of course, was still celebrated as an orthodox Jewish holiday, but they managed to incorporate new forms of worship into the Passover celebration. They fasted during the Jewish hours of Passover and then began their feast after midnight. Another interesting new development was that Jesus

---

56 Ibid, 35.

was recognized as the Passover lamb. Melito of Sardis, in his *Paschal Sermons,* noted some of rituals that the Christians in Jerusalem practiced.[57] This included celebrating until 3:00 AM, hoping that the Messiah would come on the night of Passover, as on the first Passover told in Exodus.[58]

James influence on Christianity was immense. Around 57 CE. Peter returned to Jerusalem and was confronted with a critical issue in front of the council. Questions arose over whether or not new converts to Christianity should not only be baptized but also circumcised. Peter's final decision was that only faith through baptism was required (Act 15:10–11):

> Now then, why do you try to test God by putting on the necks of the disciples a yoke that neither we nor our fathers have been able to bear? No! We believe it is through the grace of our Lord Jesus that we are saved, just as they are.

The council, somewhat in disbelief, turned to James for a response. His decision (Acts 15:19–21) would decide the future of the community, and later all of Christianity. It reads:

> It is my judgement, therefore, that we should not make it difficult for the Gentiles who are turning to God. Instead we should write to them, telling them to abstain from food polluted by idols, from sexual immorality, from meat of strangled animals and from blood. For Moses had been preached in every city from the earliest times and is read in the synagogues on every Sabbath.

---

57 Melito (died ca. 180) was the bishop at Sardis in western Turkey and is a saint in the Roman Catholic Church.
58 McNamer, *Jesus and First-Century Christianity in Jerusalem*, 37.

Chapter 2

We do not know how James would feel today about the Christian church. Many other traditions beside circumcision fell out of practice, including the eating of kosher food, and reciting the oral law or Talmud.

Around 62 CE, James was forced by a powerful man named Ananus to make a public declaration in the parapet of the Temple. He was supposed to adhere to his Jewish faith. Instead, James testified about Jesus, which only enraged the Scribes and Pharisees, who rushed at him and threw him off the parapet. The fall was about one hundred feet and should have killed James, but he survived, only to be stoned and clubbed to death. James's death came at a critical time. The Jewish-Roman war was about to erupt, and many Christians would flee when it intensified. If James's stance on Gentiles and the Jewish faith was confusing to many Jewish-Christians, then Paul's was even more perplexing.

THE APOSTLE PAUL

Pauline Christianity, an expression invented by twentieth-century scholars, was intended to display the many intricate strands of Christianity that developed shortly after the Crucifixion of Jesus. These scholars claim that Paul's writings are different from the rest of the New Testament, and it was his influence that dominated early Christianity. It can be debated how much Paul intended to separate Christianity from Judaism. Williston Walker writes, "Paul's conception of freedom from the Jewish law was as far as possible from any antinomian under-valuation of morality. If the old law had passed away, the Christian is under "the law of the Spirit of life."[59]

---

[59] Williston Walker, *A History of the Christian Church* (New York: Charles Scribner's Sons, 1970), 28.

Over time, this verse has confused Christians, because they are forced to ask to what extent Paul desired the Christians to separate themselves from Judaism. Some groups maintained that it was acceptable to be labeled a Christian while observing the Torah and Jewish traditions. And by the nineteenth-century, numerous Jewish groups emerged with the goal of converting as many Jews as they could to Christianity while retaining their culture and Jewish religious traditions.

Granting there were numerous Jewish conversions to Christianity throughout history, there was little concern for retaining Jewish traditions after the conversions. According to Dan Cohn-Sherbok in *Messianic Judaism: A Critical Anthology*,

> In 1809, however, the London Society for Promoting Christianity Amongst the Jews (LSPCJ) was established, and a number of Christians were actively involved in missionary activity. In 1813 the Children of Abraham was created... Simultaneously, in the second decade of the nineteenth century, the first translation of the New Testament was made in Hebrew.[60]

Today there are many Christians raised in Torah observant homes who still worship Jesus while observing and studying Torah Law. This movement experienced growth around the time of the turmoil and political movements of the 1960s, including the Six-Day War.[61] Several such groups

---

60 Dan Cohn-Sherbok, *Messianic Judaism: A Critical Anthology* (London: Continuum, 2000), 15.
61 The Six-Day War, also known as the Third Arab-Israeli War or June War, took place June 5–10, 1967, and ended in a decisive victory for Israel resulting in the capture of the Sinai Peninsula, Gaza Strip, West Bank, Old City of Jerusalem, and Golan Heights.

emerged during this time. One of the more well-known ones was Jews for Jesus, founded in the 1960s by Moishe Rosen, an Orthodox Jew who converted to Christianity, attended Northeastern Bible College in New Jersey, and became an ordained Baptist minister.

In his forties, Rosen became known as a youth-movement leader. According to Ruth Tucker, "He began spending time in Greenwich Village and wrote the first of his tracts ('broadsides')." Rosen and other likeminded leaders did attract many followers, and the movement did grow early on. However, the movement was not always well received. Tucker notes, "But with the horrific revelations of the Nazi Holocaust, support for Jewish evangelism declined, and ministries hesitated to confront Jews forcefully with the message of Jesus."[62]

Despite some post-Holocaust concerns, however, Messianic Jewish churches are still in existence and thriving. Unfortunately, the Messianic Jewish communities of the first century had more difficulties worshiping in and around Jerusalem than those of today, and the leadership of Paul has been questioned.

In the modern era, Paul is one of the most misunderstood of the apostles. The New Testament informs us that Paul, known as Saul before his conversion to Christianity, was a "zealous" Pharisee who intensely persecuted any followers of Jesus. Acts 3:3–9 tells us his "come to Jesus moment" occurred while traveling to Damascus under a persecution order from the high priest, when he was blinded by light and asked by Jesus, "Saul, Saul why do you persecute me?" Paul was a

---

[62] Ruth A. Tucker "An Evangelist with Chutzpah: At First Reluctant Street Preacher, Moishe Rosen, Founder of Jews for Jesus, Came to Relish Insults and Controversy," *Christianity Today* (2010): 38, *Academic OneFile*, EBSCO*host*.

Jewish-Roman, but also one of the most important leaders of the new religion known as Christianity.

Those against Paul claim that his writings undermined the authority of Torah Law in order to allow for easier gentile conversions to Christianity. Even modern philosophers have questioned Paul's motives. Friedrich Nietzsche wrote in *The Antichrist*,

> The fate of the Gospels was decided by death—it hung on the "cross." ... It was only death, that unexpected and shameful death; it was only the cross, which was usually reserved for the canaille (masses) only—it was only this appalling paradox which brought the disciples face to face with the real riddle: "*Who was it? what was it?*"—Here everything *must* be accounted for as necessary; everything must have a meaning, a reason, the highest sort of reason; the love of a disciple excludes all chance. Only then did the chasm of doubt yawn: "*Who* put him to death? who was his natural enemy?"—this question flashed like a lightning-stroke. Answer: dominant Judaism, its ruling class. From that moment, one found one's self in revolt *against* the established order, and began to understand Jesus as *in revolt against the established order.*[63]

Nietzsche, no friend of Judaism either, set out to demonstrate that Western Civilization had lost faith in God. When he said, "God is dead," he did not mean in a literal sense that God had died. It was more of a reflection of Enlightenment thinking, after centuries of being ruled by governments that controlled populations through religion and

---

63 F. W. Nietzsche, *The Antichrist* (New York: Alfred A. Knopf, Inc.,1924), 115.

Chapter 2

an aristocratic social order. Nietzsche was saying that God was no longer required, and faith useless. This included the Pharisees. Nietzsche believed it was their goal to create a ruling class first and to bring spiritual well-being to the Jews afterward. Likewise, the apostles sought to undermine the established authority of Pharisees by replacing the old order with the new order, Christianity. Nietzsche suggests that the apostles were passionate enough to even become martyrs to accomplish their overall goal. Paul becomes the main leader in his view of the conspiracy to establish the new order. Nietzsche even suggests that the Pauline Community had a problem not only with the Pharisees but with other strands of Christianity. One school, in particular, was the school of Alexandria. Again, in *The Antichrist*, he writes:

> The God that Paul invented for himself, a God who "reduced to absurdity" "the wisdom of this world" (especially the two great enemies of superstition, philology and medicine), is in truth only an indication of Paul's resolute determination to accomplish that very thing himself: to give one's own will the name of God, thora—that is essentially Jewish. Paul wants to dispose of the "wisdom of this world": his enemies are the good philologians and physicians of the Alexandrine school—on them he makes his war.[64]

Throughout the *Antichrist*, Nietzsche blames Paul for everything from the battle between science and religion, in order to control ideology, to the battle of whether or not to allow the use of philosophy within religious interpretations of Jesus. However, in recent years Paul's commitment to Judaism

---

64 Ibid, 136.

is gaining popularity. John Gager writes in his book *Reinventing Paul*, that Paul was not completely unaware of some of the charges against him. He states,

> What is more, I believe that Paul was painfully aware of this accusation against him and sought to refute it in his letter to the Romans: "Do we overthrow the law through faith? By no means! On the contrary we uphold the law." (3.31) "Is the law sin? By no means!" (7.7) "Has God rejected his people? By no means! (11.1)[65]

Therefore, Paul did not call for a complete separation between the Gentiles and Jews, only for Jews to see their error in denying Jesus as the Son of God. If there existed a competition between different ideologies within the Christian community, which is what Nietzsche suggests, then many years later, the followers of the Alexandrian school would have been disappointed, as many of their saints were latter stripped of their designations during the Middle Ages. One Church Father who is still a saint today is Saint Ignatius of Antioch.

ST. IGNATIUS OF ANTIOCH

St. Ignatius (ca. 35–ca. 108), the Bishop of Antioch, was the first Christian to describe the Christian church using the adjective "Catholic." He believed that "wherever Jesus Christ is there is the Catholic Church."[66] During the reign of Trajan (110–117), he was condemned as a Christian and sent as a

---

65 John G. Gager, *Reinventing Paul* (New York: Oxford University Press, 2002), 53.
66 Saint Ignatius, *The Ante-Nicene Father, translations of the writings of the Fathers down to A.D. 325* (Buffalo: C.L. Pub. Co., 1885), 90.

Chapter 2

prisoner to Rome to be thrown to wild beasts. In route to Rome from Antioch, he wrote a series of letters that became the central part of a later collection known as the Apostolic Fathers. These letters became an important part of Christian theology. In them, important topics are addressed: ecclesiology, the sacraments, and the duties of bishops. According to Williston Walker, "Ignatius's most original thought was that the incarnation was the manifestation of God for the revelation of a new humanity. Before Christ, the world was under the devil and death"[67]

In a sense, the concept of a new church in Jesus, and what was expected of it, did not help in uniting Christians and Jews, and the two religions only drifted further apart. Adding to the separation was that likeminded followers of Ignatius also viewed the world as evil. This more than likely upset the established Jewish religion, which further denied the importance of Jesus. Nevertheless, many early Christians embraced the concept. Even today Ignatius is viewed positively. In 2008, Pope Benedict XVI wrote the following in *The Fathers*:

> As can be seen, Ignatius is truly the "Doctor of Unity": Unity of God and unity of Christ (despite the various heresies gaining ground which separated the human and the divine in Christ), unity of the Church, unity of the faithful in "faith and love, to which nothing is to be preferred." Ultimately, Ignatius realism invites the faithful of yesterday and today, invites us all, to make a gradual synthesis between configuration to Christ (union with him, life in him) and dedication to his Church (unity with the Bishop,

---

[67] Walker, *A History of the Christian Church*, 36.

generous service to the community and to the world).[68]

A little more than a half-century after the martyrdom of Ignatius, Clement of Alexandria was beginning his ministry. The city of Alexandria was much different than many of the smaller Christian communities. Many in the cosmopolitan city were richer and better educated than people in the backwater communities throughout Judea. Clement did not appear to condemn the accumulation of wealth; in fact, many of his students were well-off. However, he did reject the excessive use of it. Many of his followers wished to become more scholarly, and learn more than just scripture; they desired more instruction on topics such as philosophy and science. This was reflected in his teachings.

ST. CLEMENT OF ALEXANDRIA

Clement of Alexandria (ca. 150–ca. 215) is the most important early Christian source for the integral idea. He was born of pagan Greek parents, and most likely spent a great amount of time in Athens. While we do not know much about his youth, he appears to have searched for knowledge and truth in many lands before finding his true religion in Christianity in Alexandria. He studied philosophy and theology under many unknown teachers, referring to them in the *Stromata* his miscellaneous studies.

Clement had the profound passions and feelings that many Christians have for their religion. But, he tended to believe that many are oblivious where he excelled the most, in

---

68 Pope Benedict XVI, *The Fathers* (Huntington, IN: Our Sunday Visitor, Inc., 2008), 17.

Chapter 2

thought and liberalism. Clement once wrote that if animals had religion, it would be mute, without words. He believed that too many Christians take this same approach and never communicate their questions, thoughts, or complaints, only knowing what they were raised on, or comfortable with, while never questioning their doctrine. Even today, the faithful watchdogs of religion, so to speak, are content with their familiar surroundings, but nonetheless dangerous when unfamiliar intruders or ideas threaten their territory.

Isaiah 8:1 states, "The Lord said to me, 'Take a large scroll and write on it with an ordinary pen: Maher-Shalal-Hash Baz [Maher-Shalal-Hash Baz is a son of the prophet Isaiah].'" Wolfson notes Clement's response in the *Stromata* to this:

> The Spirit is prophesying that through the interpretation of the Scripture there would come afterwards the sacred knowledge, which at that period was still unwritten, because not yet known, for it was spoken from the beginning to those who understand.[69]

Throughout Clement's ministry, he would use this approach to justify his calculations and translations. Clement's dates for the Nativity and Passion are one of the closest written passages from the actual time of Jesus that mentions a date for the crucifixion, which could be helpful for scholars in the future if more information is discovered. Clement plays an important role in finding an integral age of Jesus because he was one of the first to be concerned about historical dates. This was one of the few liberal ideals he was known for. He was one of the first to argue for the equality of the sexes on

---

69 Wolfson, *The Philosophy of the Church Fathers*, 94.

the grounds that salvation is extended to all mankind equally. He even went so far as to support women playing an active role in the leadership of the Church. Assisting him in his research were the vast resources of nearby centers of learning and the exchange of thought among the expanding network of the Christian Church. One place where he spent a significant amount of time, along with many seekers of knowledge, was the city of Alexandria.

During the first three centuries after Jesus, Alexandria was a center of economic and religious activity in the Roman Empire. Its excellent location as a harbor on the Mediterranean Sea transformed the city into a crossroads of trade between East and West. The city was originally founded by Alexander the Great during his conquest of Egypt and was mainly populated by Greeks. After Alexander met his death, his general Ptolemy claimed Egypt and declared Alexandria his capital. Along with Ptolemy came a large Greek population. However, the many trappings of a prosperous and rapidly growing metropolis attracted large numbers of non-Greek immigrants. Even many traditional Egyptians, who were more apt to settle farther inland along the banks of the Nile River, as well as an ample Jewish community, soon flocked to the city. A vast number of different ethnic and religious cultures populated Alexandria. Clement was influenced not only by Greek but also Jewish thought.

According to Peter Fraser, the Jews were also significant very early in the city's history; they even had their own district, along with local administration. During the reign of Philometor (ca. 186–145 BCE) two Jews, Onias IV and Dositheus, held important posts in the military. Philometor had great respect for the aptitude of Jews in military matters, and his appreciation allowed a rapid rise in power for the in-

Chapter 2

creasing numbers of immigrant Jews.[70] In this atmosphere a liberal form of Judaism developed in the metropolis. John Ferguson notes that the Jews of Alexandria spoke Koine Greek and translated the Jewish Bible into their language:

> Here developed the attempt to coordinate the Jewish faith with the philosophies of Plato and Zeno, associated above all with the name Philo. The degree of Hellenization was remarkable. Hebrew and Aramaic soon died out, and Jews even wanted to participate in athletics.[71]

However, along with the persecution under Caligula and the defeat of the Jews after the Jewish Wars with Rome in 70 CE came a decline in the political significance of Alexandrian Jews. Christians were also under persecution. This was not an uncommon occurrence; many Church leaders would leave their communities to begin a new ministry elsewhere. Clement left Alexandria around 202 CE during the persecutions under the reign of Roman Emperor Lucius Septimius Severus.[72]

It is not known for certain where Clement went after the persecutions. In 212, he was corresponding with an old pupil, Alexander, then a bishop in Cappadocia, and later Jerusalem. Alexander, in one of his letters, implied that Clement was in Cappadocia, but he may have later moved to Antioch to continue his ministry. It is known that persecution was active in this region. For a time, while Alexander was imprisoned,

---

[70] Peter Fraser, *Ptolemaic Alexandria* (Oxford: Oxford University Press, 1972), 84.
[71] John Ferguson, Clement of Alexandria (New York: Twayne, 1974), 22.
[72] Emperor Septimus Severus was a devotee of Sarapis, a god the Ptolemies derived from the Egyptian god of Memphis, Osor-Hapi. He probably worshiped at the massive temple to Sarapis, which was built by Ptolemy III and later rebuilt under Roman rule.

Talmudic Rabbis and Church Fathers

Clement fulfilled his duties in Cappadocia, during which Clement increased the number of Christian worshipers. Wherever Clement stayed in his later years, controversy over his frequent reliance on Greek philosophy may have prevented him from being recalled to Alexandria. He probably was deceased by 216, according to a reference in a letter written by Alexander.[73]

Until the seventeenth century, Clement was venerated as a saint in the Roman Catholic Church, with his feast falling on the fourth of December. His name was to be found in the Martyrologies, a catalog of the names of saints with their feast day listed in a calendar form. However, when Pope Clement VIII, pontiff from 1592 to 1605, revised the Roman Martyrology, he omitted Clement of Alexandria's name from the calendar on the advice of Cardinal Caesar Baronius, the Pope's confessor. Baronius, considered one of the most important Church historians, was the prominent leader of the revision, an epic task that included omitting all the mythological and unhistorical saints. This was difficult to achieve, because every local church had its own cluster of saints, but it was a necessary part of the Counter-Reformation of the Catholic Church.[74] Although Clement is no longer a saint, his writings still have historic value.

ORIGEN OF ALEXANDRIA

Origen (ca. 185–ca. 254), Clement's best student, stayed in Alexandria and succeeded him as teacher; if he experienced any pressure associated with stepping out from Clement's shadow, it was not apparent. In many respects, Origen's

---

73 John Ferguson, Clement of Alexandria, 16.
74 Cyriac Pullapilly, *Caesar Baronius: Counter-Reformation Historian* (Notre Dame: University of Notre Dame Press, 1975), 38.

Chapter 2

writings are more acknowledged and respected than Clement's work. Even the Neo-Platonist Porphyry, whose writings influenced Western thought, acknowledged Origen's brilliant philosophical creativity.[75] But he could not comprehend why he used such an intriguing Greek approach to a religion of such strange myths and ideas.[76] In Matthew 23:2, Jesus says to the crowds and his disciples, "The teachers of the law and the Pharisees sit in Moses's seat."[77] Wolfston notes that Origen wrote the following in response to this verse:

> I think that those who understand and explain Moses according to spiritual power, sit in Moses's seat, but are not Scribes and Pharisees, but are better than they. Such are Christ's beloved disciples, who both interpret His word through the grace of God and find out things in further meaning.[78]

This concept becomes very important in the idea of an integral age. Origen, in a sense, is justifying the Church Fathers' ways of interpreting the Bible by saying it is through the grace of God. But he is also questioning the specific authority and scholarship of the Pharisees, and perhaps Judaism in general. This newfound freedom of interpretation allowed future generations of Church Fathers to take Church

---

[75] Neoplatonism is the cross-pollination of different philosophies, including Greek and Eastern. By combining elements of these, Neoplatonism became a link between the past of Plato's morality and the emerging political power of the Christian Church. Porphyry was a student of Plotinus, the founder of Neoplatonist thought. Neoplatonists believe in one god, but a pagan one. Porphyry's work, especially his classification of species or taxonomy, became staples in university teaching during the Middle Ages.

[76] Paul Tillich, A History of Christian Thought (New York: Harper and Row, 1968), 57.

[77] Holy Bible, NIV, 547.

[78] Wolfson, *The Philosophy of the Church Fathers*, 95.

doctrine into newer roles, as the Church became not only the salvation of the Roman world but a political force as well. It can even be questioned whether some Church leaders committed fraud in their own writing or altered writings done generations beforehand.

Pope Benedict XVI speaks warmly of Origen. He believes Origen read the Bible determined to ascertain the biblical text, and then offer the most reliable version of it. He states,

> He studied extensively for this purpose and drafted an edition of the Bible with six parallel columns, from left to right, with the Hebrew characters—he was even in touch with rabbis to make sure he properly understood the Bible's original Hebrew text—then, the Hebrew text transliterated into Greek that enabled him to compare the different possibilities for its translation.[79]

Origen becomes important because of his honesty at a time when there were many different sects of Christianity not only in Alexandria but throughout the Roman Empire. Perhaps he felt that the best way to unify them was through precise interpretations of the Bible. Origin becomes a critical source in the creation of a biblical canon, although his list of scriptures comes to us through Eusebius, who may have invented the list.[80]

It does set a precedent for having an official canon at a time when many different scriptures were in circulation, including many that were suspect. This becomes critical after the reign of Constantine the Great, as the Church banned not

---

79 Pope Benedict XVI, 38.
80 Ferguson, *Encyclopedia of Early Christianity*, 170.

Chapter 2

only Christian but also Jewish scriptures, aiding in the downfall of the integral idea through the tampering of text.

ST. HIPPOLYTUS OF ROME

St. Hippolytus (ca. 170–ca. 236) was a scholar who could trace his heritage to the Greek-speaking East. He was known for disagreeing with bishops Zephyrinus and Callistus over Church doctrine. In 235, he and Bishop Pontianus were exiled by Emperor Maximinus Thrax, who persecuted Christian leaders, to Sardinia. Both soon died as martyrs under the hardships of convict life. However, before their martyrdoms, they were reconciled by the Church and their bodies brought back to Rome to be given proper burials, and Hippolytus became a saint.

Hippolytus's statue, mentioned in the previous chapter, despite errors in the Pascal calendar, becomes an important piece of evidence because it was commissioned soon after his death. Since it is in stone, it was difficult to change by future generations wanting to establish the false belief that December 25 was the chosen day of the Nativity. As a case in point, several manuscripts of Hippolytus's *Commentary on Daniel,* a work of the early third century, state, "For the first appearance of our Lord in the flesh took place in Bethlehem eight days before the Kalends of January [25 December], on the fourth day [Wednesday]"[81]

However, early twentieth-century Professor Johannes Quasten pointed out that scholars agree that although the passage would be valuable for the history of the Feast of the Nativity, it seems to be an interpolation, "though added very early."[82] In this case, researchers have two options to consider;

---

81 Quasten, *Patrology Vol 2,* 172.
82 Ibid, 173.

to agree with a likely tampered written text, or to prefer the statue commissioned shortly after Hippolytus's death. The statue informs us that Hippolytus believed the Genesis of Jesus to be during Passover. Johann Kirsch also believes that Clement influenced Hippolytus because Hippolytus was about ten years younger than Clement, and often used doctrine written by his elder in his own writings.[83] While Hippolytus was quite interested in the date of the Nativity, Clement's closer and more prominent follower Origen's dislike of celebrating birthdays may have dimmed some of the interest in the topic until Augustine's time. Unlike the Basilidians, perhaps out of bias, he chose to take theology in a different direction. Origen states in the *Homilies on Leviticus viii*,

> No one is found to have had joy on the day of the birth of his birth. No one is found to have had joy on the day of the birth of his son or daughter. Only sinners rejoice over this kind of birthday. For indeed we find in the Old Testament Pharaoh, king of Egypt, celebrating the day of his birth with a festival, and in the New Testament, Herod. However, both of them stained the festival of his birth by shedding human blood. For Pharaoh killed "the chief baker," Herod, the holy prophet John "in prison." But the saints not only do not celebrate a festival on their birthdays, but, filled with the Holy Spirit, they curse that day.[84]

---

83 Johann Kirsch, "St. Hippolytus of Rome," *The Catholic Encyclopedia*, vol. 7 (New York: Robert Appleton Company, 1910), www.newadvent.org/cathen/07360c.htm.

84 Origen and Gary Wayne Barkley, *Homilies on Leviticus, 1–16* (Washington, DC: Catholic University of America Press, 1990), 155–6, *eBook Academic Collection (EBSCOhost)*.

Chapter 2

Contributing to Origen's stance on birthdays was St. Peter Chrysologus (ca. 380–ca. 450), the Bishop of Ravenna. William Walsh, in *Curiosities of Popular Customs*, adds the following anecdote:

> "When you hear of a birthday of saints, brethren," says Peter Chrysologus, "do not think that is spoken of in which they are born of earth, in the flesh, but that in which they are born from earth into heaven, from labor to rest, from temptations to repose, from torment to delights not fluctuating. . . . Such are the birthdays of the martyrs that we celebrate.[85]

It was such that many of the saints were martyrs and their feast days fell on or near their day of martyrdom, not their day of birth. Some of this may have to do with what Jesus said in John 15:13. He states, "Greater love has no one than this, that he lay down his life for friends." Therefore, some Church Fathers were not keen on the idea of celebrating the birthday of Jesus, or anyone else, for that matter. They preferred to honor those who died as martyrs on their day of death.

One of the early admirers of the martyrs was Tertullian. In his work *Apologeticus*, he even went so far as to suggest that fleeing persecution was worse than dying for Christ. In his view Christians could, "obtain from God complete forgiveness, by giving in exchange his blood" It is from this important work one finds the phrase about the growth of the Church: "The oftener we are mown down by you, the more in

---

[85] William S. Walsh, *Curiosities of Popular Customs: Rites, Ceremonies, Observances, and Miscellaneous Antiquities* (Philadelphia: J.B. Lippincott, 1897), 119.

Talmudic Rabbis and Church Fathers

number we grow; the blood of the Christians is the seed."[86] Tertullian defends Christianity by calling for the legal toleration of the religion, and that Christians be given the same rights as the other sects of the Roman Empire.

QUINTUS SEPTIMIUS FLORENS TERTULLIAN

Tertullian (ca. 150/60–ca. 225/30), the father of Latin theology, was born in northern Africa. We know he was the son of a centurion, and was raised as a well-educated pagan. Sometime before 197, he converted to Christianity, and later wrote some of the most important apologetic works of the early Church. He is remembered for translating early Church works and the Bible from the Septuagint into Latin. This included mentioning the doctrine of the Trinity in the West. He was similar to Clement by being one of the first of the Fathers to date events in Christianity chronologically. In additional works, mainly the *Apologeticus*, he attacked Marcion,[87] the Gnostics, and others whose writing's he regarded as heresies.

To the integral existence he is significant for different reasons. They come from the work, *Adversus Judaeos* (Against the Jews), the first anti-Jewish polemic work in Latin. This story is written as a theological discussion between a Christian and a recent Jewish convert, during which they are interrupted by several ignorant bystanders. In the book, Tertullian mentions the year that Jesus was born in, but does not give a birthday or

---

86 Alexander Roberts, et al., *The Ante-Nicene Fathers: Translations of the Writings of the Fathers down to A.D. 325*. Vol. III, (Grand Rapids (MI): Eerdmans, 1957), 159.
87 Marcion, the originator of Macionism, believed that the God of Old Testament was the Creator, but was a God of rigid justice. God was inferior to Jesus, who died to save humanity from the wrath of the Creator.

month. He writes, "Let us see, moreover, how in the forty-first year of the empire of Augustus, when he has been reigning for xx and viii years after the death of Cleopatra, the Christ is born".[88] This would indicate that Jesus was born in 2 BCE. He also suggests that Augustus died in 13 AD (Augustus actually died in 14 AD). Although the dates are flawed, it informs us that for some reason Tertullian was not interested in providing a birthday for Jesus, but thought the year was an important event in his chorography of the world. Although-not-mentioned, but something else of significance that should be considered is that there may have been political motivations behind the African's silence on this topic.

Also written in the *Adversus Judaeos* are several objections to the Jewish religion. Tertullian claims that Christians have taken over from the Jews as the chosen people of God because of their denial of Jesus. Under this "New Covenant" circumcisions, observance of the Sabbath, and Temple sacrifices are no longer required. This overwhelmingly includes the Passover celebration that embraces sacrifices. Recognizing Jesus as a Jewish patriarch born on Passover would not help in this defense. Tertullian was no advocate of philosophy either. He famously said, "What does Athens have to do with Jerusalem?" This referenced the divide between man's thoughts (philosophy) and God's Words (theology). These thoughts profoundly inspired the next generation of leaders.

Despite the logistics of the 2nd century, communication among the different churches was very impressive. Most knew of each other's works. In many ways they often influenced each other. In Carthage lived another Church Father named Cyprian who was influenced by Tertullian. The Church father Jerome noted in his work *Catalogus Scriptorum Ecclesiaticorum*

---

88 Roberts, *The Ante-Nicene Fathers*, Vol. III, 159.

that, "Cyprian never passed a day without reading some portion of Tertullian's works, and used frequently to say, *Give me my master*, meaning Tertullian."[89]

ST. CYPRIAN OF CARTHAGE

St. Cyprian's (ca. 200–ca. 258) early life is a mystery. He was born a pagan into a wealthy Berber (Roman African) family of Carthage. Later in life, he converted to Christianity, giving away a large part of his wealth to the poor of Carthage. Outwardly he possessed great vigor and charisma, which enabled him to become an excellent administrator and famous orator. This African becomes an important part to the integral existence theory not because something he wrote, but because of something attributed to him. This work is today known as the *De Pascha Computus*. Written around 243, the work was either an expansion of the Paschal tables of Hippolytus or based off of the same source material. This is to some extent impressive since Hippolytus was based in Rome during times of great Christian persecution. The aforementioned persecutions led to both men's martyrdoms.

The *De Pascha Computus* is an important primary source for the birth of Jesus, and the only one linking it to the creation account in Genesis. Although Passover is not mentioned by name, the Torah indicates that its seven days are on the same dates as the seven days of creation. According to the writing, the anniversary of creation coincides with the spring equinox. At the time this was March 25/26 in the Jewish calendar; the Church Fathers believed this was March 25. But, Jesus is not born on March 25 in this analogy. He is born on March 28, the fourth day of creation/Passover and

---

89 Ibid, 5.

Chapter 2

the day God created the Sun. The passage reads:

> O the splendid and divine providence of the Lord, that on that day, even the very day on which the sun was made, the 28 March, a Wednesday, Christ should be born. For this reason Malachi the prophet, speaking about him to the people, fittingly said, "Unto you shall the sun of righteousness arise, and healing is in his wings.[90]

Contributing to the downfall of Jewish holidays, like Passover, being celebrated in Christianity was some Christian's desire to move away from honoring Full-Moon phases. On lunar cycles, Susan Roll notes in *Toward the Origins of Christmas*:

> Christians in the third and fourth centuries were highly sensitive to charges that as a result of the lunar connections with the date of Easter they were merely worshipping the sun and moon, charges by among others, the Manichaeans.[91]

Sometime between the time of Tertullian to St. Cyprian, Christians began to make a connection among Jesus and the Sun. This became official when Constantine the Great proclaimed December 25 the official date of Christmas. The Pseudo-Cyprian *De Pascha Computus* may have aided to the desire for a Christmas that occurred during a solar event, the winter solstice. This may have been because Christians wanted to distance themselves from the Talmud and Passover, which follows the spring equinox. Another well-traveled African may have further assisted this belief.

---

90 Roll, *Toward the Origins of Christmas*, 82. The verse reference is from Mal 3:20.
91 Ibid, 76.

SEXTUS JULIUS AFRICANUS

Julius Africanus' (ca. 160–ca. 240) background is little known. He may have been a Libyan philosopher. However, some scholars claim he was of Roman descent. Africanus claims himself a native of Jerusalem –which some scholars believe to be his birthplace. He traveled to Greece and Rome and went to Alexandria to study at the catechetical school sometime around the year 215. He knew Greek, Latin, and Hebrew. At one time he had been a soldier and a pagan, but wrote all his works after his conversion to Christianity. He addressed Origin personally as "dear brother." This indicates that he may have been a priest. As a close acquaintance of Origin, he was aware of Clement's writings. His five books of *Chronography* closely imitates Clement's dating in the *Stromata*.

The *Chronography* is a very difficult writing to decipher. In this writing Africanus introduced a theological variant to the popular March 25 birth of Jesus. Joseph F. Kelly best sums this up by stating:

> Sextus believed Jesus had been born precisely nine months later on December 25. This enabled Sextus to keep the sun imagery in an effective way. According to the Julian calendar, December 25 was the winter solstice, the shortest day of the year, when the sun was the weakest. Every day thereafter it grew stronger and stronger, just as a baby would.[92]

Africanus becomes important to the integral existence theory because he is one of the early Church Fathers who

---

92 Kelly, Joseph F. "The Birth of Christmas." *Baylor University.*
https://www.baylor.edu/content/services/document.php/159119.pdf.

Chapter 2

mentions March 25 as an important day in the Judeo-Christian religion. March 25 was named by different Fathers for the first day of creation, the spring equinox, Passover, the Nativity, and the Conception. This depended on the purpose for each Father's writing. Africanus' choice for a March 25 Conception may have been a compromise intended to please those who were worshiping a Passover Christmas while moving Christmas to a day that honored the Sun. This allowed it to compete with the other popular winter pagan feasts: the cult of Sol Invictus, the veneration of a Persian virility deity named Mithra, and the festival of Saturnalia.[93] By the time of St. Augustine, March 25 became the date of choice for the Conception, and the Passover birth of Jesus was now longer in favor.

Africanus also provides some early 3rd information on the Magi and the Star of Bethlehem. Although this account may be based on local legend and myths, it can still contain some truths. On the Magi he stated, "Christ first of all became known from Persia. For nothing escapes the learned jurists of that country, who investigate all things with the utmost care."[94] He further reports that when they arrived to Jerusalem, the Jews said, "How is this, say they, that wise men of the Persians are here, and that along with them there is this strange stellar phenomenon?"[95]

ST. AUGUSTINE OF HIPPO

St. Augustine of Hippo (354–430 CE), whose writings

---

93 Ibid.
94 Alexander Roberts, et al., *The Ante-Nicene Fathers: Translations of the Writings of the Fathers down to A.D. 325*. Vol. VI, (Grand Rapids (MI): Eerdmans, 1957), 128.
95 Ibid, 129.

and theologies are often listed by historians as one of the greatest influences on Western Christianity, was an early Church Father who applied dates to the lifetime of Jesus. Augustine was born in 354 CE in the small village of Thagaste in the Roman province of Numidia (today Souk Ahras in the modern country of Algeria). His mother, Monica, was Christian while his father, Patricius, had the reputation of being a hard-drinking womanizer who was prone to an occasional violent outburst. Augustine appears to have a difficult time when choosing which of his parent's legacy to fulfill in life. Christians of all eras can relate to his honesty when writing about matters of sin, and how difficult it can be to overcome the temptations of evil.

Throughout his life, Augustine struggled with the dreadful habits he picked up during those days of his youth, when he notably said, "Lord, give me chastity—but not yet." Later in life, before his conversion, he had a mistress and son out of wedlock. The matter of living a life of chastity was considered necessary for any Christian Church leader during his era, the pre-Protestant, and he defiantly struggled over the concept. However, in the end, the persistence of his overbearing mother was rewarded, and he converted to Christianity.

As in sin, he threw himself in one hundred percent to the task at hand, becoming a prominent Church bishop and prolific writer. Today, through his writings, he is remembered for helping Christians through a disturbing time in history. Augustine died of plague during the pagan Vandals siege of Hippo.

Augustine's works *City of God*, *De Trinitate*, and *Confessions* provide insight to the turbulent world in which he lived, and his concepts of "original sin" and "just war" influenced Christian thought and politics well into modern times and are

Chapter 2

subjects of debate even today.[96]

Augustine believed that Jesus lived a perfect life not only spiritually but also mathematically. Augustine obsessed over senary numbers, those who sums are perfect in Pythagorean arithmetic.[97] He wrote about the number six because it was not only the sum of 1+2+3 but also the number of days God used when creating the Earth, hence a perfect mathematical and Holy number. He speaks in *The City of God* of the order inherent in the universe:

> We must not despise the science of numbers, which, in many passages of Holy Scripture, is found to be of eminent service to the careful interpreter. Neither has it been without reason numbered among God's praises, "Thou hast ordered all things in number, and measure, and weight."[98]

Augustine even suggests that God intended the lifetime of Christ to be accordingly numbered; thus, his time on Earth was also mathematically perfect. Abbé Louis Marie Olivier Duchesne (1843–1922), the first modern scholar to theorize

---

[96] Augustine did not invent the theories of original sin and just war, but he perfected them. According to Augustine, original sin was transmitted from one generation to the next through sexual intercourse at the time of conception. This meant that newborns were already with sin because of the lust of their parents. Salvation through Jesus was important and the only way to cleanse even newborns was through baptism. The idea of just war was intended to justify war under a noble cause. Augustine said in *City of God*, "But, say they, the wise man will wage Just Wars. As if he would not all the rather lament the necessity of just wars, if he remembers that he is a man; for if they were not just he would not wage them, and would therefore be delivered from all war."

[97] Senary numbers, also known as base-6 or heximal math, uses 6 as its base. In this system all the prime numbers other than 2 and 3, when expressed in senary, have 1 or 5 as their final digit.

[98] Augustine, *Basic Writings of Saint Augustine*, vol. 2 (New York: Random House, 1948) 173.

that the idea of the Nativity and Passion occurring on the same day of the year had been common among many early Church Fathers, points to Augustine as proof. Duchesne wrote extensively about Church worship and holidays in his book *Christian Worship: Its Origin and Evolution.*

Duchesne theorized that Christmas was at first a festival unique to the Roman Church that was designed to replace a pagan festival. Christians wished to replace the holiday honoring the Sun god Mithras, which commenced after the shortest day of the year, the winter solstice. During this time, Romans exchanged gifts honoring their gods. Christians wanting to compete with the pagans turned to the birth of Jesus, which was thought to have occurred around the same time, as an alternative to the Sun worshipers. He used the following quote from Augustine's *De Trinitate* as evidence that early Christians drew a symbolical meaning from integral calendar calculations:

> For He is believed to have been conceived on the 25th of March, upon which day also He suffered; so the womb of the Virgin, in which He was conceived, where no one of mortals was begotten, corresponds to the new grave in which He was buried, wherein was never man laid, neither before nor since. But He was born, according to tradition, upon December the 25th.[99]

Even though Augustine's date of March 25 for the Passion can be easily disproved through the use of modern Moon-phase data produced by the National Aeronautics and Space Administration (NASA), it does show us through the

---

99 Ibid., 736

Chapter 2

writings of Church elders that many of them thought about the Passion and Conception of Jesus occurring on the same date of the year. Several years earlier, Clement of Alexandria, one of the best-known and important Church scholars of the early Christian church, indicated that some Christians were possibly celebrating the Nativity and Crucifixion on the same day.

LATER GREEK INFLUENCES

What one trait that many Jewish rabbis and Church Fathers did have in common was an approach to interpreting the word of God. And neither could ignore the popularity of the Greek language. Koine, or common, Greek was the dominant language in the region ever since the conquests of Alexander the Great. Ironically, while it became the language of choice for commercial and cultural communication throughout the Mediterranean world, it was also subject to alterations from the same foreigners who used it, especially in vocabulary and syntax. Not only were the Greeks philosophical, but their philosophical insights are sprinkled throughout their language.

According to Paul Tillich, remarking on the Greek concept of time, "The Greek had two words, *chronos* and *kairos*. Chronos is clock time, time which is measured ... Kairos is not the quantitative time of the clock, but the qualitative time of the occasion, the right time.[100]

The Old Testament was circulated among the Jews residing in Egypt in the Koine Greek translation, known as Septuagint, during the third and second centuries BCE. Unfortunately, its styles range from authentic translations of

---

100 Tillich, *A History of Christian Thought*, 1.

the Jewish language to false literal renderings that had to be revised later word-for-word. The Koine Greek of the New Testament, like the Old Testament, was similarly diverse. According to Kurt Eichenwald, "The Bible is a very human book. It was written, assembled, copied and translated by people. That explains the flaws, the contradictions and the theological disagreements in its pages. Once that is understood, it is possible to find out which parts of the Bible were not in the earliest Greek manuscripts, which are the bad translations, and what one book says in comparison to another, and then try to discern the message for yourself."[101]

Greek influences on Judea were felt shortly after Alexander the Great's conquests of Judea and Persia and lasted into the time of King Herod. Michael Avi-Yonah notes that Jews did accept some things Greek. He notes, "The Jews, on the other hand, seem to have accepted the Macedonian suzerain willingly; the name Alexander was admitted to the Jewish onomasticon, indicating that it might thenceforth be given to Jewish children."[102] The many accomplishments of the Greeks were not short of amazing when one thinks of the small size of the nation, lack of suitable farmland, and incredible odds against them when pitted against the prodigious Persian Empire. The geographic landscape may have created individual city-states, but when required, the city-states were able to muster a respectable fighting force.

Simply put, in ancient times Greek culture was in fashion—and no ruler could deny the accomplishments of Alexander the Great. Despite the respect the Jews had for

---

101 Kurt Eichenwald. 2015. "The Bible; So misunderstood it's a Sin." *Newsweek Global* 164, no 1; 24-41. *Business Source Premier* EBSCO*host* (accessed August 27, 2017).
102 Michael Avi-Yonah, ed., *A History of the Holy Land* (London: Weidenfeld and Nicolson, 1969), 110.

Chapter 2

him, however, they tried to resist Greek culture as much as possible, much more than the Egyptians and Persians. For Jews, restrictions on diet and polytheistic worship reminded them of the primary importance of God and to not adhere too much to any culture other than their own. This resistance turned into violence when Antiochus IV inherited the Seleucid portion of the Greek Empire in 175 BCE.

The Jews' refusal to adhere to Antiochus IV's spread of Greek ideas resulted in the robbing of the Temple and the massacre of thousands in Jerusalem by his forces, marking his place in history as a tyrannical persecutor. In 167 BCE, Antiochus IV campaigned once and for all to exterminate Judaism. Religious traditions such as circumcision and observing the Sabbath were forbidden and punishable by death. In retaliation, a Jewish priest named Mattathias of the house of Hasmon went into hiding with his five sons. Together they lead a series of successful raids, and by 160 BCE the leaders of the house of Hasmon were accepted rulers of Judea under the leadership of Mattathias's second son, Simon Maccabeus. Interestingly, the Hasmoneans appealed successfully to the Roman Senate in 161 BCE for protection against the aggression of Ptolemy and the Seleucids. Over time, the Romans increased their role in Judea to the point that Judea became part of the empire. Deals such as the Hasmoneans made with the Romans may have ensured temporary power for them, but it also opened the door for future Roman meddling.

The legacy of the ancient Greek city-states and Alexander the Great's empire reverberated long after the decline of both in the ancient world. This was no different than what occurred within the Roman Empire. The gods and ideas of democracy of Rome were similar to those of their Greek neighbors, and Greek influence over Roman culture also extended over a vast amount of time.

The Greeks had a colony on the island we know today as Sicily. The city of Syracuse was colonized as a port city in 734 BCE by the Corinthians, led by the aristocrat Archias. Over time, the city dominated the coastal plain and surrounding hill country. The next five hundred years brought civil wars and conflict with the Carthaginians and a back-and-forth domination of the area. Ironically, it was when the city finally became an ally of the Carthaginians that the Romans besieged and took Syracuse. After the fall, the city became a provincial capital.

The Roman triumph over Syracuse in 212 BCE brought the treasures of conquest back to Rome, including Greek statues and paintings, where they were quickly copied in style. According to the *Oxford Illustrated History of the Roman World*, the victories brought not only new art but also artists back to Rome as part of the spoils of war, and both art and artists were in demand.[103] Wealthy Romans craved original Greek art, which was viewed as a status symbol. Unlike other nations, Greece was far more successful in conquering the locals with its culture than its armies and navy.

Before long, Rome was looking to gain influence in Judea. When the Roman general Pompey (106–48 BCE) conquered Jerusalem in 63 BCE, he had two goals in mind— establish Roman supremacy in the East and reestablish Hellenism by bolstering the Greek city-states in the region. He was a member of the First Triumvirate of Rome along with Julius Caesar (100–44 BCE) and Crassus (112?–53 BCE), who is best remembered for defeating Spartacus. The Triumvirate was intended to keep the peace by splitting the empire, but it was

---

103 John Boardman, Jasper Griffin, and Oswyn Murray, eds., *The Oxford Illustrated History of the Roman World* (Oxford: Oxford University Press, 2001), 362.

Chapter 2

soon apparent that the empire was not big enough for the three egomaniacs. Civil war broke out between the factions of Julius Caesar and Pompey after the death of Crassus, who met his demise, along with most of his army, at the hands of the Parthians. At the time, the Parthians were the Roman Empire's greatest rival in the region, and the foremost hindrance to further Roman expansion into Asia-Minor. Rulers in the region had to select which was the best political power to align with. This was all the more confusing when Rome was embroiled in one of its many civil wars.

Such was the case when Antipater, ruler of Idumea, allied himself first with Pompey and, strategically, later with Caesar after Pompey's defeat. When Antipater was killed in 43 BCE, soon after Caesar's assignation, his sons Herod and Phasael were named tetrarchs ("rulers of fourths") of Galilee by Marcus Antonius (Mark Antony). Marcus was a friend of Caesar and theoretical an ally of Lepidus and Octavian in the Second Triumvirate, another group of Roman egomaniacs determined to destroy one another. The Parthians, main rivals of Rome in the region at the time, invaded Judea in 40 BCE in an attempt to help the Hasmoneans to regain power. After Phasael was captured and committed suicide, Herod seized the opportunity to achieve power by traveling to Rome and getting himself named king of Judea by the Roman Senate. When Marcus Antonius and his army overpowered the Parthians in 37 BCE, Herod's title became official.

Herod continued to support Greek culture by building Hellenistic temples and introducing Greek-style games and races. He sent his children to Rome to honor the Emperor Augustus and to earn an education. In return, Augustus increased Herod's kingdom. Despite his close ties to the emperor, Herod still had to compete with Greek-influenced officials in the eastern parts of the empire and quell the conventional Jews, who disliked all things Greek. The memories of the reign of Antiochus IV were still painful with many Jews, and revolts against the Roman establishment by Greek influences were always among Herod's greatest concerns. Even though Herod was Jewish first, he knew the survival of his kingdom depended on the uneasy, and sometime brutally enforced, peace between the conventional Jews and those who supported the Greeks, while adhering always to the interests of Rome. And always he had to be worried about the Parthians, as well. These dynamics placed Herod in an awkward position for his entire reign. [104]

Greek influence continued over the Jews into the times of Jesus. Some Jews are referred to as Grecians (Greek-speaking Jews) in Acts 6:1, and later in Acts 9:29, Grecians attempted to murder Paul when he tried to engage them in Christian debate. A sort of love-hate relationship developed between the Jews and Greeks. The Jews, who were forbidden by God to worship idols, were backed into a corner when it came to artistic creativity and could not help but be influenced by the Greeks.

Christians quelled the tensions between some of their own people and the Greeks by appointing the Greek-influenced leader Stephen as a deacon. Even Paul at times used a Greek style of writing to influence the many Greek-speaking Gentiles. According to *Nelson's Illustrated Encyclopedia of Bible Facts*,

---

104 The Magi from the Nativity story may have been from Parthia, an ancient kingdom centered in Iran near the Caspian Sea, or close by. The Parthians were an independent people until Cyrus the Great of Persia conquered them. But by 235 BCE, they had regained their independence and over time came to rule a large empire in the east on the edge of the Roman Empire until a Persian revolt in 224 CE overthrew the Parthian rulers. Perhaps the Parthians greatest military victory was the Battle of Carrhae against the Romans in modern-day Turkey led by Crassus. Despite being outnumbered, the Parthians used their superior horsemanship and skill with the bow and arrow to destroy the Roman infantry.

Chapter 2

It seems Paul absorbed a considerable amount of Greek wisdom during his years in Tarus, for he was able to express the gospel in terms that the Greek mind could really understand.[105]

CLASHES BETWEEN GREEK AND ROMAN CULTURE

If Christianity were to survive as a religion, it most likely would need the support of the Greek world. This became more than evident in 176 CE, when the Roman Emperor Marcus Aurelius established four chairs of philosophy at Athens, giving the teachings of Platonism, Aristotelianism, Stoicism, and Epicureanism official recognition. If the schools of philosophy had anything to worry about, it was that philosophy was becoming more of a popular fad than something that was essential to happiness in life. Ironically, Christianity would bring this about. Equally ironic was Clement's instinct to fight philosophy with philosophy, and his loss of credibility during the Middle Ages because of it. It must be taken into account that Jesus lived at a time when Greek philosophy, and philosophy in general, were highly influential. Many of Jesus' teachings have philosophical meaning, or are at least so regarded by some of the authors of the New Testament.

Greek language and ideas remained in fashion until the rise of Christianity in Rome. While Christianity had become the primary religion of the Roman Empire under Constantine, and the center of the empire was moved from Rome to Constantinople, it was Rome that became the center of the Church. Western churches accepted the Pope as the leader of the religion, while churches in the East considered him only another bishop with no more power than their own bishops.

---

105 J. I. Packer, Merrill C. Tenney, and William White, eds., *Nelsons Illustrated Encyclopedia of Bible Facts* (Nashville: T. Nelson, 1995), 160.

Western churches gradually changed the Greek canons into Latin. Other areas of Church policy became issues. Rulers in the East—Russia for example—had far more independence from the Church, and Church protocol was moving in different directions between the two regions. These subtle changes over time slowly created a rift between the Eastern and Western churches. The Greek-speaking churches of the Byzantine Empire, which became the Orthodox Church, officially split from the Catholic Church in the schism of 1054. Along with this slow split between East and West came an increasing disdain in the West for many things Greek, including philosophy and scientific reason.

CONCLUSION

Hillel the Elder went on to become one of the most esteemed Jewish scholars of his time. Likewise, Augustine also became one of the most respected early Church Fathers. Although living about 400 years apart, their approaches toward their respective religions were similar. Rabbis and Church Fathers both believed that their interpretations of their holy books were given to them by God. Both guided their respective religions into the diverse directions they believed God wanted them to. By using allegorical interpretations[106] of the Bible, the rabbis and Fathers were able to find various levels of meaning and new insights. Some were more willing to focus on these areas, and some were more orthodox. Clement in particular was not afraid to write about things as he saw them, while Rabbi Yahushua was more conservative in his

---

106 The practice of allegory is much older than the first century CE. The Stoics employed it in interpreting ancient Greek literature, and in Alexandria, Philo applied it to Jewish scriptures. An allegory is a story or poem that can be interpreted to reveal a moral or political lesson.

Chapter 2

interpretations.

Rabbi Yahushua was the first to remark in writing on the ancient oral concept of prophets being born and dying during Passover. Since he was born after Jesus' death, he would have been aware that it occurred at Passover. Other than Yahushua noting the integral idea, not much more was written or said about the topic. Why did it receive less attention? Either Yahushua believed that Jesus was not the Messiah, Passover death notwithstanding, or it was best for Judaism that Christians not make more use of the integral idea. Both sides viewed conversions and marketing as important for survival. In any event, the topic of the integral existence of Jesus received little attention from either Christians or Jews. Aiding to the separation was Tertullian's criticism over some Jewish religious practices, including sacrifices. Julius Africanus and the Pseudo-Cyprian author of *De Pascha Computus* also contributed to the rift by emphasizing the importance of the Sun over the Passover Moon during the birth of Jesus.

Augustine also had the opportunity to link the two faiths closer. In *De Trinities, Book 4, Chapter 5*, he stated that Jesus was conceived on March 25. However, he lists no source, mentioning only that it was based on belief: "For He is believed to have been conceived on the 25th of March." On the topic of Christmas, he mentions only that its date was based on tradition. He states, "But, He was born, according to tradition, upon December 25th."[107] At the time it set the official Church date for Christmas on December 25, or nine months after March 25. Augustine, a man who obsessed over numbers and time, did not mention the integral concept, or

---

107 Augustine, *On Trinity*, trans. Arthur West Haddan, in From Nicene and Post-Nicene Fathers, First Series, vol. 3, ed., Philip Schaff (Buffalo, NY: Christian Literature Publishing Co., 1887), revised and edited for New Advent by Kevin Knight, www.newadvent.org/fathers/130104.htm. (Accessed August 26, 2017).

any reference to the Talmud. It must be kept in mind that by the time of Augustine, the Talmud was on the Christian banned-book list.

Clement also had the opportunity to mention the Talmud alongside the beliefs of the Basilidians, who recognized the birth and death of Jesus as occurring on the same date of the calendar. But, as with Yehoshua, precise evidence is lacking as to why Clement did not mention it. He might not have been aware of the verse in the Talmud, or perhaps he chose not to compare a Jewish book to Christian sources. Whatever the reason, he did not have a problem comparing the Bible to Greek mythology to prove the Bible older and more valid.

Clement did write of the relationship of Jesus to important events in Jewish traditions, such as the birth of Adam or the life of Moses. In the *Stromata,* Clement draws parallels between the events in Jesus' life, significant dates in Jewish history, and important occurrences in the Roman Empire. Although Clement was a Christian during a time of great by the Roman authorities, it did not stop him from matching significant dates in Roman history with what he considered important Judeo-Christian events. This was not unusual; many subjects of the Roman Empire used the reigns of the emperors to mark significant non-Roman dates.

However, Clement's best student, Origen, and his likeminded followers downplayed the significance of birthdays. This was mainly because the greatest threat to Christianity in his lifetime, the Roman Empire, celebrated the emperor's birthday, as well as astrology, which requires knowing one's birthday, and was becoming more popular. Another tradition in Christianity at the time was to celebrate the day a saint died, mostly through martyrdom, instead of his birth.

In another century, the birthdate of Jesus became more important, and Christians would more and more come to

Chapter 2

regard his birth, free of sin, as a gift from God that deserved to be celebrated. However, this would not take place until a century after the actual birth of Christ, and that passage of time only made finding an actual birth date more difficult. By then, Christian leaders were not interested in understanding the Jewish calendar better.

Finding evidence from the time Christians did celebrate lunar cycles is challenging, but not impossible. In 1551, a real-life Indiana Jones moment occurred when a 3rd century statue of Hippolytus of Rome was unearthed in Rome that proves the importance of Passover celebrations to Christians of that time. The statue indicates that Jesus was born during Passover.

Figure 2.1 Statue of Hippolytus of Rome

St. Hippolytus statue, courtesy of www.catholicworldnews.com

CHAPTER 3
THE JEWISH CALENDAR AND PASSOVER

Father Raymond E. Brown (1928–1998), American Roman Catholic priest, was one of first modern theologians to attempt to date the Crucifixion. By using methods similar to his, scholars today have an excellent formula for calculating a plausible solution to this question. Brown was regarded as one of the preeminent biblical scholars of the United States during his lifetime. His theories and work were groundbreaking because he always did an excellent job of interpreting the biblical texts, on the assumption that they are candidates for historical reconstruction. This was very similar to what some of the early Church Fathers did.

The Bible states that Jesus was crucified during the time of Passover, an ancient Jewish holiday that has not changed much over history. Since the Crucifixion occurred during Passover, we know that half of the integral idea is true.

Chapter 3

According to Brown, the Gospels all point to some basic facts: The discussion of this issue makes sense only if we assume that the evangelists are reliable for the minimal chronological references that they all supply, namely, that Jesus died in Jerusalem on a day before the Sabbath at Passover time during the prefecture of Pontius Pilate.[108]

Keys to determining this date would include finding the day of the week or the date of the month, evaluating the evidence that the canonical books provide, and understanding the Jewish calendar and celebration dates. The investigation of the Crucifixion will be examined in Chapter 7, but the intricate workings of the Jewish calendar must come first.

This thesis in this book practices the recommendations of Brown by not only examining the written accounts of the evangelists but also the known scientific data. Brown's written account of the dating of the Crucifixion is significant because scholars know who Jesus was and can easily place dates, after proper research, on some of the other events Brown wrote of in his historiography of the Crucifixion.

THE PASSOVER CELEBRATION

The Jewish calendar has 12 months but is lunar based. The first day of the month begins when the first sliver of the new Moon is viewable after dark. The problem with strictly lunar calendars is that there are approximately 12.4 lunar months in every solar year, so a 12-month lunar calendar is about 11 days shorter than a solar year and a 13-month lunar

---

108 Raymond E. Brown, *The Death of the Messiah: From Gethsemane to the Grave: A Commentary on the Passion Narratives in the Four Gospels*, vol. 2 (New York: Doubleday, 1994), 1350.

The Jewish Calendar and Passover

calendar is about 19 days longer than a solar year. The months drift around the seasons on such a calendar: on a 12-month lunar calendar, the Jewish month of Nissan, which is intended to occur during the spring equinox, would occur 11 days earlier in the season each year, eventually occurring in the winter, the fall, the summer, and then the spring again. On a 13-month lunar calendar, the same thing would happen in the other direction, and faster. To compensate for this drift, the Jewish calendar uses a 12-month lunar calendar with an extra month occasionally added.

The month of Nissan occurs 11 days earlier each year for two or three years, and then is moved forward 30 days, balancing out the drift. In ancient times, this month was added by observation: The Sanhedrin observed the conditions of the weather, the crops and the livestock, and if these were not sufficiently advanced to be considered "spring," then the Sanhedrin inserted an additional month into the calendar to make sure that Pesach (Passover) would occur in the spring. It was referred to in the Torah as Chag he-Aviv, or the Festival of Spring.

The Jews wanted to keep Passover on the first Full-Moon, or Nissan 15, after the spring equinox, hence the extra months in certain years to make up for the differences in the solar and lunar cycles. According to Mordell Klein, Passover is the most ancient of all Jewish festivals and extremely popular, both a national and an agricultural festival. Every spring for a period of seven days (seven in Israel, eight in the diaspora) Jews commemorate the anniversary of the Exodus from Egypt over three thousand years ago.[109] Passover celebrates God's sparing of the eldest son during the plagues of Egypt and the birth of Israel after the Exodus. It is also a time of prayer for a

---

109 Mordell Klein, *Passover* (New York: Leon Amiel, 1973), 1.

Chapter 3

good harvest. The Jews were not astronomical experts, they did not have the knowledge or instruments of the Greek or Egyptians, but their calendar and careful observations of the sky kept Passover festivals on a fairly accurate schedule. Even though lunar cycles and solar cycles are totally unrelated, both calendars can be compared when calculating Passover, since the spring equinox, a solar calendar marker, was used by the Jews as a starting point in determining the time of Passover. Aspects of both calendars, such as phases of the Moon and days of the week can therefore be used to research the Gregorian date of the Crucifixion of Jesus.

ANCIENT PASSOVER CELEBRATIONS

According to the Book of Exodus, Moses, on a divine mission from God, asked Pharaoh to release the Israelites from bondage. When Pharaoh refused, God responded with a number of plagues. The ten plagues of Egypt told in Exodus included the Nile turning into blood, frogs, lice, insects, pestilence (killing of the livestock), boils on man and beast, hail and fire, locusts, darkness, and the death of the firstborn. It was after the last plague that Pharaoh released the Israelites. This plague is the one from which Passover takes its name, when the angel of death passed over the Jewish households that had marked their doorposts with the blood of a lamb, as God had instructed, thus sparing the firstborn.

During the first century CE, Jewish observers informed the Sanhedrin when the first sign of a new Moon became visible. This was most likely affirmed by more than one witness for accuracy. The Sanhedrin comprised the ancient Jewish Supreme Court of the land, meeting in the Hall of Hewn Stones inside of the Temple. According to tradition, they were given the Oral Torah after Moses, the elders, and

The Jewish Calendar and Passover

the prophets. Besides having the task of setting the calendar, they also decided difficult cases involving capital punishment. However, under Roman rule, the Sanhedrin lost their authority to give the death penalty.

After the Sanhedrin were informed of a new Moon by nighttime observers, they then sent messengers throughout Judea announcing that the new month had begun. Several factors may have caused inaccuracies, such as cloudy or rainy nights, or starting times of the phases of the Moon that occurred during the day. Nevertheless, they were still in charge of determining the commencement of the new month and the celebrations that followed. There were two Sanhedrins, the Great Sanhedrin or Supreme Court in Jerusalem and the Lesser Sanhedrins chambered in municipalities throughout Judea. In the New Testament, it was the Great Sanhedrin who conspired to put Jesus to death but did not have the Roman authority of executing prisoners. Hence, the sentence of death for Jesus derived from Pontius Pilate's final decision. It should also be noted that the New Testament mentions Nicodemus and Joseph of Arimathea, members of the Sanhedrin, as followers of Jesus, so not all of the Sanhedrin were in favor of Jesus' sentence of death.

Before the first Passover, as mentioned, every Israelite household was commanded to slaughter a lamb and mark their doorposts with its blood to protect their firstborn. As Klein points out, following this instruction was not without risk: "His was an act of faith because the lamb was a holy animal for the Egyptians who could be expected to be provoked in rather the same way that Hindus in India are when Muslims there slaughter cows."[110]

Over time, the Passover celebration became more

---

110 Ibid, 12.

Chapter 3

elaborate. The sacrifice was to be a year-old male sheep or goat without any defects. On the fourteenth day of the month, all of Israel was to slaughter the sacrificial lamb at twilight. After the slaughter, the Israelites were given strict instructions for the preparation of the Passover meal from the sacrifice. That same night the whole lamb was to be roasted over fire until it was completely cooked, and was consumed. Any meat left over was to be burned the next morning. Complementing the meat were bitter herbs and unleavened bread. The yeastless bread was to be consumed for the next seven days of the Passover festival, with the harsh penalty of excommunication for those who broke the command. These rules and regulations were still in effect during Jesus' lifetime. The fact that a one-year-old male sheep was to be sacrificed has an uncanny similarity with the story of Jesus. His ministry lasted one year according to the Gospels, and both were killed during the Passover feast.

The Temple in Jerusalem was designed for the sacrifices, which were not to be brought elsewhere. Since all males were to appear three times yearly before God, one being Passover, Jerusalem was densely crowed during the festival. The Jewish historian Josephus estimated that 3,000,000 Jews attended the last Passover just before the war with Romans in 70 CE.[111] However, it must also be noted that Josephus's numbers were sometimes inflated. Whatever the true number, it most likely was a large gathering.

After the destruction of the Temple by the Romans, the Passover sacrifice could no longer be brought there ending the practice. However, a controversy developed, and still exists today, with many Jews arguing that a sacrifice should still be offered, even without a Temple. Klein notes:

---

111 Ibid, 25.

The Jewish Calendar and Passover

Although the Temple, the focal point of Jewish worship, was destroyed, the rabbis ensured that Jewish religious practice would continue. They stressed the idea that every man was to turn himself into a temple; prayers were to be offered up instead of sacrifices.[112]

Once again, there is an uncanny similarity between Jesus and the sacrificial lamb. Jesus leaves the Earth after his Crucifixion, and the sacrificing of the lamb ceased after the destruction of the Temple by the Romans. Christians waited for the return of Jesus, while some Jews waited for the rebuilding of the Temple to begin sacrificing again.

The hit and miss method in the calculation of the calendar would not last. Most scholars agree that by the time of the second century BCE, a Greek mathematician named Hipparchus was able to calculate the positions of the Moon and Sun with an instrument known as an astrolabe. It was not until around 127 CE that Ptolemy of Alexandria provided models and tables that could be used to calculate the position of the Moon, Sun, and some planets. His scientific treatises later became of continued importance to Arabic and European astronomers. However, even by the fourth century the Jews, because of their lack of interest or desire to have an accurate calendar, were still in need of one based on astronomical calculations.

MODERN PASSOVER CELEBRATIONS

Today, Passover dates are no longer based solely on traditions and visual observations. In the middle of the fourth

---

112 Ibid, 28

Chapter 3

century CE, Hillel II wanted a calendar that informed Jews outside of Judea when to begin Jewish festivals. The system of sending messengers over hostile territory was not only dangerous but also unreliable. Hillel II used mathematical and astronomical calculations to establish the modern Jewish calendar. Graetz informs us that Hillel's calendar, published in 359 CE, was most likely based on an even older one designed by Samuel bar Abba (Samuel).[113]

Samuel (ca. 165–257 CE), a Jewish Talmudist, lived in Nahardea, Babylonia, and was a teacher of halakha (Jewish law), and an astronomer, judge, and physician. He learned many astronomical techniques from Persian sages, believing in the importance of knowledge of the heavens in order to become closer to God. Samuel used his astronomical expertise to design a calendar for the purpose of informing the Babylonian Jews, far from Judea, when the exact days of Jewish festivals fell. However, he kept the calendar secret from the public out of respect for the Elders of the Sanhedrin and time-honored tradition, so it was not until Hillel II that a usable system was finally in place.

After the destruction of Herod's Temple, what to do about the sacrifices came into question. During that time, the Sanhedrin were led by Gamaliel II. He decreed that the sacrifices should continue in family homes, with each family sacrificing its own goat or sheep. An article in the Israeli newspaper *Haaretz*, explains the eventual demise of the practice:

> Other rabbis believed that the Passover sacrifice, like all the other sacrifices, could only be conducted by the priests in the Temple and that like the other

---
113 Graetz, *History of the Jews*, 574.

The Jewish Calendar and Passover

sacrifices, should not be conducted until the Messiah comes and the Temple is rebuilt. . . . Within about two generations, the practice ceased when the anti-sacrifice camp assumed control and threatened to excommunicate those who practiced it. So, sometime in the second century C.E., Jews stopped the practice.[114]

Today, in place of the sacrifices, a set of scriptural and Rabbinic passages relating to the Passover sacrifices are recited after the Mincha (afternoon prayer) on Nissan 14, and a lamb-shank bone or chicken wing, known as the zeroa, which is not eaten, is placed on the Passover Seder plate to remind the Jews of the sacrifices from the time of the Temple. However, some modern Jews are attempting to bring back the ritual sacrifices.

Shortly before the 2017 Passover, Jack Moore reported in an article for *Newsweek* that Israeli police and veterinary services oversaw the first ritual sacrifice to occur within the walls of the old section of Jerusalem in nearly 2,000 years. The activist behind the ritual, the Temple Mount Institute, paid 36,000 shekels to proceed with the event. Although the sheep was sacrificed in the Jewish Quarter, near the Hurva Synagogue, it was a rehearsal for an actual sacrifice that was to occur during the following Passover near the Temple Mount. Moore states:

> In recent years there has been a growing movement from within the Israeli religious right for Jews to be allowed to perform rituals and pray at the site, regardless of the status quo. The religious Jewish

---

[114] Elon Gilad, "Why Jews Stopped Sacrificing Lambs and Baby Goats for Passover," April 24, 2016, http://www.haaretz.com/jewish/features/.premium-1.716147.

Chapter 3

activists see the sacrificial killing of goats and sheep as a mark of their claim of ownership of the religious site.[115]

The police did stop the group from conducting the planned Passover sacrifice, but only time will tell if support for the group continues to increase or decreases. Despite the desires of some Jews to return to the times of sacrifice, in a similar article on the *Times of Israel* website, an Israeli-based news service, many readers responded negatively in the comments section. Calling the ritual, "barbaric in nature" and admonishing that "as long as there are those who would bring animal sacrifices, Hashem (God) will not allow the rebuilding of His Bais Hamikdah (temple)."[116]

In the future, if there are more movements for Christians to observe Jewish celebrations such as Passover, for example, then they must decide how authentically to observe them. This might be a challenge for some. Many would agree that the killing of animals for sacrifice is immoral while others would argue that the Bible commands it. The question then remains, Was the commandment by men voicing God or was it by God through the voice of men? Perhaps the best way to decide would be to ask what Jesus would want of us. We live in a new age, and perhaps some of the old traditions are in need of revision, but some of the old traditions might also need to stay. The use of sacrifices will remain controversial in any attempt to rebuild the Temple.

---

115 Jack Moore, "Why Do Jewish Activists Keep Trying to Sacrifice Goats in Jerusalem's Old City?" *Newsweek*, April 18, 2017, www.newsweek.com/why-do-jewish-activists-keep-trying-sacrifice-goats-jerusalems-old-city-583433.
116 Times of Israel Staff, "In Modern First, Passover Sacrifice to Take Place in Old City," The Times of Israel, April 5, 2017, www.timesofisrael.com/in-first-passover-sacrifice-to-take-place-in-old-city/.

The Jewish Calendar and Passover

LUNAR VS. SOLAR

Today's most widely used calendar, the Gregorian, is solar-based, calculated using the time it takes the Earth to orbit the Sun. The Jewish calendar is based on three astronomical phenomena: the rotation of the Earth about its axis (a day); the revolution of the Moon about the Earth (a month); and the revolution of the Earth about the Sun (a year). These three phenomena are independent of each other, so there is no direct correlation between them.

On average, as we have noted, the Moon revolves around the Earth in about $29\frac{1}{2}$ days. The Earth revolves around the Sun in about $365\frac{1}{4}$ days, that is, about 12.4 lunar months. Extra days, leap days, are added to make up for the difference between the lunar and solar lengths. Since the Jewish calendar cannot have months that are exactly $29\frac{1}{2}$ days long, two Jewish months, Cheshvan and Kislev, have either 29 or 30 days depending on the year. This keeps the first of the month on a New-Moon phase, and the fifteenth on a Full-Moon phase.

Also significant is the Alexandrian Egyptian calendar mentioned in Clement's writings. It began as a lunar calendar, but Egyptians started to use stars instead of just the Sun and the Moon in calculating time, counting up the seconds, minutes, hours, days, weeks, months, years, centuries, and even millennia. They invented a new sidereal calendar, which is considered the oldest invented calendar on Earth. Some argue that this calendar is actually the most accurate one because it depends on the rising of the star Sirius (or Sopdet, as the ancient Egyptians called it) which, as observed from Earth, allows for a more precise measurement than using just the Sun and the Moon. According to H. E. Winlock, "In 2773 BCE he [Djoser, founder of the Third Dynasty] dropped his

Chapter 3

New Year's observations and took up the 365 day year, which actually brought his seasons back into their original places only once again during his whole history."[117] In 238 BCE, Ptolemy III introduced the Alexandrian calendar, a reformed solar calendar. Therefore, the Egyptians were using a solar calendar by 2773 BCE, while the Jews are still using a lunar one.

Clement may have stumbled in the same places that modern scholars do, on the differences between the canonical books. The first three canonical Gospels place the Last Supper as a Passover meal, while John informs us that the Last Supper was the Passover preparation meal (John 19:14). The reasons for this dispute may be that the author of Mark simply produced an error, then the authors of Matthew and Luke used Mark as a source—or perhaps the author of John desired Jesus to become a Passover sacrifice for more dramatic reasons, so facts were slightly altered. Many scholars have suggested that Mark was the first Gospel written, and was then used as a source for Matthew and Luke, so any errors in Mark will most likely appear in Matthew and Luke.

Disagreeing with the synoptic gospels, the Gospel of John informs us that Jesus was tried on the Friday morning before Passover, crucified and entombed that afternoon, hence paralleling the sacrifice blood of the Passover lamb. All the Gospels agree that Jesus later disappeared from the tomb on a Sunday morning, after being crucified on a Friday. It also becomes significant at this point to understand how the Jewish days of the week relate to the Roman Julian calendar. Today the Georgian calendar, although based on the Julian calendar, follows the traditional seven-day Jewish week, not the tradetional Roman week.

---

117 H. E. Winlock, "The Origin of the Ancient Egyptian Calendar." *Proceedings of the American Philosophical Society* 83, no. 3 (1940): 447-64. http://0-www.jstor.org.rosi.unk.edu/stable/985113.

THE DAYS OF THE WEEK

Gartenhaus and Tubis noted the following: "The first day of Rosh Hashanah, the first of Tishri, cannot be on a Sunday, Wednesday, or Friday. (This singular requirement is to satisfy the religious constraints that Hashanah Rabah on the 21st of Tishri cannot fall on the Sabbath, and that Yom Kippur on the 10th of Tishri not fall on a Friday or Sunday. As an aside, it is a consequence of the first of these requirement that Yom Kippur can never fall on a Tuesday."[118]

Passover can fall on any day of the week, which makes finding a date for the Crucifixion easier, since the Gospels tell of a Friday Crucifixion. Leofranc Holford Strevens notes that the week as we observe it today has components from two different calendars: "The week as we know it is the fusion of two conceptually different cycles: the planetary week, originally beginning on Saturday, derived from Hellenistic astrology, and the Judeo-Christian week, properly beginning on Sunday."[119]

The Romans created the yearly universal calendar similar to the one in use today in the Western world. They abandoned the lunar calendar sometime around 400 BCE, changing to a solar calendar. They had an eight-day week, with the last day, the nundinae, being a designated market day. According to Holford-Strevens, "In Roman almanacs the eight days of this cycle were marked with the letters A to H. On the nundinae, country folk went to town, auctions were held, and legal disputes settled."[120]

---

118 Solomon Gartenhaus and Arnold Tubis. "The Jewish Calendar--a Mix of Astronomy and Theology," *Shofar*, no. 2 (2007): 110, *Literature Resource Center*, EBSCO*host*.
119 Leofranc Holford-Strevens, *The History of Time: A Very Short Introduction* (Oxford: Oxford University Press, 2005), 64.
120 E. G. Richards, *Mapping Time: The Calendar and its History* (Oxford, Oxford University Press, 1998), 208.

Chapter 3

By the time of Emperor Constantine, the weeks were on a seven-day calendar. Duncan Steel describes the putting aside of Sunday for rest: "Constantine legislated in A.D. 321 for unnecessary work to be forbidden on a Sunday. That is, in fine weather essential agricultural tasks could be conducted, but otherwise the good Roman (who was effectively being instructed to adopt Christian practices) was supposed to set aside one day in seven as a day of rest. Upon this law stands the legality of the week which we have inherited."[121]

Constantine's decision made sense because he desired to connect his former ties to the Sun and his new ties to Christ. This may also have been an attempt to establish a day of the week just for Christians, similar to the Jews' Sabbath. Sunday was the day of the resurrection of Jesus, so this particular day could be used not only as a day of rest but also a day of worship for the Christians. After the decree of Constantine, the Christians, similar to the Jews, now enjoyed their own day. Unfortunately for scholars, Constantine's degree of 321 CE, which led to the combining of the Jewish week and Roman calendar, came almost three hundred years after the Crucifixion of Jesus. If it had happened earlier, scholars might now have an easier task of calculating the date of the Crucifixion.

It must also be considered that it was under Constantine's rule that the Edict of Milan was decreed in 313 when he ruled the Western Roman Empire. This gave legal toleration toward Christian worship only ten years after Constantine's predecessor Diocletian had passed an edict persecuting the Christians. Steel notes: "In A.D. 386 Theodosius I, the emperor of the Eastern Roman Empire, decreed that Sunday, the Lord's day, was holy; he abolished the Roman festival

---

121 Duncan Steel, *Marking Time: The Epic Quest to Invent the Perfect Calendar* (New York: John Wiley & Sons, Inc., 2000), 86.

The Jewish Calendar and Passover

calendar, marking the final overthrow of the pagan state religion and the establishment of Christianity as the official creed of the empire."[122]

Figure 3.1 shows the Hebrew name of the day of week and its meaning. The Jewish system of a seven-day week goes back long before the Christian era and may be one of world's oldest continuous religious practices. One may assume that the seven-day week, according to Jewish traditions, has never been altered or broken. If this is true, then this would also include the time of Jesus.

Figure 3.1 The Jewish Calendar in Days

Weekday Name	Hebrew "Name"	Hebrew Meaning
Sunday	Yom Reeshone	First day
Monday	Yom Shaynee	Second day
Tuesday	Yom Shlee´shee	Third day
Wednesday	Yom Revee´ee	Fourth day
Thursday	Yom Khah´mee´shee	Fifth day
Friday	Yom Ha´shee´shee	Sixth day
Saturday	Shabbat	Rest

The next step in the calculation of the Crucifixion is to find a plausible Passover date that would allow for Jesus to die on a Friday. Passover, in both ancient and modern times, begins after sunset and is always close to a Full-Moon phase. It

---

122 Ibid, 86–7.

Chapter 3

always occurs on the 15th day of Nissan in the Jewish calendar, which falls between March 21 and April 30 in the Gregorian calendar. Historians need to examine the years around 27 CE to 34 CE, the timeframe during which most historians think Jesus died, in order to determine the year. This must then be followed by finding a Passover that corresponds to a Full-Moon phase that occurred on a Friday or Saturday night and then comparing the information from the New Testament for any discrepancies.

Although no simple task, NASA has calculated the dates for all the phases of Moon from ancient to modern times. The United States Navy has created the Julian Date Converter, which reveals the weekday of any date since antiquity; these two services have made a near impossible task much easier.

Christians desire to celebrate Easter on a Sunday, this also contributes to its being on a different date each year. If Christians celebrated Easter on Passover, then Easter would start with a Full-Moon. These anomalies also further separated Christianity from Judaism. Most of the time the two celebrations are close to each other on the calendar, but still on different dates. If Passover begins with a Thursday or Friday Full-Moon then Easter for that year could fall on the third day of Passover, a Sunday, similar to the first.

There are 12 months in the Jewish calendar, with an extra month added every two or three years to make up for the .4 lunar differences between the Jewish calendar and the Gregorian calendar, which is solar based. Nineteen solar years are equal to 6939.602 days, while 19 Jewish years, or 235 lunar months, are equal to 6939.688 days. It requires seven Jewish leap years, or years with 13 months, to balance the two different calendars. These are the same calculations used in the configuration of the modern Jewish calendar, set during the fourth century CE. This becomes challenging because of the

The Jewish Calendar and Passover

difference between a lunar and solar calendar. Figure 3.2 shows the Jewish month and its Gregorian equivalent. Jewish holidays often fall on a different Gregorian day of the month, or even in a different month, because of the difference between the lunar calendar and the solar calendar. Notice that Easter can either be in the month of March or April depending on when the first Full-Moon occurs after the spring equinox.

Figure 3.2 The Jewish Calendar in Months

Hebrew Months	Jewish Holidays	Secular Months
Nissan	Passover, Yom HaShoah	March-April
Iyar	Yom HaZikaron, Yom HaAtzmaut, Lag BaOmer	April-May
Sivan	Shavuot	May-June
Tammuz		June-July
Av	Tishah B'Av	July-August
Elul		August-September
Tishri	Selichot, Rosh HaShanah, Yom Kippur, Sukkot, Simchat Torah	September-October
Cheshvan		October-November
Kislev	Hanukkah	November-December
Tevet		December-January
Sh'vat	Tu BiSh'vat	January-February
Adar	Purim	February-March

Chapter 3

Quite often Jewish months fall during different months of the Gregorian calendar. This is why sometimes Christians in the west celebrate Easter in the month of March, and sometimes in the month of April unlike Christmas that is always December 25. Since Christians desire to celebrate Easter on a Sunday, this also contributes to it being on a different date each year. If Christians celebrated Easter on Passover, then Easter would start three days after a Full-Moon. But, because it does not it separated Christianity further from Judaism. Most of the time, unless the Passover Full-Moon begins on a Thursday, the two celebrations are close to each other on the calendar, but still on different dates.

CONCLUSION

Time has different meanings. The older I become, the more I value my time not being wasted. I have come to a point in my life that time is more important than money, as I move away from the midlife and approach old age. Time can mean the indefinite, continued progress of existence referring to the past, present, and future conveniently regarded as a whole. But, it is also a point of measurement, in minutes, hours, days, years, decades, centuries, etc. Fortunately, there are signs in nature that help us keep track of time. Solar days and years, lunar cycles, and the position of constellations in the sky.

At this date, absolutely proving the theory of the integral existence is difficult until more primary sources surface. Nevertheless, a well-designed historical theory can allow future historians and researchers to strongly infer from empirical evidence that the theory is most likely correct compared to what is known through primary sources. After examination of the Jewish calendar, and having a better grasp of what

The Jewish Calendar and Passover

Passover is, several things need to be established in order to support the integral idea: (1) the seven-day week needs to be proven to be continuous to the time of the Crucifixion of Jesus; (2) valid phases of the Moon, through computer programs, must be available; (3) existing competing theories that are false must be disproven; and (4) a reason or reasons for Jesus living an integral life should be produced. All of these concerns will be addressed in the following chapters.

We know that the seven-day week goes back to ancient history. We also know that Passover must fall on a Full-Moon, which can be determined by NASA, and it must be the first Full-Moon after the spring equinox. Further, a date for the Crucifixion must fall on a Thursday or Friday, as reported by Matthew, Mark, Luke, and John in the New Testament. Although not an easy task, this puzzle will be explored in Chapter 7, where specific dates will be verified.

The ancients, despite living in simpler times, did keep track of weeks, months, and years. This was mainly because of religious practices, but calendars such as the Roman nundinum also provided some order. Although the Jews practiced a lunar calendar, today with the use of computers we can easily compare it to the solar calendar. This was something much more difficult for the Church Fathers. The difficulty, in fact, may very well have frustrated some to the point of not even trying to search for accurate dates for the birth and death of Jesus.

If we truly desire to learn more about Jesus, then we need to understand the Jewish holidays he celebrated. By learning more about these holidays, we can learn more about his life, death, and Resurrection. For example, we know that Jesus was crucified during a Full-Moon phase. The Last Supper, perhaps the most important meal in the New Testament, was a Passover preparation meal. Maybe Christians should ask why

Chapter 3

we are not following the example of Jesus and doing the same in honoring Passover. We know that the month of Nissan was important to the Jews because they believed it important to God. Exodus 12:2 informs us that God said to Moses and Aaron (his brother), "This month is to be for you the first month, the first month of the year." Therefore, Nissan has been very significant politically and religiously. Jesus died during Passover, as the New Testament informs us. The Talmud mentions that the prophets were born and died during Nissan. According to the Rosh HaShanah Tractate, "In Nissan our ancestors were redeemed from Egypt, and in the same month we shall be redeemed." It would make sense for Jesus to have been born and resurrected during this Jewish month.

PART II

THE PASSOVER BIRTH

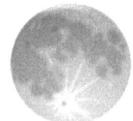

CHAPTER 4
THE NATIVITY

According to the *Encyclopedia of Early Christianity*, the purpose of the Gospels was not to provide historical insight. Rather,

> The New Testament writings appear to have not been written as sacred literature, but only to "settle disputes and address the life and ministerial needs of the Church." From the early second century, some New Testament writings were called "scripture" or used authoritatively alongside the Old Testament in supporting the faith and ministerial practices of the Church ...[123]

---

123 Ferguson, *Encyclopedia of Early Christianity*, 170.

Chapter 4

Therefore, they were not originally intended to be records of important dates. Early Christians were worried more about preparing for the return of Jesus than they were about the spiritual well-being of future generations of Christians.

Of the four Gospels, only two, Matthew and Luke, chronical the birth of Jesus, and both provide conflicting narratives at times. The first critical difference is the appearance of an angel of the Lord to signal the coming of Jesus. In Matthew 1:20–24, an unnamed angel appears to Joseph in a dream. In Luke 1:26–38, the angel Gabriel appears directly to Mary. This event later became known as the Annunciation but is also referred to the as the Annunciation to the Blessed Virgin Mary, the Annunciation of Our Lady, or the Annunciation of the Lord.

In both Luke and Matthew, Jesus is born in Bethlehem, but each gives a different account of the reasons the holy family with the yet-to-be-born Jesus arrived in the city. In Matthew 2:1–12, Jesus is born in a house and visited by Magi from the East. In Luke 2:1–16, Jesus is born and placed in a manger, and the main witnesses are the shepherds from the fields and angels. It has even been suggested that Jesus, who was from Nazareth, was conveniently said to be born in Bethlehem to fulfill an old Jewish prophecy that predicted that the coming Messiah would be born in that city.

Interestingly, in many accounts of the Nativity (Nativity displays, Christmas cards, and Christmas plays) both narratives are combined into one scene, and sometimes donkeys and sheep appear. As to when this occurred, the only evidence available is from Luke, which informs us that the shepherds were in the fields. This has caused many historians to speculate that the Nativity occurred during the springtime, and not during the winter months of the Northern Hemisphere when Christmas traditionally occurs. Further, it is thought that

The Nativity

if there were no rooms in Bethlehem, only six miles from Jerusalem, then some important event was occurring there. Passover would fit this description, because Jews from across the country came to worship during this time, and it occurs when the shepherds are in the fields.

One interesting aspect of the accounts that is not mentioned is why Mary, pregnant with child, traveled to the town of Bethlehem when she was so close to delivery. Luke mentions that Caesar Augustus issued a degree that a census should be taken of the entire Roman Empire. This required everyone to register in his town of origin. Matthew gives no account of a Roman census. But, if this were also the time during Passover, it might explain why Mary would travel at such a critical time in her pregnancy. In order to align with the integral idea, Jesus' birth would have had to occur around Passover during the month of Nissan, and Joseph and Mary would have visited the Temple during the Passover worship. To the Jews, Passover was the most important holiday, and the Temple the most sacred site in Israel.

According to the Bible, the First Temple was built by King Solomon around 957 BCE. Deuteronomy 12:2–27 says that the Temple replaced the Tabernacle in the Sinai Desert constructed by followers of Moses, becoming the sole place of sacrifice in Israel. In 586 BCE, the Babylonians sacked Jerusalem and destroyed the Temple. In 536 BCE, King Cyrus of Persia ordered the rebuilding of the Temple. Around 20 BCE, during the reign of Herod, the Temple was renovated and expanded, becoming known as Herod's Temple. In 70 CE, the Temple was destroyed by the Romans during the Jewish War. In 691 CE, after the Muslim conquest of Jerusalem, a Muslim shrine, the Dome of the Rock, was constructed on the Temple Mount and remains there today.

The Talmud mentions that pregnant women were close

Chapter 4

enough to the Temple during times of worship that they could smell the sacrifices. In Avot 5:8, it is acknowledged, "Ten miracles were wrought in the Sanctuary: No woman miscarried from the scent of the holy meat, and the holy meat never stank ... and a man never said to his fellow, "The place is too strait for me to lodge in Jerusalem."[124] Hence, according to this passage, even women close to birth had a special place to worship. Never too strait refers to the fact that rooms to stay in were always available. Therefore, women were an important part of Temple worship, as shown in Figure 4.1.

Figure 4.1

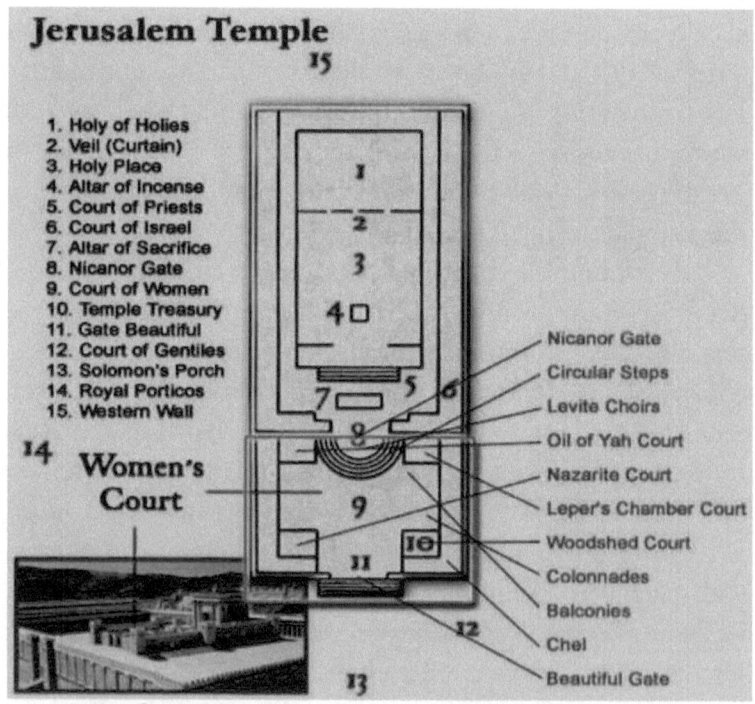

Image Credit Bible History Online www.bible-history.com/court-of-women/illustration.html

---

124 Rodkinson, *New Edition of the Babylonian Talmud*, 2765.

The verse is from Rabbi Nathan, although scholars believe the commentary was not written by him, only attributed to him, just as many books of the New Testament are thought to be attributed. The commentary suggests that pregnant women were part of the celebration, even though it was believed that the smell of burnt meat could cause a miscarriage. There were even special areas were the women met. The Temple included several courts, one for gentiles, one for women, one for men, and one for the Priest, and of course above the Court of the Priest from the Heikal (Temple) was the Holy of Holies, or Debir, where the Ark of the Covenant once stood.

This passage from the Talmud also informs us that rooms were available in Jerusalem throughout holy weeks, something Luke disagrees with. Therefore, if the Nativity occurred during the holy week of Passover, it was possible for Joseph and Mary to find a room in nearby Bethlehem, as recounted in Matthew. The city of Jerusalem was always full of people at Passover. James Charlesworth informs us in the introduction to *Jesus and Temple: Textual and Archaeological Explorations,* "The thousands of priests and the treasures demanded a Temple police. They also controlled the crowds that could become mobs during the festivals, especially at Pesach (Passover), when Jerusalem frequently tripled in size."[125]

This could also explain why Joseph and Mary were in Bethlehem, somewhat away from the possible Passover crowds, since Matthew does not give a precise reason for the young couple to be in Bethlehem, like the census spoken of in Luke. Tradition, although questioned by some scholars, holds that Joseph was from Bethlehem, and this might further explain why the young couple were in that town.

---

125 James H. Charlesworth, Ed., *Jesus and Temple: Textual and Archaeological Explorations* (Minneapolis: Fortress Press, 2014), 10.

Chapter 4

It was demanded in the Torah (Deut. 16:16, Exod. 23:14) that every Jew make a pilgrimage to the Jerusalem Temple three times a year—at Passover, 50 days later at Shavuot (also known as Pentecost or Feast of the Weeks), and in the autumn at Sukkot (also known as Tabernacles or Festival of the Booths). Jews living far away, or in Galilee, were required to make a pilgrimage only once a year. If the account given in Matthew did happen during a Passover celebration, and Joseph did own property in the city, this might explain why Jesus was born there. We may never know for sure. This missing information, or lack of information, by the authors of Luke and Matthew later affected the date for the Nativity.

THE HISTORIOGRAPHY OF CHRISTMAS

Abbé Louis Marie Duchesne was the first modern theologian to recognize the belief of early Church leaders that the Conception or Nativity and Passion occurred on the same date of the calendar year. In his book *Christian Worship: Its Origin and Evolution,* Duchesne points to Augustine as proof of his theory that this belief was common among the Fathers:

> Augustine blames the Jews for having transgressed against the command *non coues agnum in lacte matris suae* [Latin: a lamb in its mother's milk does not Coues] The lamb is Jesus Christ, crucified the 25th of March, that is, on the same day in which His mother began to have milk; "Dicuntur enim feminae ex quo conceperint lac colligere" [Latin: The day she was said to have conceived] (*In Heptat.*, ii. 90).[126]

---

[126] L. Duchesne and M. L. McClure, *Christian Worship: Its Origin and Evolution: A Study of the Latin Liturgy Up to the Time of Charlemagne* (London: Society for Promoting Christian Knowledge, 1910), 264.

The Nativity

In this verse, Augustine chastises the Jews for not acknowledging Jesus as the lamb and points to March 25, the date of the Crucifixion, as the same date as the Conception, or the day that Mary "began to have milk." This could also explain the Church stance on abortion. Therefore, sometime after Hippolytus of Rome, the Roman Church decided to honor the birth of Jesus in December, nine months after Augustine's date for the Conception. More precisely, this became accepted sometime between the death of Hippolytus and the reign of Constantine I. Therefore, between the third and fourth century, the Church began to take a greater interest in setting an official date to celebrate the Nativity.

Duchesne theorized that Christmas was at first a festival unique to the Roman Church, designed to replace a pagan festival; Christians wished to replace the holiday honoring the Sun god Mithras, which commenced after the shortest day of the year, or the winter solstice. During this time, Romans exchanged gifts honoring their god. Christians wanting to compete with the pagans turned to the birth of Jesus, which was thought to have occurred around the same time, as an alternative to Sun worship.

December 25 was chosen to replace the pagan Roman holiday *Natalis Solis Invicti,* which means "Birthday of the Unconquered Sun."[127] This belief has only added confusion to dating the Nativity, because it is now assumed by many scholars that the Church Fathers were only creating a new day to celebrate, and not selecting one based on records. Fortunately, we have other sources that predate even Augustine that point to a much longer Church tradition of celebrating the Nativity. Interestingly, these sources predate even the emergence of Christianity as the official religion of the Roman

---

127 Ibid, 261.

Chapter 4

Empire. Therefore, whether or not Christians were trying to compete with pagan festivals must be questioned.

PAPAL AUTHORITY AND CHRISTMAS

Regrettably, sometimes even Church sources can be considered unscrupulous. The earliest record of a December 25 Nativity is from a book, the *Liber Pontificalis*, a biography of the Popes. It was created in the third century and updated through the ensuing years. It suggests that Pope Saint Telesphorus (reigned 126–137) was the first to preach a Christmas Midnight Mass on December 25. It states, "He appointed at the season of the nativity of our Lord Jesus Christ, and that at the season of the Lord's nativity masses should be celebrated during the night."[128] As Louise Loomis, who translated the book from Latin into English in the early 20th century, stated in his footnotes, "The night mass at Christmas is still a feature of the Roman ritual. The author of the Lib. Pont. is the earliest writer to allude to it. It can hardly have been instituted before the date of the Nativity was fixed during the fourth century."[129] Today the Liber Pontificalis is considered by many modern scholars as early Church propaganda to establish papal authority.

Other early sources point to December 25 as an established Church tradition. But, once again these sources may have been tampered with for similar reasons. We can also read the following words of Theophilus (115–181), Catholic bishop of Caesarea in Palestine from *Magdeburgenses*: He states, "We ought to celebrate the birthday of Our Lord on what day

---

128 Loomis, Louise Ropes, *The Book of the Popes (Liber Pontificalis)* (New York: Columbia University Press, 1916). 12–13.
129 Ibid.

so ever the 25th of December shall happen."[130] Theophilus lived almost two hundred years before Christianity became the official religion of the Roman Empire and the mass persecutions of Christians ended. However, the *Magdeburgenses* was written in the sixteenth century, and cannot be considered a valid primary source for Theophilus. In fact, the first valid recorded date of Christmas being celebrated on December 25th was in 336, during the time of Emperor Constantine.

Not mentioned by Duchesne or Loomis, but something else to consider is the fact that most Christians were illiterate, and received most of their instructions on faith directly from the Church and those who interpreted the New Testament. This brings into question the extent to which the limited few who interpreted the New Testament produced errors in their work, or indirectly, through copying older texts into newer editions. If so, Christianity would be taken in undesired, for better or worse directions. Bart Ehrman explores the problem in his book *Misquoting Jesus*. Citing William Harris, a professor at Columbia University, he maintains that in the best of conditions the literacy rate may have been lower than ten to 15 percent of the population.[131] Ehrman adds,

> One of the factors contributing to scribes' alterations of their text was their own historical context. Christian scribes of the second and third centuries were involved with the debates and disputes of their day, and occasionally these disputes affected the

---

130 *Magdeburgenses*, Cent. 2. c. 6. Hospinian, *De origine Festorum Chirstianorum.*
131 Bart, D. Ehrman, *Misquoting Jesus* (New York: HarperSanFrancisco, 2005), 37.

Chapter 4

reproduction of the texts over which the debates raged.[132]

These debates could have altered even the dates of an important Christian holiday, like Christmas, shifting it to December and not March or April. Making matters worse, some of the most important Church Fathers erred at times. Even Clement, in calculating his chronology of the world, misquoted Luke 3:1–3 to cite Jesus' age as 30 exactly when the author of Luke states he was approximately 30. Further complicating the problem is that many of the original manuscripts written by the early Christians have been lost to the ravages of time.

Ehrman notes that Origen, one of the most important early Church Fathers, even wrote of the erroneous practice displayed by some of the copyists around the end of the second century. According to Origen, the true author's meaning was at the mercy of scribes who either through error or pure audacity were altering the original texts. He wrote the following to complain:

> The differences among the manuscripts have become great, either through the negligence of some copyist or through the perverse audacity of others; they either neglect to check over what they transcribed, or, in the process of checking, they make additions or deletions as they please.[133]

If this was the case, the manuscripts Origen and Clement were using may have had errors similar to those that Origen complained of. Unfortunately, the original manuscripts Origen

---

132 Ibid, 88.
133 Ibid, 52.

The Nativity

used no longer exist. The earliest known intact Christian codices are from the fourth century, close to the rule of Roman Emperor Constantine the Great, around three hundred years after Jesus and a century after the death of Clement. Nevertheless, the first four books of the New Testament are the closest historical evidence in existence pertaining to the life of Jesus. What limited knowledge we have about the Nativity and the life of Jesus comes from them. But, can the Gospels be trusted? They must be examined and compared for common themes.

THE FOUR GOSPELS

The definition of gospel is derived from the two Old English words *god*, meaning "good," and *spell*, meaning "tidings" or "news," thus good news. The Gospels are attributed to St. Matthew, St. Mark, St. Luke, and St. John, who have become acknowledged as evangelists, or bringers of good news. The first three gospels have become recognized as the Synoptic Gospels because they give a synopsis of the life of Jesus. The Synoptic Gospels recount Jesus' teachings mainly in Galilee, while John tells of Jesus' teaching in Judea. Each book, while concentrating on a narrative of Jesus, gives a unique personal biography of him all its own. Henrietta C. Mears neatly sums up the significance of having four different accounts of Jesus when she writes:

> He is presented as: King in Matthew, Servant in Mark, Son of Man in Luke, and Son of God in John. Each of the writers is trying to present a different picture of our one Lord.[134]

---

134 Mears, *What the Bible Is All About*, 221.

Chapter 4

Consequently, each of the Gospels has its own perspective, and scholars must somehow separate bias form fact in order to find evidence of the integral existence. It must also be remembered that the authors of the Gospels were describing only the everyday life of Jesus. Clement, Hippolytus, Origen, and Augustine, who came later, were the ones who attempted to find deeper and greater philosophic insight into Christianity.

According to Diarmaid MacCulloch, in *Christianity: The First Three Thousand Years*, the Gospels describe Jesus' interactions with the poor and uneducated:

> Biographies were not rare in the ancient world and the Gospels do have many features in common with non-Christian examples. Yet these Christian books are an unusually 'down-market' variety of biography, in which ordinary people reflect on their experiences of Jesus, where the powerful and the beautiful generally stay on the sidelines of the story, and where it is often the poor, the ill-educated and disreputable whose encounters with God are most vividly described.[135]

Therefore, the Gospels become more about how Jesus interacted with individuals and God and less about the logistics of the future of Christianity. That was left to the Apostles and future Church Fathers. They decided what doctrine to follow. This resulted in many rifts between the leaders. These rifts led to new denominations, each with different bylaws and religious procedures.

---

135 Diarmaid MacCulloch, *Christianity: The First Three Thousand Years* (New York: Penguin Books, 2009), 77.

THE GOSPEL OF MATTHEW

Even though Matthew is the first book of the New Testament, it is not the oldest. R. T. France places the Gospel of Matthew after the destruction of the Temple:

> The current majority view that Matthew's Gospel was written in the fourth quarter of the first century depends mainly on three argument: (a) that its setting reflects the period of final separation between the Church and the synagogue, probably around AD 85, (b) that it is written in the light of the experience of the Roman capture of Jerusalem and the destruction of the temple in AD 70, and (c) that it is dependent on the Gospel of Mark, which some scholars also date after AD 70, others shortly before.[136]

This timing placed the author of Matthew in the awkward position of having to decide how much to separate Christianity from Judaism. But he still mentions important customs and celebrations, such as the Passover meal and Joseph, Mary, and Jesus visiting the Temple 31 days after the Nativity.

Most Bible scholars agree that the Gospel of Matthew was not composed by the Apostle Matthew but only named in his honor. The original version of the book was written in Greek, not Hebrew. According to Randel Helms in *Who Wrote the Gospels?* whoever wrote Matthew most likely used the Gospel of Mark as a source:

> Of the 661 verses in Mark, some 600 appear in

---

136 R. T. France, *The Gospel of Matthew* (Grand Rapids, MI: Wm. B. Eerdmans, 2007), 18.

Chapter 4

Matthew, most of them rewritten but containing, in hundreds of instances, the same words in the same order; that there is a literary relationship between the Gospels of Mark and Matthew has been recognized since at least the time of St. Augustine of Hippo.[137]

While many New Testament scholars presume Matthew and Luke used Mark as a source, some believe in a Two-Source Theory—that Matthew and Luke had another common hypothetical source other than Mark. German scholars give the hypothetical Gospel or source the abbreviated name of *Q*, for *Quelle*, German for "source." *Q* was probably lost to time after scribes halted its production, preferring Matthew and Luke, the updated versions, to the old source. Eventually, the existing copies of *Q* crumbled or were purposely destroyed. Perhaps *Q* disappeared because it was thought to be just a gospel of Jesus' sayings, lacking any significant narratives.

Since no other such texts with only sayings of Jesus existed, it is easy to criticize the supporters of the *Q* hypothesis. However, such a lost gospel was discovered in 1945 in Egypt, known as the Gospel of Thomas. It was eventually translated from the Coptic language. According to Helms, "Thomas is exactly what *Q* was said to be, a collection of sayings of Jesus with no narrative context, no 'gospel story,' at all."[138] While the discovery of Thomas does not totally prove *Q* was a real source for Matthew and Luke, it does without a doubt prove such a text could have existed. We will know more about the Gospels in the future as more of recently discovered ones are restored.

---

137 Randel Helms, *Who Wrote the Gospels?* (Altadena, California: Millennium Press, 1997), 41.
138 Ibid, 102.

THE GOSPEL OF MARK

The Gospel of Mark is the briefest of the canonical books, but arguably may also be the earliest, thought to be written around 70 CE. It mentions nothing of the birth of Jesus. The author of Mark describes the many miracles performed by Jesus early on in the text. While brief, Mark still narrates the miracles with a passionate but direct attitude. By the second century, Church scholars assumed the author of Mark was not a personal eyewitness of Jesus. But, according to Helms, "Most of the Gospel of Mark is a collection of what had previously been unconnected fragments about Jesus, units of oral tradition, and brief written stories and sayings that reveal a long history of transmission before they reached Mark; the collection looks nothing like the "reminiscences of Peter."[139]

This breaks with Eusebius's belief that the author of Mark was an interpreter of Peter. In his *Ecclesiastical History (iii.39)*, Eusebius writes from the account of Papias, bishop of Hierapolis, about whom we really know little. It is known that he worked during the first half of the second century, and only fragments of his writings remain. According to Eusebius,

> This also the Presbyter used to say, "When Mark became Peter's interpreter, he wrote down accurately, although not in order, all that he remembered of what was said or done by the Lord. For he had not heard the Lord nor followed Him, but later, as I have said, he did Peter, who made his teaching fit his needs without, as it were, making any arrangement of the Lord's oracles, so that Mark made no mistake in

---

139 Ibid, 3.

Chapter 4

thus writing some things down as he remembered them."[140]

Eusebius may have been wrong in thinking that the author of Mark was an interpreter for Peter, but if the Gospel was written in 70 CE, there would still have been enough witnesses around to tell the story of Jesus, especially the facts of the Crucifixion. It must be remembered that Passover was a large celebration, with large number of Jews attending. Although it was 40 years later, there would likely have been witnesses still alive who watched Jesus walking the streets of Jerusalem bearing the cross, and able to report it accurately.

THE GOSPEL OF LUKE

According to F. F. Bruce, Luke was not a local eyewitness to the events of Jesus' ministry:

> Luke was a physician by profession, and according to a tradition, which can be traced back to the second century, was a native of Antioch in Syria. Some support is given to this tradition by the internal evidence of his writings.[141]

Brooke Westcott adds to our understanding of Luke by stating, "The Gospel of St Luke, it is then said, stands third in order [in the canon], having been written by "Luke the physician," the companion of St Paul, who, not being himself

---

140 Eusebius, Pamphili. *Ecclesiastical History, Books 1-5: Fathers of the Church, a New Translation, v. 19*, New York, Fathers of the Church, Inc., 1953), 206.
141 F. F. Bruce, *The New Testament Documents: Are They Reliable?* (Grand Rapids, Michigan: William B. Eerdmans, 1981), 80.

an eyewitness, based his narrative on such information as he could obtain, beginning from the birth of John."[142]

Luke (1:1–4) suggests he used accurate research skills when he begins the verse by stating that he has investigated his sources, and written an account of what he learned—not typical of a New Testament writer. It states,

> Many have undertaken to draw up an account of the things that have been fulfilled among us, just as they were handed down to us by those who from the first were eyewitnesses and servants of the word. Therefore, since I myself have carefully investigated everything from the beginning, it seemed good also to me to write an orderly account for you, most excellent Theophilus, so you may know the certainty of the things you have been taught.

Interestingly, Luke is mentioning that he wrote while using primary sources who were direct acquaintances of Jesus. However, the primary sources used by Luke have been lost. Ehrman points out the following:

> One of the earlier accounts may have been the source that scholars have designed Q, which was probably a written account, principally of Jesus' sayings, used by both Luke and Matthew for many of their distinctive teachings of Jesus (e.g., the Lord's Prayer and the Beatitudes).[143]

Bruce brings to the forefront the issue of Luke's use of

---

142 Brooke Westcott, *A General Survey of the History of the Canon of the New Testament*, 7th ed. (London: Macmillan, 1896), 217.
143 Ehrman, *Misquoting Jesus*, 24.

Chapter 4

sources. He points out, "Whatever his sources were, Luke made good use of them. And he sets his story in the context of imperial history. Of all the New Testament writers, he is the only one who so much as names a Roman emperor." [144] In fact, he mentions three, Augustus, Tiberius, and Claudius. Luke is sometimes referred to as the only true Church historian until Eusebius, informing us of valuable information no other early Christian writer bothers to mention.

THE GOSPEL OF JOHN

Some scholars date John to the second century. R. V. G. Tasker notes, "Cement of Alexandria, for example, who died in 212, states on the authority of the elders of an earlier age that John wrote the Gospel last of the evangelist . . . Irenaeus states that John survived till the reign of Trajan, which began in AD 98."[145]

The Gospel of John, like Mark, makes no mention of the birth of Jesus or the Star of Bethlehem. The original author of the Gospel of John never fully discloses his identity. John himself is referred to only in the third person as the "disciple Jesus loved," and the reader is never informed for sure that this is John. He leaves several clues pointing to his identity as John, son of Zebedee, who was also the brother of James, son of Zebedee, another of the original Twelve Disciples. However, even this is uncertain, because in many cases throughout the Bible a book was named after a famous biblical person, and not necessarily the author.

The Gospel of John can lead readers to believe that perhaps John was a direct witness to many of the miracles of

---

144 Bruce, *The New Testament Documents,* 81.
145 R. V. G. Tasker, *The Gospel According to St. John: An Introduction and Commentary* (Grand Rapids, MI: Wm. B. Eerdmans, 1965), 20.

The Nativity

Jesus, and of the Crucifixion, during which Jesus asked the disciple he loved to take care of Mary, his mother (John 19:25–27). This also implies that John knew what year Jesus was crucified. However, there is no historical proof of this. The New Testament also informs us that John was a friend to Peter; both were fishermen, and Jesus sent the two of them together to prepare for the Passover meal (Luke 22:7–13), and both ran together to the tomb of Jesus when Mary Magdalene told them Jesus was missing (John 20:1–9). Both were early disciples of Jesus.

Scholars have intensely debated whether John had an original unknown source, perhaps John himself, or was a collaboration of several of John's followers known as the Johannine community. Most scholars agree that the source known as *Q* was not a source for John. Whoever the true author or authors of John were, they provide an ample amount of historical information that can be used in an attempt to date the Crucifixion, a topic that will be debated later in the book. Also absent from John is mention of the Magi. Although much of what we know of them comes from Matthew, there are small clues from other historical sources. The next chapter will explore the possible origins and motives of the Magi. Over time they become steeped in legend. Called wise men, Christians respect them because they were the first to worship Jesus, and came from great distances to do so.

CONCLUSION

Analyzing the four Gospels, and making sense of the differences between each one when investigating the Nativity is a very daunting task. Each author could be compared to a different witness at a crime scene or accident. They may have been at the same place and interviewed other witnesses

Chapter 4

themselves, but each has a different view or motive in telling their story. Luke left out details that Matthew believed important, while John mentions nothing about the Nativity, and Mark appears to be a good source for Matthew and Luke but is missing many important events.

Matthew and Luke appear to be genuine and honest. Despite the difference in their narratives, they seem to believe in the sources that lead to the information they gathered. Luke appears to be thorough in the way he collected and noted evidence, but Matthew's story matches better with clues found in the Talmud. For example, the Talmud mentions that there were rooms available in Jerusalem during Passover, leading one to believe that Jesus could not have been born in a stable unless his parents were poor. Matthew mentions that the Magi visited Jesus in a house. There are more similarities and differences. It must also be considered that if these Gospels were written after 70 CE, then the primary sources for them would be 75 years old or older. If they were second-generation secondary sources, they would have been somewhere around 50 years old. The following list shows some of the similarities and differences between Matthew and Luke.

Similarities between Matthew 1–2 and Luke 1–2

1. Jesus' birth is related to the reign of Herod the Great (Matt 2:1; Luke 1:5).
2. Mary, a virgin, is engaged to Joseph, but not living with him (Matt 1:18; Luke 1:27, 34).
3. The names of the parents of Jesus are Mary and Joseph (Matt 1:18; Luke 1:27).
4. Joseph belongs to the house of David (Matt 1:1–16; Luke 1:27).
5. Jesus is recognized as a son of David (Matt 1:17, 25;

The Nativity

Luke 1:27, 33).
6. An angel announces the birth of Jesus (Matt 1:18–25; Luke 1:26–38.
7. Jesus is conceived through the Holy Spirit; an angel announces this to Joseph (Matt 1:20) or Mary (Luke 1:35).
8. Jesus' Conception does not involve Joseph (Matt 1:18–19; Luke 1:34–35).
9. "Jesus" is the name given by the angel before the birth (Matt 1:21; Luke 1:31).
10. An angel identifies Jesus as savior (Matt 1:21; Luke 2:11).
11. Jesus is born after Mary and Joseph come together to live (Matt 1:25; Luke 2:5–7).
12. Jesus is born in Bethlehem (Matt 2:1; Luke 2:5–7).
13. Outsiders (the Magi in Matthew and shepherds in Luke) see a sign in the night sky (star or angels).
14. There is external testimony to Jesus (Magi in Matt 2:1–12; Simeon and Anna in Luke 2:25–38).
15. Joseph, Mary, and Jesus settle in Nazareth (Matt 2:23; Luke 2:39).
16. Jesus is referred to either as King of the Jews (Matt 2:2) or as the one who will inherit David's throne and reign eternally over Jacob's house, and have an unending kingdom (Luke 1:32–33).
17. An angel appears to a male figure (Joseph in Matt 1:20; Zechariah in Luke 1:11).
18. Herod or Zechariah is afraid (Matt 2:3; Luke 1:12).

Events Found Only in Matthew

1. Joseph resolves to divorce Mary (1:19).
2. The Magi visit the family from the East (2:1–12).

Chapter 4

3. The family escape Herod by fleeing to Egypt (2:13–15).
4. Herod orders the slaughter of the male children (2:16–18).
5. An emphasis on fulfilled prophecies (1:22–23; 2:5–6, 15, 17–18, 23).

Events Found Only in Luke

1. The angel that visited Mary is named Gabriel (1:26–38).
2. Mary sings a song of praise (1:46–55).
3. Angels visit the shepherds (2:8–21).
4. Mary and Joseph take the newly born Jesus to the Temple (2:22–38).
5. At the Temple, Simeon and Anna, the daughter of Phanuel, of the tribe of Asher, foretell that Jesus will become the redemption of Jerusalem (2:25–35).[146]

The last two events listed above, from Luke, reference Joseph and Mary taking the month-old Jesus to the Temple. In Jewish tradition, this was not uncommon; in fact, it was customary for parents to take their firstborn males to the Temple. This is because in Exodus 13:1–2 "the Lord said to Moses, 'Consecrate to me every firstborn male. The first offspring of every womb among the Israelites belongs to me, whether man or animal.'" This meant that every firstborn son was to become the family priest, in charge of sacrifices for

---

[146] This list is drawn from Raymond E. Brown in *The Birth of the Messiah* (rev. edition; New York: Doubleday, 1993; 34–35); Joseph A. Fitzmyer in *The Gospel According to Luke I–IX* (Anchor Bible 28; New York: Doubleday, 1981; 307); and Patricia M. McDonald for Jeremy Corley, *New Perspectives on the Nativity* (London: T & T Clark International, 2009), 200–1.

The Nativity

every member of the family. But, after the Exodus from Egypt, the Israelites committed the serious sin of the Golden Calf, in which only the tribe of Levi were not guilty. Numbers 3:11–12 informs us that, because of this, God decreed that the Levites were his and were to take the place of the firstborn sons of Israel. In Numbers 18:15, the Lord ordered that that the firstborn of any woman not from the tribe of Levi or a priest had to be redeemed from service to God by paying five shekels of silver one month after birth to a Temple priest.

Thus, as tradition called for, Jesus, who was from the tribe of Judah, was to undergo the Pidyon HaBen, meaning "the Redemption of the firstborn son." In the traditional ceremony, Joseph brought Jesus to the Temple 31 days after birth. He would next have to respond to a ritual set of questioning indicating that this was Mary's firstborn son. This also required him to redeem the newborn Jesus by paying the five silver shekels to the Temple priest, followed by a sacrifice of two young pigeons.

By preforming this ritual and receiving the five shekel offering, the Levites took the place of Jesus as a priest. Later it was the Levites who offered Jesus to the cross. The irony is that Jesus could never be a Temple priest or preform important day-to-day rituals there because he was not a Levite, but his death in 30 CE and the destruction of the Temple in 70 CE allowed him to become more than a priest. Jesus now had something other than the role of high priest to aspire to.

Perhaps it was a combination of the testimony of the visiting Magi, Simeon and Anna at the Temple and Old Testament prophesy that inspired the young Jesus to become a prophet himself. If Simeon and Anna, who were elderly and worshiped on a regular basis at the Temple, were aware of the integral existence mentioned in the Talmud, then they also would have been aware of any future prophets being born

Chapter 4

during Passover and presented to the priest as part of the redemption of the firstborn son only 31 days after the Passover celebrations. Thus, their testimonies are important and they are the perfect witnesses. There must have been something special about Jesus; he more than likely did not have a halo over his head as depicted in Renaissance paintings, and probably would have looked like any other 31-day-old newborn, but the presence of signs in the night sky, the fact that Jesus was born in Bethlehem, and the prophesy found in the Talmud may have aided Simeon and Anna in making their prediction of great things for Jesus.

Finding more precise evidence of a Passover Nativity would enhance the integral concept. However, other theories may hurt this idea. In the future there will be other concepts with different dates for the Nativity and Crucifixion. Many of these are flawed. Unfortunately, once the flawed information gets out, it is echoed across the world in a matter of seconds and takes on a life of its own. Quite often Christians are good natured and accept whatever is posted in a positive way, such as evidence as the existence of Jesus, as true because the name Jesus is mentioned. As a historian I do not.

For example, there is currently a September birth theory based on Luke 1: 5-26. From this verse, it is learned that Jesus is 6-months younger then John the Baptist. While working in the Temple, John's father, Zacharias was told by Gabriel that his wife, Elizabeth, would become pregnant. She was baron, and could not have children. This is where things get misconstrued. Based on information from the Talmud, we know that Zacharias's Temple duty was over in late June. But, Luke only mentions that "after these days" Elizabeth became pregnant. Therefore, as a historian I cannot use this as evidence for when Jesus was born. Was "after these days" intended to mean days, weeks, or months. Unfortunately, some have calculated a Passover birth for John, and a September birth for Jesus, and some have accepted this.

CHAPTER 5

THE MAGI

*M*atthew is the only one of the Gospels to mention the Magi and the Star of Bethlehem. The author mentions both very early in the Gospel, and not much is known of either outside of Matthew. Matthew 2:7–12 states the following:

> After Jesus was born in Bethlehem in Judea, during the time of King Herod, Magi from the east came to Jerusalem and asked, "Where is the one who has been born king of the Jew? We saw his star in the east and have come to worship him.". . . Then Herod called the Magi secretly and found out from them the exact time the star had appeared. He sent them to Bethlehem and said, "Go and make a careful search for the child. As soon as you find him, report to me,

Chapter 5

> so that I too may go and worship him." After they had heard the king, they went on their way, and the star they had seen in the east went ahead of them until it stopped over the place where the child was. When they saw the star, they were overjoyed. On coming to the house, they saw the child with his mother Mary, and they bowed down and worshiped him. Then they opened their treasures and presented him with gifts of gold and of incense and of myrrh. And having been warned in a dream not to go back to Herod, they returned to their country by another route.

The two most likely places for the Magi to have come from are Babylonia or Persia, but Arabia is gaining support. Both make an excellent choice because of their long history of astronomy and the fact that large Jewish populations were living in those regions at the time. The Greek geographer Strabo of Amasia (64 BCE–ca. 23 CE), who was alive during the birth of Jesus, gives a description of the life of the Babylonian astronomers in *The Geography of Strabo 16:1-6*:

> In Babylon a settlement is set apart for the local philosophers, the Chaldaeans, as they are called, who are concerned mostly with astronomy; but some of these, who are not approved of by the others, profess to be genethlialogists (writers of horoscopes). There is also a tribe of the Chaldaeans, and a territory inhabited by them, in the neighborhood of the Arabians and of the Persian Sea, as it is called. There are also several tribes of the Chaldaean astronomers.[147]

---

147 Strabo, *The Geography of Strabo Vol. 7,* (Cambridge, MA: Harvard University Press, 1961), 203.

The Magi

Accordingly, we know from Strabo that there were several settlements from around the time of the Nativity that specialized in astronomy that would have been aware of new celestial occurrences. It is intriguing, too, that there were also Jewish settlements close to the Chaldaeans' settlements. Paul Johnson, in, *A History of the Jews*, writes the following:

> As Greek ideas about the one-ness of humanity spread, the Jewish tendency to treat non-Jews as ritually unclean, and to forbade marriage to them, was resented as being anti-humanitarian; the word 'misanthropic' was frequently used. It is notable that in Babylonia, where Greek ideas had not penetrated, the apartness of the large Jewish community was not resented—Josephus said the anti-Jewish feeling did not exist there.[148]

Therefore, the Jews living in the East had a much easier time getting along with local governments than the Jews living in the heavily Roman-influenced Judea. This was most likely because they considered Judea as their chosen land and the Romans as intruders.

Further enhancing the relationship between the Jews and current rulers of Babylonia and Persia, the Parthians, was the fact that the Jews were not on friendly terms with the Parthians rivals in the region, the Romans. Accordingly, the enemies of Rome became short-term allies of the Parthians. As mentioned in Chapter 2, the Parthians dealt a humiliating defeat to the Roman leader Crassus, killing him in the process at the battle of Carrhae in 53 BCE, and halting Roman imperial expansion into Mesopotamia.

---

148 Paul Johnson, *A History of the Jews* (New York: Harper & Row, 1987), 134.

Chapter 5

The Parthians were also attracted to some of the traditional concepts of Judaism. The Magi more than likely practiced Zoroastrianism. Judaism and Zoroastrianism are closely related and may have influenced each other. S. P. Hildreth noted this in 1852:

> It is a remarkable circumstance that the Magi themselves, although never speaking of Zoroaster as the author of their religion, repeatedly in their writings attribute this honor to Abraham. Sharistani tells us that "Persian kings, in general, adhered to the religion of Abraham, and their subjects were always of the religion of their prince... The common people, while the religion of the Magi prevailed in Persia, invariably ascribed their doctrines to Abraham; styling their faith, at all times, Kish Abraham."[149]

Unlike the Greeks, who practiced the worship of many gods, the Zoroastrians worshiped only one god and had a dualistic world view, a belief in good versus evil. [150] Perhaps this why the Parthians and Jews were able to work and live side-by-side. Looking at Judaism and Zoroastrianism, George Carter noted the following:

---

149 S. P Hildreth, "The Wise Men from the East, no. 4, *Family Visitor* 3, no. 6 (June 15, 1852): 42, *Agricultural Periodicals from the Southern, Midwestern, and Western U.S., 1800–1878*, EBSCO*host*.
150 Zoroaster, Old Iranian Zarathushtra, or Zarathustra (born ca. 628 BCE, probably Rhages, Iran, died ca. 551 BCE, site unknown), was an Iranian religious reformer and founder of Zoroastrianism, or Parsiism, as it is known in India. Some Christians claim he borrowed the savior idea from the older Book of Isaiah. Some scholars believe he may have lived much earlier, perhaps around 1500 BCE.

Each was proclaimed by a prophet. Each worshipped one God. Each believed in an evil power. Each forbade images. Each laid emphasis on a moral act. Each was intolerant toward other systems. Each developed priestly cults, and emphasized ceremonial cleanliness. Each had something like a synagogue worship. Belief in angels and demons and in the future life were ideas common to both.[151]

Not mentioned by Carter but of equal importance was the emphasis on prophets and the respect that Persian rulers had for Judaism. Hence, the teachings of Jesus and a belief in salvation and an inner life would have been met with acceptance by the followers of Zoroaster. Consequently, they would have been interested in the affairs of Judea.

When Marco Polo made his epic 24-year journey through the Middle East to China in 1271, he passed through what is modern-day Iran. During this time, he was greeted by the citizens of Sabā. He was told that their town had been the point of origin of the Magi. A. V. Williams Jackson notes the following:

> It has long been recognized that the names "Saba" and "Ava" of Marco Polo are probably to be identified with Savah, some 50 miles southwest of Tehran, and with Avah, a village about 16 miles southwest of Savah. The third city, called "Cala Ataperistan" by the Venetian traveler and said to be "three days' journey" from Sabā, has not identified, although Marco Polo is correct in his statement that

---

151 George William Carter, *Zoroastrianism and Judaism* (New York: AMS Press, Inc., 1970), 38.

Chapter 5

the name means 'Castle of the Fire-Worshippers,' for it represents the Persian Kalah-i Atasparastan.[152]

Thus, more than one town claimed to have some connection to the Magi's narrative, which may contribute to the theory that three Magi did, in fact, make their epic journey. Marco Polo, in his book *The Travels of Marco Polo*, writes about visiting this region of Iran while traveling to China:

> In Persia, there is the city which is called Saba, from whence were the three Magi who came to adore Christ in Bethlehem; and the three are buried in that city in a fair sepulcher, and they are all three entire with their beards and hair. One was called Baldasar, the second Gaspar, and the third Belchior. Marco inquired often in that city concerning the three Magi, and nobody could tell him anything about them except that the three Magi were buried there in ancient times. After three days' journey you come to a castle which is called Palasata, which means the castle of the fire-worshippers; and it is true that the inhabitants of that castle worship fire, and this is given as the reason.[153]

It is intriguing that there exists evidence from Iran that the Magi did travel from that location to pay homage to Jesus. Polo later even references the Magi's gifts of gold, frankincense, and myrrh. Thus, the inhabitants of the region were at least aware of the narrative. Polo also gives an account of an

---

152 A. V. Williams Jackson. "The Magi in Marco Polo and the Cities in Persia from Which They Came to Worship the Infant Christ," *Journal of the American Oriental Society* 26 (1905): 79–83, doi:10.2307/592877.
153 Marco Polo, *The Travels of Marco Polo* (New York: Orion Press, 1958). 35.

unusual gift that Jesus gave the Magi when they left:

> When they went away, the infant gave them a closed box, which they carried with them for several days, and then becoming curious to see what he had given them, they opened the box and found in it a stone, which was intended for a sign that they should remain as firm as a stone in the faith they received from him. When, however, they saw the stone, they marveled, and thinking themselves deluded, they threw the stone into a certain pit, and instantly fire burst forth in the pit.[154]

Although the Magi were at first disgusted by the gift from Jesus, they soon found out it was more than a stone. The stone transforming itself is, of course, a metaphor for a simple carpenter who turns out to be a Messiah. It also proves that Jesus was respected by some in Iran well into the thirteenth century. Marco Polo reports that the Magi brought some of the fire with them back to their Church, where they worshiped it as a god by offering it sacrifices. Marco Polo believed this to be the reason the inhabitants of Persia worshiped fire.[155] His account, therefore, points to somewhere in first-century Parthia as the best choice for the origin of the Magi, even though this source is one thousand years after the birth of Jesus. It also indicates that the Magi were more than likely aware of Jewish prophecy and religion, since they were in close proximity to the Jewish community in Babylonia.

If the Magi came from Persia or Babylon, they were more than likely well-adept astrologers, astronomers, and philosophers. This required them to spend many hours each day

---

154 Ibid, 34.
155 Ibid.

Chapter 5

learning from ancient manuscripts and experienced teachers and ample amounts of time in the evenings observing the sky. They managed their own astrological charts over the centuries; unfortunately, none survive today. The charts documented when the planets and celestial bodies rose and the paths they followed. Celestial bodies were the subjects of intensely serious study by these wise men. Their proficiency in astronomy required them to watch the movements and alignments of the celestial bodies to predict important events. According to Mark Kidger, in his book *The Star of Bethlehem: An Astronomer's View*,

> If the Magi did indeed come from Babylonia, as is tacitly accepted by many people, then the distance they would have had to travel to get to Jerusalem was around 550 miles... The journey would have been made in a camel train, or possibly, on horseback... If the camel train traveled at around two miles per hour and for around eight hours per day, the journey would have taken close to a month and a half.[156]

From Persia, where the Magi may have originated, to Jerusalem was a journey of between 1000 and 1200 miles. Such a distance may have taken anywhere between 3 and 12 months by camel. Besides the time of travel, there were probably many weeks of preparation, which would include gathering the gifts and readying the animals for the journey. Depending on how hostile the area was, they may have needed guides and bodyguards.

If the Magi were Zoroastrians from Persia, they would have been intrigued by the Jewish idea of a savior bringing

---

[156] Mark Kidger, *The Star of Bethlehem: An Astronomer's View* (Princeton University Press: Princeton, NJ, 1999), 29.

The Magi

justice and happiness to the world. The linkage between a new star and a savior went far back into the Zoroastrian past. They would have known of Balaam, who in Numbers 24:15–19 is described as living in the Mesopotamian city of Pethor and being ordered by the king of Moab to curse the Israelites. Instead, tongue-tied by God, he blessed them and prophesied the coming of a great king out of Israel. Balaam said that there shall be seen a star out of Jacob and a scepter shall rise out of Israel. Zoroaster predicted the advent of a savior known as the Saosyant, who would bring justice and happiness to the world. Thus, the Saosyant and the Star out of Jacob work together as evidence.

According to Carter, the Saosyant denotes a figure who is a combination of priest, deliverer, and saint. Carter writes from the ancient text of Zoroastrianism:

> The victorious Saoshyant with his helpers shall restore the world, which henceforth never will grow old and never die, never decaying and never rotting, ever living and ever increasing, and master of its wish, when the dead will rise, when life and immortality will come, and the world will be restored at its wish . . . In bringing to pass the wonderful and happy future, Saoshyant will be assisted by 15 men and 15 damsels. Together they perform a final sacrifice, the virtue of which will bring about the resurrection and the blessings of immortality. There will be a long conflict with evil but Saoshyant will be victorious.[157]

Maneckji Nusservanji Dhalla noted in his book *Zoroastrian*

---

157 Carter, *Zoroastrianism and Judaism*, 77–8.

Chapter 5

Theology that Persian rulers, guided most likely by political expediency, often built or restored the temples of conquered people, including built temples honoring Jewish, Egyptian, Babylonian, and Greek divinities:

> He notes, "Their empire was made up of various nationalities of diverse faith, and the Achaemenian rulers were always tolerant toward the religions of these subject races. . . . Cyrus ordered the restoration of the temple at Jerusalem, and Darius, the devout worshipper of Auramazda, favored its rebuilding as decreed by Cyrus.[158]

Carter further noted, it was even proclaimed on an ancient cylinder inscription that, "Cyrus was the shepherd and the anointed of Yahweh in Judea."[159]

We still do not know the Magi's reason for visiting Jesus. Was it a pilgrimage to honor Jesus, or more of a political junket to ensure a future alliance between Parthia and Judea? The Magi may not even have known that Jesus was to become a future prophet or ruler, and it is quite possible they believed he would be a combination of both in the image of David or Moses.

When the Magi entered Palestine, they went first to see Herod, the current ruler. Herod was unaware of any new king of the Jews being born, but being the egomaniac that he was, he became extremely jealous. He wanted to know more about this new potential rival and how best to dispose of him. However, he was careful not to let the Magi in on his plan and asked them to return after they found Jesus, so he too could worship the new king. The Magi told Herod when the star first

---

158 Maneckji Dhalla, *Zoroastrian Theology* (New York: AMS Press, 1972), 73.
159 Ibid.

appeared, and then left to find Jesus on their own. Matthew says that Herod told them only to go to Bethlehem. It is unclear why the Magi started their search for Jesus in Jerusalem. It may have been the most logical choice, since Herod was there and it was customary to honor the local ruler when in a new land, or perhaps the weather conditions hampered their astrological skills, forcing them ask for assistance. Once in Bethlehem, the star went before them once again, and led them to Jesus.

Indeed, if the Magi were from western Iran, their astrological skill and knowledge of astronomy may have been lacking compared to that of their neighbors to the west, the Babylonians. It also calls into question the type of astrological object were following, a matter that will be addressed in the next chapter. According to David Pingree in the *Encyclopædia Iranica,*

> We have no direct evidence, however, that would clarify the nature of Iranian astronomy during the Achaemenid period. In the Parthian period, however, we do find evidence from eastern Iran that Babylonian mathematical astronomy and astral omens continued to be studied and that Indian concepts had begun to be influential.[160]

Another popular theory is that the Magi may have been Chaldaeans. Chaldea was a Semitic-speaking nation that existed in the southeastern region of Mesopotamia along the banks of the Euphrates River. For a brief time, during the

---

160 David Pingree, "Astrology and Astronomy in Iran," *Encyclopædia Iranica*, vol. 2, E. Yarshater, ed. (New York: Routledge & Kegan Paul, 1987) 858–871http://www.iranicaonline.org/articles/abul-hasan-ahwazi-astronomer-fl, www.iranicaonline.org/articles/abul-hasan-ahwazi-astronomer-fl.

Chapter 5

sixth century BCE, they came to rule Babylonia, but over time they were absorbed into other nations. The Chaldaeans of the first century CE were much better at astronomy than the Zoroastrians and even practiced astrology with horoscopes, something the Zoroastrians did not do until later centuries.

According to Lindsay Jack in his book *Origins of Astrology*, "The Mesopotamians used the mixture of imaginative reverie and systematic space-division in dealing with the sky as with the entrails of victims. There was nothing unusual in attaching a name to bright and impressive stars, or in grouping several together in some pattern. What was new was the extent to which an anxious and persistent imagination was brought to bear on the earthly or heavenly event."[161]

If the Magi were Chaldeans from Babylonia, they would have been very interested in the activities that were occurring in the sky from 7 BCE to 4 BCE. Because of their closeness to Jewish settlements, they may have known of the Jewish prophecies of a savior and were aware of Jewish customs and rituals. Perhaps they even gave advice or readings to some of the more liberal Jews, or studied the Torah, or they may have been Jewish themselves. The Magi certainly knew of Jesus, the soon-to-be-great king, from some source of information, and astrology and astronomy were around for long time before the life of Jesus. But, as with so much about the Star of Bethlehem, evidence is lacking. An aspect of the problem is determining just how adept the Babylonians were at astrology. According to Zolar in *The History of Astrology*,

> Alexander Marshack, writing in the November 6, 1964, issue of *Science*, thought that the nicks cut in certain reindeer bones and in mammoth ivory during

---

161 Jack Lindsay, *Origins of Astrology* (London: Frederick Muller Ltd, 1971), 24.

the Upper Paleolithic period represent notations of lunar sequences. Thus, some ten thousand to twenty-five thousand years ago man was observing and reporting the cycles of the Moon.[162]

The Mesopotamians believed that the stars and planets were actually gods and goddesses who could use their divine will to influence the lives of humans. Because of this, they became expert astronomers and were able to predict the movements of the starts quite accurately. The development of the Zodiac, with its 12 signs, came next, followed by the casting of personal birth charts. The first horoscopes were naturally for members of the royal family, with the oldest known Babylonian horoscope for a person dating to 409 BCE.[163]

JEWISH ASTROLOGY

In one of the earliest verses in the Old Testament, the author of Genesis leads readers to believe that the stars have a divine purpose. Genesis 1:14 states, "And God said, let there be lights in the firmament of the heaven to divide the day from the night; and let them be for signs, and for seasons, and for days, and years." But, many Christians today believe that looking to the stars for spiritual guidance or horoscopes is immoral. Whether or not the Bible condemns the practice of astrology is a matter of debate. The only thing for sure is that the Bible contradicts itself when it comes to the use of astrology for prediction. In the Old Testament, Isaiah 47:13–14 clearly states that astrologers are evil and will be condemned:

---

162 Zolar, *The History of Astrology* (New York: Arco, 1972), 3.
163 Ibid, xi.

Chapter 5

> Let now the astrologers, the stargazers, the monthly prognosticators, stand up, and save thee from these things that shall come upon thee. Behold, they shall be as stubble; the fire shall burn them; they shall not deliver themselves from the power of the flame: there shall not be a coal to warm at, nor fire to sit before it.

However, Luke 21:25, states, "and there shall be signs in the Sun, and in the Moon, and in the stars." This contradiction has led many followers of the Bible to think it best to avoid the issue altogether, reasoning that is it better to be safe than sorry. It is true that throughout history charlatans have used the celestial bodies for their own personal gain without acknowledging the Creator. Perhaps this is why the Bible vilifies the use of astrology—the Holy Book has a problem with humans taking full credit for predicting the future, or falsely using God's work. Nevertheless, there is evidence that the celestial bodies are here as signs to humans. Whatever the case, astrology became only a small part of the Bible and its stories.

Perhaps skills in astrology were lacking among the Magi, the most famous astrologers in history. We know they lost track of the star and "rejoiced" when it reappeared. The Wise Men, as they also came to be known, were from somewhere outside of Judea and quickly returned there after paying homage to the infant Jesus, in order to escape the wrath of King Herod. But their profession was not new and dates to a much earlier period than Jesus.

As time went by in many ancient civilizations, astrology became an essential part of religion; very often astrologers became respected priests, with a status just below that of the royal family. There were many types of astrologers in practice during this time; it is important to know what these were in order to help explain the extent of the astrological knowledge the Magi had.

PTOLEMAIC AND GREEK ASTROLOGY

Because of proximity, the early Christians of Egypt may have had some influence on the Christians of Judea with the practice of astrology. This also may have strengthened the legend of the Magi when Christians read Matthew, or it may have inclined the author of Matthew to write about the Magi following the Star of Bethlehem in the first place. The Egyptians became expert astronomers, using the celestial bodies to align their temples and pyramids. They were also concerned about the effects of the heavens on humans, and are thought to have learned astrology from the Greeks, who learned it from the Babylonians. There is evidence that the Egyptians, under the Ptolemaic Greeks, were charting the zodiac before the time of Jesus. On the sandstone ceiling of the pronaos of the Temple of Hathor in Dendera was a carved relief that represented a map of the sky. According to Ramaden Hussein,

> The image of the sky represented eternal cycles, not only the death, rebirth, and resurrection of Osiris, but also the planting, harvesting, and replanting of crops and the life, death, and rebirth of the people of in the afterlife ... Based on the positions of the planets in relation to the constellations and references to eclipses, the zodiac has now been dated precisely to 50 B.C.[164]

---

164 Ramadan B. Hussein, "A Visit to Denidera," *Calliope* 21, no. 3 (November 2010): 20, *MasterFILE Complete*, EBSCO*host*.

Chapter 5

This becomes very significant when you think of how near Egypt is to Israel. Although Egypt is west of Jerusalem and the Magi came from the East, one cannot rule out the possible influence Egyptian astrology had on Matthew when he wrote about the Magi and the Star of Bethlehem. Another influence on Matthew may have come from Greece.

When Alexander the Great conquered much of the known world, Babylonian astrology was absorbed by the conquered areas of his empire and brought back to Greece and Egypt by Ptolemy. This makes sense, because the Chaldean priests influenced the Greeks in ways other than just astrology; after all, they were also very adept in medicine and science. It was in Greece that astrology became more personal, however, due to the fact that the Greeks were more humanistic than their eastern neighbors. Their gods and goddesses were very much like humans, and while the gods were in control of the heavens, at times humans could use them for personal motives. In a lot of Greek mythical lore, humans go head to head against the gods, and at times get the better of them. Astrology allowed the Greeks, in minor ways, to manipulate the gods. Zolar writes the following:

> Both Plato and Aristotle defended the divinity of the stars, but they did not ask the heavens for prediction of the future. This is true, despite Aristotle's saying; "This world is inescapably linked to the motions of the world above. All power in this world is ruled by these heavenly motions." This attitude nevertheless allowed for popular beliefs in prediction by astrology.[165]

---

165 Zolar, *The History of Astrology*, 56.

The Magi

Greek astrology was based on Babylonian astrology. The main difference between them was their spheres of influence. Greece was at the crossroads of Europe, Asia, and Africa. Greek was becoming the universal language of the region, and most nations felt the Greek influence on everything from theology to science. Like Egypt, Greece most likely did not have a great influence on the Magi themselves, but it may have influenced the writers of the New Testament, who sometimes wrote in Greek instead of Hebrew.

ROMAN ASTROLOGY

Through their conquest of Greece, the Romans were also influenced by the Greek style of astrology. As Greek slaves journeyed into Roman houses, they brought their practice of astrology with them. Tamsyn Barton notes that the rise of astrology in Rome paralleled the shift in how Rome was ruled:

> I argued that the timing of astrology's rise in profile at Rome just as the old Republican oligarchy gave way to the rule of one man, was no coincidence, in connection with the monarch. The old system, in which power was diffused among a small ruling class, needed diviners under firm control of the state.[166]

Since emperors and generals were individuals, and personal horoscopes are for individuals who want to know what the future looks like, the practice of astrology was popular with the elites. Emperors wanted to predict the future because of the occupational hazards of their profession, including the far too frequent assassinations that ended many

---
166 Tamsyn Barton, *Ancient Astrology* (Routledge: London, 1994), 62–3.

Chapter 5

of their reigns. Every now and again an upstart general would also seek out the skills of a good astrologer. Perhaps the most famous of these imperial forecasts to come to pass was the advice given to Julius Caesar to beware of the Ides of March.

At times, the practice of astrology was subject to strict laws imposed by the Republic and later emperors. Between 8 and 13 decrees expelled astrologers during the time between the deaths of Julius Caesar in 44 BCE and Marcus Aurelius in 180 CE. The decrees often came as the result of civil unrest and times of great peril. Examples of this were the civil war fought between Augustus and Marcus Antonius, or the trial of Marcus Sribonius Libo Drusus, a young man with imperial lineage, who was consulting astrologers and other mystics to help him overthrow Tiberius. However, Barton informs us that, "Libo committed suicide before he could come to trial. The Senate immediately passed two decrees against astrologers and diviners, and two men, either astrologers or magicians, were executed publicly, one being thrown off the Tarpeian Rock and the other beaten to death with rods to the sound of bugles."[167]

One can only imagine the effect these executions had on would-be professional astrologers. None the less, many wealthy Roman citizens consulted them, and these incidents prove that the use of astrology could be an important instrument of propaganda against the general public when used under the right circumstances.

Perhaps the low point in the relationship between the Roman Empire and astrology coincides with the rise of Christianity. This started to unfold around the time St. Augustine began a campaign against the practice of astrology. In 358 CE, laws connecting magic and divination were finally

---

167 Ibid, 44.

formalized. By then, they were regarded as one and the same—and punishable by death. This included prominent members of the imperial court when Constantius II (317–361) became concerned over his entourage practicing divination.[168] In response, he warned that even those of high rank were subject to death.[169] During these early years of Christianity, those mainly in charge, emperors and high bishops, did not want to compete with any forms of pagan worship, and for a time this included astrology, which therefore became unfashionable throughout the Christian realm for a short while.

CONCLUSION

An early 3rd century source for the Magi coming from Persia comes from Julius Africanus (mentioned in Chapter 2). Perhaps, the best evidence of the Magi's origins is from Marco Polo, although it dates to over a thousand years after their journey. He strongly indicates that they came from northwest Persia. When theorizing about the astrological skillset of the Magi, it might be best to under- rather than overestimate. First-century Roman astrology was deficient when compared to the later, pre-Renaissance period, when astrology was part of the required curriculum at many European universities. It was similarly deficient in Persia. Astrology was practiced more in Egypt, Greece, and Babylonia. Although Roman emperors around the time of Jesus had their horoscopes done, they were used more as instruments for propaganda than anything else.

---

168 Constantius II was the son of Constantine the Great and Fausta. He ascended to the throne along with his brothers, Constantine II and Constans, upon the death of their father.
169 Barton, *Ancient Astrology*, 64.

Chapter 5

Therefore, would-be psychics had to be careful to support their clients and not tell them anything negative, or present their findings in the wrong way.

Richard Trexler writes in his book *Journey of the Magi* that the early Christians were embittered by the overwhelming rejection of the Jewish establishment toward the upstart religion. To make matters worse, they further believed that because of persecution from the Romans, their best hope for survival was the non-Jewish world of the Gentiles. Because of this, Trexler believes that Matthew had probably already identified the Magi as representatives of the Gentile world:

> Indeed, Matthew probably already thought of the Magi as representing that gentile world. Augustine would establish the notion of the Magi as the "first fruits" of the gentiles, while Luke's Jewish shepherds, converted over time into the polar opposite of the rich, intelligent Magi, soon stood for all Jews. When had the Jews received such a legation as that of the Magi to Jesus, asked Augustine triumphantly. Even the queen of Sheba had come only to hear Solomon, not to adore him as the Magi adored the king of the Jews.[170]

Overtime the Magi came to represent something more than ambassadors. They did not represent kings or rulers of other nations but became "wise men" who set out to honor the new king. Their journey to Bethlehem to worship Jesus parallels the journey of everyday Christians who seek out the wisdom of the Lord. Their journey to Jesus was long and filled with potential harm from Herod; however, through the help

---

170 Richard Trexler, The Journey of the Magi: Meanings in History of a Christian Story (Princeton, Princeton University Press, 1997), 15.

of God, they returned safely home. It is believed that they were not Jewish—they were perhaps the first non-Jews to worship Jesus, but their journey may have been influenced by Jews living in Babylon. In the past, historians have focused on the astrological and astronomical skillset of the Magi while overlooking their political motives. Marco Polo leads us to believe that the Magi themselves may have been kings. If they were not, they were must likely ambassadors for a king of Parthia or local regional ruler. Long before the birth of Jesus, Parthia and Rome had clashed over the territories in between the two ancient powers. Since Herod was a puppet ruler of the Roman Empire, the rulers of Parthia would have relished the idea of Herod being deposed by a new king of the Jews. We know that the Jews rejected Jesus as the Messiah because they were searching more for a warrior king, similar to David, who would free Judea from Roman tyranny. It should not be much of a stretch to believe that the Magi similarly hoped for a Jewish revolution. Although it is not often mentioned, the motives of the Magi may have been political as well as religious.

It must also be remembered that Herod and his brother were named as tetrarchs by the Roman leader Marcus Antonius to support Hyrcanus II. Hyrcanus was later deposed by his nephew Antigonus, who had help from the Parthians. Herod then bribed Marcus Antonius to not only restore him to tetrarch, but to make him king of Jews. G. A. Williamson states, "Herod was never at a loss for appropriate gifts, which in his approaches to Antonius were on a vast scale. Antonius had a political motive too: Rome could never tolerate a Jewish king who owed his throne to their most dreaded enemies, the Parthians."[171]

---

171 G. M. Williamson, *The World of Josephus* (Boston: Little, Brown and Company, 1964), 78.

Chapter 5

Therefore, Rome helped Herod defeat Antigonus, who was executed, and the Roman senate named Herod king of the Jews. Thus, Magi from Parthia or Babylonia most likely would have raised Herod's suspicions even if they were not official state ambassadors. The Magi may have had other motives than worshiping Jesus. As far as we know, they did not return to honor Jesus after the first visit. The true reasons behind this remain suspect. Nevertheless, Matthew does inform us that Herod allowed the Magi to visit Jesus in order to determine his location, so Herod could later have him murdered. It remains unknown how upset Herod was when the Magi did not return, but more than likely he was not happy, and would perhaps have executed them if he could have. The only real clue that remains of the motives of the Magi are the gifts that they brought to honor Jesus.

It is written in Matthew that the Magi "bowed down and worshiped him" before presenting him with gifts of gold, frankincense, and myrrh. Isaiah 60:6 prophesied that gold and frankincense would be given to the king as gifts. Gold was always a symbol of wealth and royalty, and was not an unusual form of gift. Frankincense is a yellow gum that comes from the frankincense tree. When heated, it gives off a sweet scent. It was a common ingredient in the holy anointing oil used by priests. Myrrh comes from a shrub that exudes a yellow-brown oily resin that is highly fragrant and used to anoint the dead.

Since myrrh was used in anointing the dead, many Christians assume the gift was intended to foreshadow the coming sacrifice Jesus would make. But, it must be remembered that myrrh has other medicinal and religious uses. The Greeks and Romans used it for many different ailments, from lesions of the mouth to hemorrhoids. Winston Craig notes that the herb was one of the ingredients of the anointing oil used in the Jewish tabernacle and served as incense in religious rituals centered on ancient gods. It was proved effective as a fumigant for homes and temples of the Old Testament.[172]

Why the Magi worshiped Jesus remains unknown. Some have suggested that they desired to worship the future religious icon. We know that the Jews were expecting more of a deliverer from Rome and less of a prophet. Therefore, it must be questioned why the Magi would be seeking something other than the general consensus. Regardless of false propaganda, Persian kings were not considered gods by their subjects. According to Lindsay Allen,

> Although the Persian kings strongly associated themselves with certain gods, there is no sign that a state religion was used as a tool for drawing all kinds of subjects into a ritual relationship with the monarch. Despite the implications of overweening ideas about divinity suggested by some Greek authors, the Persian kings were not perceived as divine in their own milieu (the mantle of divinity descended only where regional kingship traditions, as in Egypt, required it)."[173]

By the time of the Parthian Empire, kings had even less of authority than the Persian kings three hundred years earlier. If the Magi practiced the Zoroastrian religion, then they, like the Jews, would have been very uncomfortable worshiping another god, since their religion was monotheistic. But, their religion also includes such features as messianism and the

---

172 Craig, Winston J. "Myrrh: Nature's Ancient Anti-Inflammatory Agent," *Vibrant Life* (2008): 20, *Academic OneFile*, EBSCO*host*.
173 Lindsay Allen, *The Persian Empire* (Chicago: University of Chicago Press, 2005), 126.

Chapter 5

concept of heaven and hell. Thus, they would have been spiritually in tune with the teachings of Jesus. It is my belief that the journey of the Magi may have had political motives. If they thought Jesus was the future king of the Jews, they may have wanted to recruit him before the Romans did. However, like many Jews, the Magi may have failed to realize that Jesus was unique. The New Testament does not mention any other visits by the Magi.

Another possibility, that will be examined greater in Chapter 6, is that the Magi assumed Jesus was in peril. A particularly interesting Passover Full-Moon eclipse occurred close to the believed time of Jesus' birth. Centuries before Jesus, Magi believed lunar eclipses were an evil omen for their king. When one occurred special prayers, religious amulets, and rituals were required.

The Magi believed the light of the Moon was important. At the end of the month, when the Moon was not visible, hostile powers of the night temporarily gained the supremacy in heaven. During this time the king was responsible to perform special rituals. Needless to say, a total lunar eclipse was an extremely dangerous time for the king. These belief lead to the Magi charting and predicting eclipses. Over time they were able to accurately forecast lunar eclipses.

Eclipses were among the most the important celestial events in Babylonian astronomy. Even the Moon-god Sin was not safe during a lunar eclipse. Sin was responsible for the illumination of Moon that lighted the night time heavens while protecting the world from the seven demons. Over time not only was Sin in danger, but also the ruler. Sin was associated with cattle because the waxing Moon appears similar to the horns of that animal. An association to him and fertility devolved due to the Moon's connection to cattle and the similar lengths between lunar and menstrual cycles.

The Magi might have, although evidence is lacking, viewed the lunar eclipse occurring at the exact same time as the Star of Bethlehem as an attack on Sin and the infant Jesus. One demon in particular, Lamashtu, becomes the main suspect. She was an evil she-demon, daughter of the god Anu, who attacked unborn children and infants.

Mesopotamian infants were protected in the mother's womb against Lamashtu though the use of magical amulets. The amulets often depicted the demon on one side and a spell exorcising it on the other. The child was still in danger from Lamahtu for the next two to three years, who was held responsible for infant mortality. According to Jane McIntosh,

> Amulets and spells or incantations were used against such known dangers, and representation or symbols of benign spirits were placed above or beside the openings into houses—doors, windows, and even pipes—to prevent evil spirits from entering. Unforeseen ills were dealt with by exorcism or magic, a sorcerer driving away the demon responsible, using spoken formulae and ritual gestures and procedures, and attempts were made to avoid them by using divination.[174]

It is my strong belief that the Magi viewed two events at the same time, the Star of Bethlehem and a Passover eclipse. The Star informed them of the birth of Jesus. The eclipse, according to Babylonian religious beliefs, lead them to believe that Jesus was in peril and needed protection, or the current leader Herod was dying. One of the many misconceptions about the Magi was that they were Christians or Jewish. They

---

174 Jane R. McIntosh, *Ancient Mesopotamia: New Perspective* (Santa Barbara, CA: ABC-CLIO, 2005), 216.

Chapter 5

were trained Magi who believed in the ancient Babylonian magic and religious practices. The main purpose for their visit to Jesus may have been to present him with a special amulet to protect him from Lamashtu. Another theory was that it was to honor him as the savior told of in the Zoroastrian religion. It was not to worship him as Christians would. Many scholars have totally overlooked this fact. In their Star of Bethlehem theories, the Magi use Old Testament prophecy as reasons to recognize Jesus as the king of the Jews without even considering the obvious fact that the Magi practiced the Babylonian religion.

Overlooking Babylonian beliefs and religious practices is a crucial, but a common mistake. Figure 5.1 is an obsidian amulet. It displays Lamashtu on the front with a magical formula on the back that rendered the demon's power worthless. Sometimes the demon Pazuzu was displayed on the amulets. Pazuzu, although a demon also, was so feared by Lamashtu that he drove her and her powers away, therefore protecting the mother and infant. Perhaps a similar amulet was the Magi's gift of gold to Jesus.

Figure 5.1

Lamashtu demon amulet, ca. early 1st millennium B.C., Mesopotamia or Iran, courtesy of the Metropolitan Museum of Art

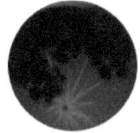

CHAPTER 6

THE STAR OF BETHLEHEM

In 1870, German archeologist Heinrich Schliemann directed major excavations at the city of Troy. Located in the modern nation of Turkey, Troy is in the far northwest of the Anatolian peninsula, which is also the farthest western protrusion of the Asian continent. Before Schliemann's discovery, Troy and the Trojan war were consigned to the realm of legend. Nevertheless, the location of ancient Troy had always been the subject of interest and speculation, and many archeologists were determined to find the lost city. Much of what was known about Troy came from the narrative set in Greek poems, in particular the *Iliad,* which is attributed to Homer.

Chapter 6

In the *Iliad*, many of the characters take on godlike qualities, and the gods even take sides during the war. But, even though the Greek historians, Eratosthenes, Herodotus, and Duris of Samos all provided dates for the war, later historians were quick to dismiss both the city and war as legend. Contributing to this was that little was known about the historical Homer. Historians date the completion of the *Iliad* to around 750 BCE, during a period known as the Epic Cycle of narratives that were written in the sixth century BCE from older oral traditions. Attitudes toward Homer as a historian changed after Schliemann's discovery and proved that sometimes myths do have historical value. According to Michael Wood, from *In Search of the Trojan War*, the oral traditions are shrouded in the mists of time:

> Oral tradition, especially in the shape of Homer, was all they had to rely on, because, as Josephus points out so many years ago in his preface to the *Jewish War*, "it was late, and with difficulty, that they came to the letters they now use." In terms of 'archaeology' the Comparable Greeks also had little sense of the ancient past . . . [175]

Just as they were by Troy before its discovery, historians are baffled by the Star of Bethlehem. Troy and the Star are similar in other ways as well: The Greeks were not skillful in written history before Homer. The *Iliad* contained many unbelievable events, and not much is known about Homer. Similarly, the Jews were not skillful in astronomy, the Gospel of Matthew contains many unbelievable events, and less is

---

[175] Michael Wood, *In Search of the Trojan War* (New York: Facts on File, 1985), 29.

known about the author or authors of Matthew than is known about Homer.

Academia offers several diverse theories, countless probabilities, and sometimes heated debate on the topic of the Star among self-proclaimed experts and well-informed amateurs. Despite this, and the unlimited possible outcomes for what the Star was, it is best to limit the debate to only a few of the more probable hypotheses. The authors of the New Testament could be accused of falsifying events to match with prophecy from the Old Testament. Figure 6.1 shows this.

Figure 6.1

Figure 6.1 Prophecies of the Coming of Jesus	Old Testament Scripture	New Testament Fulfillment
The Messiah would be born of a woman.	Genesis 3:15	Matthew 1:20 Galatians 4:4
The Messiah would be born in Bethlehem.	Micah 5:2	Matthew 2:1 Luke 2:4-6
The Messiah would be born of a virgin.	Isaiah 7:14	Matthew 1:22-23 Luke 1:26-31
The Messiah would come from the line of Abraham.	Genesis 12:3 Genesis 22:18	Matthew 1:1 Romans 9:5
The Messiah would be a descendant of Isaac.	Genesis 17:19 Genesis 21:12	Luke 3:34
The Messiah would be a descendant of Jacob.	Numbers 24:17	Matthew 1:2
The Messiah would come from the tribe of Judah.	Genesis 49:10	Luke 3:33 Hebrews 7:14
The Messiah would inherit King David's throne.	2 Samuel 7:12-13 Isaiah 9:7	Luke 1:32-33 Romans 1:3
The Messiah's throne will be anointed and eternal.	Psalm 45:6-7 Daniel 2:44	Luke 1:33 Hebrews 1:8-12
The Messiah would be called Immanuel.	Isaiah 7:14	Matthew 1:23
The Messiah would spend a season in Egypt.	Hosea 11:1	Matthew 2:14-15
A massacre of children would happen at Messiah's birthplace.	Jeremiah 31:15	Matthew 2:16-18

Chapter 6

PIOUS FICTION VS. PROPHECY

Figure 6.1 (previous page) displays some of the uncanny similarities mentioned in the Old Testament that were then fulfilled in the New Testament with the birth of Jesus. In order to legitimize the prophecy, however, solid scientific evidence is required. An important piece of evidence is the Star of Bethlehem.

One possible theory about the Star of Bethlehem is that it was a miracle of God, something never seen before or after in the nighttime skies over Judaea. This reflected two schools of theology, those who did not believe in miracles from God and those who did. One of the great riddles for scholars is which came first, those who lamented pious fiction or those who shouted hallelujah to fulfilled prophecy. The former viewed Matthew's Nativity narrative as an apologetic account invented after the fact to establish the Messianic status of Jesus. Their opinion is that since the Star of Bethlehem does not occur in any of the other Gospels or anywhere else in the New Testament, it was pure fiction. One scholar, R. M. Jenkins, concludes that there exists no generally accepted answer to what the Star of Bethlehem was. It could have been a fictional story invented by Matthew, or it may have been inspired by the appearance of Halley's Comet in 66 CE, shortly before the Gospel of Matthew was written. According to Jenkins, "Matthew may have invented the star completely or it may have been based on oral stories of some manifestation in the heavens that occurred by chance at around the same time. This significance could either have been astronomical or astrological or both."[176]

---

[176] R. M. Jenkins, "The Star of Bethlehem and the Comet of AD 66," *Journal of the British Astronomical Association* 114 (December 2004): 336–42, *Academic Search Premier*, EBSCOhost.

The Star of Bethlehem

Jenkins also points out that one likeminded professor, William Phipps, also prefers the explanation of Josephus that the Magi visited Herod in 10 BCE and Comet Halley influenced the author of Matthew. But, this is questionable. Josephus wrote that when Herod completed Caesarea Sebaste, he celebrated the new capital of Judea by commanding that a great festival take place. This festival attracted ambassadors from other nations. Josephus stated in *Antiquities of the Jews* *16.5.1*, "Now, when a great multitude had come to that city to see the shows, as well as the ambassadors whom other people sent, on accounts of the benefits they received [from Herod], he entertained them all . . ."[177]

It has been suggested that ambassadors and Magi were the same in order to "influence" Matthew, but are ambassadors literally the same as Magi, and did Herod really benefit the rulers of Parthia? Many of the cities he dedicated and temples he rebuilt were in Greece or Syria, and Herod was ruler of Judea, thanks to his support and political alliance with Rome, not Parthia. Therefore, even the pious fictionist can be accused of fabricating stories.

If a valid candidate for the Star of Bethlehem can be found, this would give more credit to biblical prophecy and show that the Star was more than a miracle. Numbers 24:17, interestingly reads, "I see him, but not now, I behold him, but not near, A star will come out of Jacob; a scepter will rise out of Israel."

ASTROLOGY VS. ASTRONOMY

In the last chapter, it was mentioned that the practice of astrology became less popular after Christianity became the

---

177 Flavius Josephus, *The Complete Works of Flavius Josephus, the Celebrated Jewish Historian* (Philadelphia: John E. Potter, 1870), 495.

Chapter 6

official religion of the Roman Empire. It was close to dying out altogether in the West when the empire began to weaken, as wave after wave of barbarian invasions occurred a couple of hundred years before the final fall of the empire. But, because the Magi were from Babylonia or Parthia, it raises the question of what was more important in aiding the Magi in their quest—astrology or astronomy, or was it a healthy combination of the two?

Several years after Jesus, as the decline of the Roman Empire unfolded, astrology in the Arab world continued to play a significant role among the established sciences. Writings of the famous Arab astrologer Albumassar (805–886 CE) and others soon found their way into European centers of learning once Europe had begun to recover from the fall of the empire; astrology was added to the curriculum of many European universities. In fact, Thomas Aquinas (1225–1274 CE), one of the most influential Church leaders and writers, became an admirer of astrology. Through him, astrology became acceptable again to the Church and was considered the cause of all advents that take place on Earth. By the Renaissance, even the Popes had astrologers as members of their papal staff, and astrology came into fashion again, along with the return of other Greek ideas and culture. The *Catholic Encyclopedia* informs us that many Catholic rulers went to astrologers for advice:

> Emperors and popes became votaries of astrology—Charles IV and V and Popes Sixtus IV, Julius II, Leo X and Paul III. When these rulers lived astrology was, so to say, the regulator of official life; it is a fact characteristic of the age, that at the papal and imperial courts ambassadors were not received in audience until the court astrologer had been con-

The Star of Bethlehem

sulted ... Thus had astrology once more become the foster-mother of all astronomers. In the judgment of the men of the Renaissance—and this was the age of a Nicholas Copernicus—the most profound astronomical researches and theories were only profitable insofar as they aided in the development of astrology.[178]

However, with the Renaissance also came the Enlightenment and the Scientific Revolution, and an eventual decline in the importance of astrology. Once again, it was viewed as unnecessary and a form of witchcraft. Ironically, it was one of astrology's greatest admirers, Johannes Kepler (1571–1630), who also played a major role in its decline and near end during this era.

Kepler, one of the world's best-known astronomers, was born in the modern nation of Germany in 1571. At the University of Tübingen, he excelled in mathematics. He wished to become a minister but was persuaded to teach mathematics and astronomy at what is today the University of Graz. It was here that he began to develop his theories for the eponymous laws of planetary motion. David Love reports that in 1599, he sent a letter to his friend Herwart von Hohenburg that reads,

> How does the face of the sky affect the character of a man at the moment of his birth? It affects the human being—- for as long as he lives—- in the same way as the knots which the peasant haphazardly puts around the pumpkin. They do not make the pumpkin grow, but they decide its shape. So, does the sky: it does

---

178 Charles G. Herbermann and Edward A. Pace, *The Catholic Encyclopedia* (New York: Appleton, 1907), 18–25.

Chapter 6

not give the human being morals, happiness, children, fortune and wife, but it shapes everything in which the human begin is engaged.[179]

Love sums this up by stating, "In other words, he saw astrology in much the same way as we now see our genes—not as a complete determinate of all our actions but as a strong and inescapable influence on us.[180]

Kepler believed that astrology had a strong influence on humans. In his preface to the *Rudolphine Tables*, published in 1627, he states, "Although one may deny that events of human affairs depend on the stars, nevertheless he is certainly forced to recognize some effects on human affairs."[181] But Kepler is, unfortunately, said to have contributed to the downfall of astrology on the university level when his laws provided one of the foundations for Isaac Newton's theory of universal gravitation. After Newton and the scientific revolution, astrology was no longer part of academic life in Europe. It returned to popularity during the early twentieth century but outside of mainstream religion, where it remained part of the occult. Scientific revelations made astrology and astronomy into separate, unrelated subjects, but if one explores the mindset of the Magi and manages to keep the hold the two subjects together, several possible celestial objects rise to the challenge of being contenders for the Star of Bethlehem. Occultations could fit this. An astronomical occultation is when one astrological object moves in the front of, or occults, another.

---

179 David Love, *Kepler and the Universe: How One Man Revolutionized Astronomy* (Amherst, NY: Prometheus Books, 2015), 118.
180 Ibid.
181 Ibid, 120.

THE DOUBLE OCCULTATION OF BETHLEHEM

Astronomer Michael R. Molnar, who is retired from the Physics and Astronomy Department at Rutgers University, has made a detailed case for his theory that the Star of Bethlehem, may have been a pair of astrologically significant lunar occultations. An occultation occurs when the Moon passes in front of another body, making it disappear from the sky. He writes of the Moon's occultations of Jupiter in Aries on March 20 and April 17, 6 BCE, in his book, *The Star of Bethlehem: The Legacy of the Magi*. According to Molnar, the occultations signaled to the Magi that a "King of the Jews" was about to be born in Palestine. Hence, they soon embarked on one of the epic treks of the New Testament, with gifts in hand for the new king.

Corresponding with Molnar, this was possible because astrologists, or Magi in this case, would view the Moon passing in front of Jupiter, a planet associated with royalty, while in Aries the Ram (the ram being the ancient symbol for Judea), indicating that a new king of Judea was about to be born, and under such rare circumstances, an important one.

Molnar's theory connects somewhat well with the integral idea in that April 17, 6 BCE, would fall during the month of Nissan, the month in which the prophets were born and died, according to the belief from the Talmud, but it would not fall during the Passover celebration that commenced on April 4 of the year. One would have to decide how precise the integral idea needs to be, either by the exact month or by the exact Passover week to accept Molnar's date. He does have his critics though. Mark Kidger points out many problems with the March 20 and April 17 occultations of 6 BCE. In this case, it was the planet Jupiter that the Moon moved in front of. If the Moon passes in front of a planet or star, when the celestial

Chapter 6

body suddenly reappears at the border of the Moon, particularly at the border of the Moon's disk, which creates a shadow, the result is an amazing sight to behold. But Molnar's occultation may not have been amazing. According to Kidger:

> Although the March and April occultations were theoretically visible from Jerusalem, we must also consider practicality. The April 17 occultation occurred near the heliacal rising of Jupiter, with the Moon exactly one day before New, when it is unlikely to be visible ... Furthermore, the occultation occurred around midday in Jerusalem and Babylon, and a thin crescent Moon would be totally invisible in the sky so close to the Sun during daylight ... This occultation would thus have been totally invisible. The March 17 occultation occurred after sunset. It was not visible in Babylon because Jupiter had already set there at the time, but it was visible in Jerusalem, if only marginally ... For Molnar's theory to be tenable, we must assume that the Magi were able to interpret correctly an event that they could not have seen.[182]

Consistent with a few of Kidger's concerns is Arron Adair, who wrote the following in an article for *Sky & Telescope*:

> When the book came out, the news media reported this idea as a major historical breakthrough. Ancient Babylonian tablets, however, state that this type of event foretold the *death* of a king. Talk about

---

182 Kider, *The Star of Bethlehem*, 106–9.

interpretive flexibility! Besides, the occultation was invisible, taking place in the daytime near the Sun."[183]

There are a few other issues with Molnar's historical research. A significant part of his theory revolves around the purchase of coins from the region that show the zodiac Aries the Ram looking back at a star. The coins were supposedly issued to honor the rare occultations of 6 BCE and the coming of a new king in Judea. However, several other Roman coins from the time also show zodiacs with a star above them. Molnar admits that Aries the Ram is often displayed as looking backward. He states, "The lore says that Aries is looking backward for Helle, and another interpretation says that Aries is admiring his Golden Fleece, not a star.[184] Therefore, a Roman coin is more likely to portray Aries looking backward at a Golden Fleece, not the occultation of Jupiter. Perhaps Molnar gave too much significance to the coin with the imprint of Aries. Today, his theory provides readers only with questions about his true motives and research methods.

The two coins in figure 6.2 show that zodiacs on coins was not unusual. The first coin struck in 14-16 CE is from Antioch.[185] It displays the Roman god Zeus on the front and Aries the Ram on the reverse. I will leave it up the reader to speculate what the desired result was by the Roman authorities issuing this coin, but it is a far strength to imagine it had anything to do with the 6 BCE occultation. The second coin is

---

[183] Aaron Michael Adair. "Science, Scholarship, & Bethlehem's Starry Night." *Sky & Telescope* 114, no. 6 (December 2007): 26. *MasterFILE Complete*, EBSCO*host*.
[184] Michael Molnar, *The Star of Bethlehem: The Legacy of the Magi* (New Brunswick, New Jersey, Rutgers University Press, 2000), 50.
[185] Photograph courtesy of ForumAncientCoins.
/www.forumancientcoins.com/gallery/displayimage.php?pos=-56925

Chapter 6

from Cypress (ca. 27 BCE– ca. 14 CE).[186] It shows that zodiacs, in this case Capricorn and Scorpio, with stars was nothing more than, a zodiac and a star to remind the common people that they were constellations in the heavens, and not Earth animals.

Figure 6.2

Top Photograph: Antioch of Syria under Augustus courtesy of forumancientcoins.com

Bottom Photograph: Cyprus Time of Augustus 27 B.C.- 14.A.D. courtesy of Athena Numismatics/ vcoins

---

186 Photograph courtesy of Athena Numismatics/ vcoins.com
www.vcoins.com/en/stores/athena_numismatics/18/product/cyprus_time_of_augustus_27_bc__14_ad_two_zodiac_signs_in_one_coin_and_probably_the_finest_/607630/Default.aspx

THE CONJUNCTION OF BETHLEHEM

Perhaps if St. Augustine, whose influence on Western thought is as great as anyone's, had not had such a love-hate relationship with astrology, then more Christians would take a more liberal approach to it and not cast it as an instrument of the Devil. It has been suggested by many scholars searching for a meaning to the Star of Bethlehem that is was not a "star" at all, but an astrological sign or a planet, perhaps Venus or Jupiter. But, there are problems with this theory. The Magi more than likely would have been very familiar with these and would not have mistaken them for a "star." However, there is a case to be made that the Star was a conjunction of two or more planets. Conjunctions occur when planets travel roughly along the same circle and pass each other.

Conjunctions are rather common and would not seem to be a significant enough event to send the Magi on a five-hundred-mile, or much longer, trip to Jerusalem. However, a triple conjunction may have excited the Magi. This occurs when a planet appears to travel backward in the sky in a movement known as retrograde motion. In retrograde motion, two planets pass each other, then one backs up and they pass each other again, and finally, they pass each other a third time as normal forward movement is resumed. The triple conjunction hypothesis appealed to many scholars because in Matthew the star somehow stood over Bethlehem to guide the Magi. This could indicate that it was an object in retrograde.

Retrograde motion may seem like a difficult subject to understand. But it is a natural occurrence. The next time you pass a car on the highway you will notice from your vantage point that the car, while traveling in the same direction as you, appears for a moment to be traveling backward. This is retrograde or retrogradation. The same phenomenon may be

Chapter 6

observed with planets, except that instead of watching from your car, you are watching from the Earth. Christopher Crockett neatly sums up the concept in an online article for *EarthSky.org*:

> Typically, the planets shift slightly eastward from night to night, drifting slowly against the backdrop of the stars. From time to time, however, they change direction. For a few months, they'll head west before turning back around and resuming their easterly course. Their westward motion is called retrograde motion by astronomers. Though it baffled ancient stargazers, we know now that retrograde motion is an illusion caused by the motion of the Earth and these planets around the sun.[187]

A triple conjunction between Jupiter and Saturn occurred in 7 BCE and has been mentioned as a possible candidate for the Star of Bethlehem. Making the display even more impressive was a massing (a massing is when several planets move into close proximity in the sky) of Mars, Jupiter, and Saturn that immediately followed the conjunction. The conjunctions and massing also occurred in the constellation of Pisces, which was often identified with the Jews.

In December of 1996, Craig Chester wrote in an article for *Imprimis* about the possibility of a conjunction being the Star of Bethlehem:

> According to him, "In 3 B.C. And 2 B.C., there was a series of close conjunctions involving Jupiter, the planet that represented kingship, coronations and the

---

187 Christopher Crockett, "What is retrograde motion?" EarthSky, February 6, 2017, http://earthsky.org/space/what-is-retrograde-motion.

birth of kings. In Hebrew, Jupiter was known as *Sedeq* or "Righteousness," a term also used for the Messiah.[188]

In September of 3 BCE, Jupiter came into conjunction with Regulus (the star of kings), the brightest star in the constellation of Leo. Although Chester does not force the issue with an exact date for the Nativity, he does think in the article that the events were enough to signal the Magi to travel to Judea. In order for his theory to hold up, he needs to go against the consensus of most historians and move the death of Herod from 4 BCE up to 1 BCE.

One of the problems with conjunctions is how they explain the accounts in Matthew of the star standing over Bethlehem. Chester points out that conjunctions do appear to move when they exhibit a retrograde loop, showing both backward and forward movement. In order to give the article a feel-good Christmas mood, Chester notes that, "We do know for certain that Jupiter performed a retrograde loop in 2 B.C. and that it was stationary on December 25, interestingly enough, during Hanukkah, the season for giving presents."[189]

More recently, Rick Larson, a lawyer from Texas, has added to the hype created by Chester. Larson has done an ample amount of research on the Star of Bethlehem and found a new and somewhat convincing contender for it by extending the assumed date of Herod's death, thought by conservative scholars to be 4 BCE, by three years. Like Chester, he points to other scholars, Andrew Steinmann in particular, who studied old manuscripts of Josephus and found that the date of Herod's death might have been copied incorrectly or

---

188 Craig Chester, "Star of Bethlehem." *Imprimis* 22(12) (December 1993): 1–7.
189 Ibid.

Chapter 6

wrongly calculated and may have occurred in 1 BCE, not 4 BCE.

As noted earlier, inept copyist and mathematical errors were common until the invention of the printing press and computers. This was sometimes on purpose, and sometimes just negligent. If this theory is correct, then it contributes to an already confusing matter by adding three more years to account for in determining the date of the Nativity.

According to Larson, the first conjunction in September of 3 BCE was the Conception of Jesus, and nine months later, in June of 2 BCE, Jesus was born.[190] This would also allow for the Magi visiting Jesus around December 25, when he was six months old. Nonetheless, Larson does contribute some interesting thoughts to the problem and makes valid points.

Traditionally, scholars believed that Herod died in 4 BCE because Josephus mentions that Herod died in the interval between a lunar eclipse and the following Passover. This is tantalizing, because if the death of Herod is ever proven, it would narrow down a birthdate for Jesus. For centuries, the accepted date of Herod's death has been following the lunar eclipse of March 13, 4 BCE.

NASA can verify that an eclipse did occur at this time. Recent calculations, however, showed that this eclipse was only partial (40 percent total and fairly hard to detect), and that the events narrated by Josephus to have occurred between this eclipse and the Passover that followed are nearly impossible to fit in if one believes the 4 BCE date as the death of Herod. The total eclipses of January 9–10, 1 BCE, and December 29, 1 BCE, however, eliminate this problem.

Assisting Larson in his theory of the Star of Bethlehem is the work of Steinmann. Steinmann examines the time between

---

190 Rick Larson, *The Star of Bethlehem*, DVD, Stephan Vidano, Stephen Vidano Films, Mpower Pictures. 2009.

the death of Herod and his funeral before the year's Passover. According to him, several scholars began to advance a 1 BCE rather than a 4 BCE date.[191] Josephus gives a precise account of Herod's funeral and all the events that led up to it. The main event was the eclipse that occurred shortly before his death. Some of the other events during this time include the day before the eclipse, when Herod has two Jewish rabbis burned alive for prematurely celebrating his death by tearing down a golden eagle (the symbol of the Roman Empire) over the Temple's eastern gate. A day later, Herod's health worsened, and he was advised by his physicians to travel from Jericho to Callirrhoe to bathe in the mineral waters there. After the remedies failed, Herod, admitting he was dying, sent for Jewish elders from throughout the kingdom to place them in custody until his death, and to be executed afterward. This was in order to ensure that there was mourning (instead of celebration) following his demise. After the elders arrived, he received letters from Rome giving him authority to execute his son Antipater for the murder of Pheroras and other acts of treason (Antipater was killed immediately). Finally, five days later, Herod died.[192]

Herod had ordered an elaborate funeral procession and a seven-day period of mourning following the funeral. The procession traveled about 23 miles from Jericho to his grave at Herodium and included the crown jewels, which were brought from Jerusalem and spices to treat the body, requiring 500 domestics to carry them. All of this, we know, occurred before Passover.[193]

---

191 Andrew E., Steinmann. "When Did Herod the Great Reign? " *Novum Testamentum* 51 (2009), 1–29, *JSTOR Journals*, EBSCO*host*.
192 Ibid, 13.
193 Ibid, 13–4.

Chapter 6

Steinmann estimates that allowing for the shortest possible time for each event, a minimum of 41 days would have to have elapsed after the eclipse of 4 BCE for all events to occur, not enough time between the eclipse and Passover. But if Herod died during the 1 BCE eclipse, this would have allowed 92 days for all the events to have occurred, which would be much more reasonable. The next closest eclipse occurred on January 10, 1 BCE, which Steinmann believes was enough time. If he is correct, this also opens the window for Jesus to have been born earlier, perhaps as early as 2 BCE.[194]

But Steinmann ignores one important fact mentioned by Josephus, a fact that Steinmann himself lists: "The Passover came, and immediately afterward, Herod Archelaus left for Rome to have his authority to rule confirmed by Augustus.[195] Most historians prefer 4 BCE as the death of Herod because that is when his son' reigns began. Steinmann's theory revolves around the surmise that the sons of Herod began their reigns before Herod died. But according to Josephus, Herod Archelaus was not an official ruler until after Herod's death. Steinmann sidesteps this fact by insisting that Herod Archelaus dated the start of his reign to 4 BCE because this was when he was named Herod's successor.[196] This would be highly unusual. Most of the time, the new king or queen becomes ruler on the death or deposal of the old ruler, and dates his reign to then, not before. Herod would have had to have three sons for this to be possible.

Therefore, Steinmann desires Herod Archelaus's reign to coincide with Herod's, so that Herod could die in 1 BCE instead of the expected 4 BCE; nevertheless, nothing is revealed about Herod's younger sons Herod Antipas and

---

194 Ibid, 16.
195 Ibid, 14.
196 Ibid, 20.

Philip the Tetrarch, whom Augustus had also named as rulers. After the death of Herod, Herod Archelaus ruled Galilee and Perea, and Philip the Tetrarch ruled Iturea and Trachonitis, but both began their reigns in 4 BCE. Did Herod have three sons as co-rulers while still alive? Nothing is known of this.

Despite this information, Larson examined conjunctions occurring after 4 BCE. He found through a modern computer software program named Starry Night that there was a triple conjunction of Jupiter and the star Regulus (which is in the constellation of Leo the Lion), followed by a conjunction of Jupiter and Venus in Leo ninth months later. Six months after that, Jupiter "stops" (goes into retrograde) in Virgo. It would have been possible for the Magi to detect this conjunction, and perhaps it was also a significant enough celestial display to inspire them to visit the newborn king.[197]

According to Larson, this triple conjunction started on September 11, 3 BCE, which he believes is the Conception of Jesus. This is the first meeting of Jupiter and Regulus (looking east). Regulus is the brightest star in Leo and thought to be very special. The nation of Israel is often referred to as the "Lion of Judah," so this meeting would have been important. Then, nine months (the duration of a pregnancy) later, on June 17, 2 BCE, Jupiter and Venus (the planet of mothers) met in Leo (over Israel this would have been in the west), and it would have been a very bright "star" indeed. This would have marked the birth of Jesus. Then on December 25, 2 BCE, if you were in Jerusalem looking south toward Bethlehem, Jupiter would be "standing" in Virgo, the constellation of the Virgin (Mary being a virgin). Larson believes that this was the day the Magi would have visited the baby Jesus. Molnar, and later Larson, bring up many questions about astrology because

---

[197] Frederick A Larson, "Setting the Stage," The Star of Bethlehem (n.d), http://www.bethlehemstar.net/stage/stage.htm. (accessed August 28, 2017

Chapter 6

both of their calculations would have been detected and interpreted by the Magi using some form of astrology.

The problem with Molnar's and Larson's royal configuration and occultation theories is that the Star of Bethlehem is not a star at all, only a conjunction or occultation. These are not unusual astrological events and would not take on the unique features mentioned in Matthew. The author or authors of Matthew should be given some consideration when they call a star a star that moved. Going against the integral theory, that prophets were born during Passover, Molnar's date of April 17, 6 BCE, is too late to have occurred during the seven days of Passover of that year, which commenced around the Full-Moon of April 4, and Larson's date of June 17, 2 BCE, is far from the Passover Full-Moon that occurred on April 19 in that year.

THE SUPERNOVA OF BETHLEHEM

Another possibility is that the Star of Bethlehem may have been a nova or supernova. Nova means "new" in, referring to what appears to be a very bright new star shining in the sky; the prefix *super* distinguishes supernovas from ordinary novas, which are far less luminous. Supernovas are more than a nova. Sir Colon Humphreys softens the theory:

According to Sir Colin Humphreys, "The first suggestion that the star of Bethlehem was a nova or a supernova was made by Foucquet in 1729, and possibly earlier by Kepler in 1614... A nova or supernova satisfies the requirement that the star of Bethlehem was a single star which appeared at a specific time, but cannot account for the star moving through the sky. Similarly, all other suggestions for the star of

The Star of Bethlehem

Bethlehem (e.g. that it was Venus, etc.) can be ruled out except one, a comet.[198]

Nova are relatively frequent appearances of a "guest star." They turn on and off over a period of years. Novas occur in binary star systems in which one star is a normal star while the other is a compact white dwarf. A dwarf star is the remnant of the death of a star like the Sun, in which about half of the mass of the Sun has been compressed to a millionth of its volume, making a dense object about the size of the Earth. Hydrogen-rich gas pours from the normal star into an accretion disk around the white dwarf and then builds up a shell of material on the surface of the white dwarf. As this material accumulates, it becomes hotter and denser. Eventually, it ignites into a thermonuclear explosion, which causes the star to light up for days or weeks as material is ejected from the star. Figure 6.3, from NASA, shows one.

Figure 6.3

Image Credit: NASA

---

198 Colin J. Humphreys, "The Star of Bethlehem—a Comet in 5 BC—and the Date of the Birth of Christ," *Quarterly Journal of the Royal Astronomical Society* 32 (1991), 389–407.

Chapter 6

The word supernova was coined by Walter Baade and Fritz Zwicky in 1931 to describe a stellar explosion that briefly outshines an entire galaxy, radiating as much energy as the Sun or any ordinary star is expected to emit over its entire life span before fading from view over several weeks or months. After supernovas explode, they collapse into objects far more condensed than white dwarfs and far less luminous, or into neutron stars or black holes that provide no brightness to the galaxy. Isaac Asimov describes the effect of supernovas on the universe:

> Supernovas contribute to the dust and gas supply of the universe, and are important to star formation in three ways. 1. They add to the raw material, of course. 2. The shock wave of the explosion may initiate a wave of compression in a cloud of dust and gas that may happen to exist near the supernova. That sets in motion the formation of a star, or even the formation of a whole cluster of stars. 3. The dust and gas of the supernova is rich in massive atoms that formed at the core of the star, and these are crucial to the eventual formation of life.[199]

Supernovas are rare events and can occur at any time. People living from 1572 to 1604 were fortunate enough to witness two supernovas in our galaxy. They can be the brightest star in the sky before fading and can be observed during the day if bright enough. The last directly observed supernova in our galaxy, the Milky Way, was Kepler's Star of 1604 (SN 1604); remnants of two more recent supernovas have been found retrospectively. Nevertheless, observations in

---

199 Isaac, Asimov *Exploring the Earth and the Cosmos* (Crown Publishers, Inc.: New York, 1982), 222.

other galaxies indicate that supernovas occur on average about three times every century in the Milky Way, making our galaxy well overdue for one.

The ancients were not welcoming toward new objects in the sky, according to Asimov:

> The Greek philosopher Aristotle (384–322 B.C.) felt this changelessness of the sky to be a law of nature. On Earth, he believed, all things changed and decayed, were first formed and then destroyed, while all things in the sky were changeless, perfect, and perm-anent."[200]

Objects such as clouds, comets, meteors, and the weather were considered inside the Earth's atmosphere, and outside the realm of the sky. This belief, along with the popularity of Aristotle, placed astronomers in a difficult position whenever new objects, such as supernovas, were discovered in the Greek and Roman dominions. Asimov continues:

> Once astronomers got the fixed idea that there was no change in the heavens, they would grow very reluctant to report a change. They would fear being disbelieved and worry that their reputation might suffer... Eventually, to report such a change might even have come to involve sacrilege.[201]

Comets, meteors, and supernovas were considered bad omens most of the time in the ancient world. Many scholars use this fact to dismiss the possibility that the Star of

---

200 Isaac, Asimov, *The Exploding Suns: The Secrets of the Supernovas* (Truman Talley Books: New York, 1985), 2–3.
201 Ibid, 13.

Chapter 6

Bethlehem was a supernova or comet. But it must be remembered that the Jews were not astronomers, and because they used a lunar calendar were primarily focused on the phases of the Moon, not celestial omens, despite Genesis 1:14 informing us that there will be signs in the sky. It must also be remembered that we do not know the true political motives of the Magi. They might have very well embraced bad omens if they opposed the Roman Empire or its close ally Herod.

It was only during the last five hundred years that normal astrological events have been viewed as just that. Due to resistance from the Catholic Church, Western astronomy required time to develop. This resistance slowly began to recede after 1543, when Polish astronomer Nicholas Copernicus (1473–1543) published a book describing the mathematics necessary to predict movements of the planets. This book was so controversial at the time that it was published only his deathbed; legend has that he was handed a copy shortly before expiring. Copernicus assumed that the Earth, along with the other planets, revolved around the Sun, a very controversial theory during this time in history. Many people were unwilling to believe that the Earth was traveling through space at an enormous speed and was not stationary, at the center of the universe. It would take at least another half-century before astronomers began to accept the heliocentric theory.

Three years after Copernicus's book was published, Tycho Brahe (1546–1601) was born in the south of Sweden, which at the time was part of Denmark. When he was about 14, he observed an eclipse of the Sun and became interested in astronomy. Then, on November 11, 1572, he observed a new star in the constellation Cassiopeia that was brighter than any of the others in that popular constellation. He continued to watch the star while it remained bright for a relatively brief period and then began to fade. In all, he observed the star for 485 days. Interestingly, using a similar timeframe, this would have been enough time for the Magi to notice the star, travel to Judea, and meet with Herod. It is assumed that Herod ordered the slaughter of all newborns under the age of two based on the Magi's report of when the star first appeared in Babylon/Persia.

Johannes Kepler, a student of Brahe, was one of the first modern astronomers to debate about what identifiable astronomical phenomenon could be linked with the Star of Bethlehem. In December of 1603, he became curious after he witnessed a conjunction of the planets Jupiter and Saturn with Mars followed in the same area by a supernova in the constellation Ophiuchus. According to A. J. Sachs and C. B. F. Walker, this was a triple conjunction:

> In medieval times the conjunction of Jupiter and Saturn, known as the "great conjunction" (recurring only once every 1986 years on average), was regarded as of great astrological significance. Kepler calculated that a similar conjunction with Mars moving into the vicinity soon after had occurred in the year 7 B.C. = Julian year 39. On that occasion, the conjunction had been a triple conjunction, a very much rarer event than the normal single conjunction.[202]

Kidger notes that the triple conjunction theory is mistakenly attributed to Kepler:

---

202 A. J. Sachs and C. B. F. Walker, "Kepler's View of the Star of Bethlehem and the Babylonian Almanac for 7/6 B.C.," *Iraq* 46 (1984): 43–55, doi:10.2307/4200210 (accessed August 28, 2017).

Chapter 6

Kepler in fact, believed that the Star of Bethlehem was a nova similar to the one he had just observed. Despite this, most discussions of the Star incorrectly attribute the triple conjunction theory to Kepler. In fact, the first serious suggestion that the triple conjunction theory was the Star of Bethlehem was not made until 1825.[203]

It has been suggested that a supernova or nova could not be the Star of Bethlehem because the death of a star was not considered a good omen by the ancients. But taking a philosophical approach, the death of an old star, or regime, could also activate the creation of new stars—a new regime. It must be remembered that Jesus was not well received by the old regimes; in fact, it was the Romans who crucified him, only to later succumb themselves to Christianity, and it was the Jewish authorities who denied him, only to have their power weakened in later generations by the Christians, now more powerful with support from the Gentile world. However, there are still other celestial objects that the Star of Bethlehem could have been.

THE COMET OF BETHLEHEM

Origen was one of the first theologians to suggest that the Star of Bethlehem may have been a comet or had comet-like qualities. He speaks of this in *Contra Celsus, Book I, Chapter 58*:

> He writes, "The star that was seen in the east we consider to have been a new star, unlike any of the other well-known planetary bodies, either those in

---

203 Kidger, *Star of Bethlehem*, 204.

the firmament above or those among the lower orbs but partaking of nature of those celestial bodies which appear at times, such as comets, or those meteors which resemble beams of wood, or beards, or wine jars, or any of those other names by which the Greeks are accustomed to describe their varying appearances. And we establish our position in the following manner.[204]

Figure 6.4

Image Credit: NASA

Interestingly, the Chinese similar to the Greeks in naming them by their appearance in everyday object, called some comets "brooms." Comets (Figure 6.4) are celestial snowballs composed of ice, frozen gases (carbon dioxide, ammonia, methane, and more), rock, and dust that together form a nucleus as large as several miles across. Astronomers believe that they are left-overs from the gas, dust, ice, and rocks that initially formed the solar system around 4.6 billion years ago. When a comet's orbit approaches the Sun, it heats up and

---

204 Origen, *The Ante-Nicene Father, Translations of the Writings of the Fathers down to A.D. 325 Vol 4*, (Buffalo: C.L. Pub. Co., 1885), 422.

Chapter 6

spews dust and gases into a giant glowing head that can form a cloud called a coma, which expand out to 50,000 miles. The dust and gases from the tail of a comet can stretch away from the Sun for another 600,000 miles.

According to Humphreys,

> Comets probably have the greatest dramatic appearance of all astronomical phenomena. They can be extremely bright and easily visible to the naked eye for weeks or even months. Spectacular comets typically appear only a few times each century. They can move slowly or rapidly across the sky against the backdrop of a star, but visible comets usually move through the star background at about 1 or 2 degrees per day relative to the Earth.

Humphreys also reminds us that the identification of the Star of Bethlehem as a comet originated with Origen in the third century, and was popular among Renaissance painters, including Giotto, in their depictions of the Nativity.[205]

To date, the most valid candidate for the Star of Bethlehem is a celestial body from actual Chinese records. They report that an object of interest was observed in 5 BCE for more than 70 days. The 5 BCE date for the Star of Bethlehem also fits well with the textual evidence for the length of stay of Jesus and his family in Egypt. According to Matthew 2:13–15, after the Magi left Bethlehem, Joseph was warned that Herod planned to kill Jesus, so the family left for Egypt (a classic refuge for those trying to flee the tyranny of Palestine) and returned after Herod died. Both Origen and Eusebius state that Jesus and his family were in Egypt for two

---

205 Humphreys, "The Star of Bethlehem," 392–3.

The Star of Bethlehem

years and they returned in the first year of the reign of Herod Archelaus, one of Herod the Great's sons, whose reign began when Herod died.

Therefore, if Herod died at the end of March, 4, BCE, the first year of the reign of Herod Archelaus would have been from April 4 BCE to April 3 BCE. Jesus and his family probably left for Egypt shortly after the Magi left Bethlehem, about April–June 5 BCE. If they stayed in Egypt a reasonable time after the death of Herod, to be absolutely sure of the news, they might have returned to Israel on, say, March 3 BCE, when traveling conditions would be good, in the first year of Herod Archelaus, having spent about two years in Egypt. Accordingly, the 5 BCE Chinese object is consistent chronologically with both Herod's massacre of the infants and the two-year stay in Egypt, and it is the only celestial object the ancients recorded that would fit the description of the Star of Bethlehem.

Isaac Asimov notes that the Chinese reported objects in the cosmos that the Roman and Greeks did not bother with:

> Between 500 B.C. and A.D. 1500, China was far ahead of the West in science and technology. Throughout ancient and medieval times, Chinese astronomers kept a close watch on the sky and recorded anything unusual that happened anywhere. They were not hampered by dogmatic beliefs of perfection, and theirs was a relatively secular society in which fear of supernatural beings did not unduly restrict their thinking.[206]

---

206 Asimov, *The Exploding Suns: The Secrets of the Supernovas,* 14.

Chapter 6

Asimov adds that the Chinese were interested not only in scientific research but also astrology. They regarded heavenly events as omens of earthly occurrences like wars, plagues, and the death of important people. They also recorded any new "guest stars" that appeared briefly among the permanent stars. Many of these too were missed by Western astronomers. Before long, Korean and Japanese astronomers were using technology learned from the Chinese.[207]

Naturally, the Chinese and other Far Eastern records have been closely examined to find if any of their observations reveal celestial objects that were discovered around the time of Jesus. Two events do exist that could very well be the Star of Bethlehem. The first, a possible comet or nova, is found in a book called the *Ch'ien-han-shu,* which, according to Kidger, states the following: "In the second year of the period of Ch'ienp'ing, the second month, a *hui-hsing* appeared in Ch'ie-niu for more than 70 days."[208] The second month in the Chinese calendar is equivalent to the period from March 10 to April 7, 5 BCE. Ch'ien-nui is the Chinese constellation that included Alpha and Beta Capricorni. *Hui-hsing* literally means "broom stars." These were bright comets with tails that swept through the sky with their movement. Seventy days would have given the Magi enough time to reach Judea, meet with Herod, and find Jesus.

The second account is from Korea. *In the History of the Three Kingdoms—-the Chronicle of Silla* reports: "Year 54 of Hyokkose Wang, second month, (day) Chi-yu, a *po-hsing* appeared in Ho-Ku." Ho-Ku is the Chinese constellation, or asterism, that includes Altair and various stars of the south of Aquila (the Eagle). The problem with this account that has confused scholars is that Chi-yu did not exist in the second

---

207 Ibid, 14–5.
208 Mark Kidger, *The Star of Bethlehem*, 235.

month. Mark Kidger notes, "Chi-yu really should be "I-yu," a character written in an almost identical fashion... the chronical really states: "Year 54 of Hyokkose Wnag, second month, (day) I-yu, a *po-hsing* appeared in Ho-Ku." (the Korean characters are very similar). This would translate to a date of March 31, 4 BCE."[209]

This would also mean that the Korean object, most likely a nova, would have been viewable during Passover of that year. However, the fact that both celestial objects were observed in the same vicinity as Capricorn only a year apart has led astronomers to theorize that they were the same event and that one sighting was erroneously reported. It is most likely that the Chinese observation is more accurate because the Chinese had been keeping records longer and have a long history of detailed bookkeeping.

In 1978, A. J. Morehouse claimed in an article for The Journal of The Royal Astronomical Society of Canada that the Star of Bethlehem was actually a sequence of events:

> He stated, "I propose here, however, that the "Christmas Star" was actually three unrelated events ... The first of these was a series of conjunctions which, altogether, covered a period of 11 months and which began with the first of a triple conjunction of Jupiter and Saturn. The second was a passive nova which appeared around March 24, 5 BCE, about 11 months after the end of the conjunctions. This nova appeared near the winter solstice point of that date, perhaps close enough to be of importance to the astrologically-minded Magi. The third event, which occurred almost 11 months to the day after the

---

209 Ibid.

Chapter 6

second one, was the appearance of another nova . . . It is still debatable whether the object was a nova or comet."[210]

The 5 BCE object makes an excellent "Star of Bethlehem," and the other worldly signs would have only added to the significance of the nova. Of all the possibilities listed to date, by far the best choice for the celestial candidate that explains the Star of Bethlehem is the Chinese object observed during the Passover of March 23, 5 BCE. Making this celestial object an even more attractive candidate for the Star is that comets are connected to the reign Roman Emperor Augustus Caesar.

AUGUSTUS' COMET

Augustus Caesar appears to have a political fondness for comets. There exist two ancient sources that tell of Augustus' use of comets for propaganda. The first is from Pliny the Elder (CE 23–79). He was a Roman author, naturalist and natural philosopher, a naval and army commander of the early Roman Empire, and a friend of the emperor Vespasian. Pliny wrote in the encyclopedic *Natural History* about Augustus' use of a very brilliant comet observed shortly after Julius Caesar's assassination in 44 BCE, and just before Augustus dedicated the Olympic games to Venus. Augustus used this comet to connect its appearance with his family in their claim of divine honor, as being directly descended from Venus. Pliny writes:

In one only Place of the whole World, namely, in a Temple at Rome, a Comet is worshipped: even that

---

[210] A. J. Morehouse, "The Christmas Star as a Supernova in Aquila." *Journal of the Royal Astronomical Society of Canada*, vol. 72 (April, 1978): 65-7.

The Star of Bethlehem

by *Divus Augustus Caesar* himself was judged fortunate to him. Who, when it began to appear, acted in Person as Overseer in those Games which he made to *Venus Genetria*, not long after the Death of his father, *Caesar*, in the College by him erected.[211]

Similar to the United States dollar today, ancient coins were a form of identification and propaganda for Roman rulers. Augustus used the image of a comet on the reverse of many of his coins to assert the deification of Julius Caesar. Image 6.5 below shows Augustus' use of comets to justify his reign by placing them on the reverse of some of his coins.

Image 6.5

Photograph: Augustus silver denarius with comet tail pointing upwards 19-18 BCE courtesy Roma Numististics

Augustus also placed the image of Capricorn, his zodiac sign, on many of this coins. Image 6.6, next page, shows Augustus use of his zodiac Capricorn by placing one on the reverse of his coins. This one shows Capricorn with the globe at his feet with a ridder and cornucopia on its back.

---

211 Pliny the Elder, Holland, Philemon, *Pliny's Natural History in Thirty-Seven Books* (London: Barclay, 1847-49), 65.

Chapter 6

Image 6.6

Photograph: Augustus silver denarius with Capricorn c. 16 BCE courtesy of A. Marinescu, Vilmar Numismatics LLC

It must be remembered that Julius Caesar was never officially proclaimed emperor. Therefore, he took advantage of the 44 BCE comet to proclaim his legitimacy. This belief is reinforced through the writings of Ovid. Named Publius Ovidius Naso (43 BCE–17/18 CE), he was a popular Roman poet who lived during the reign of Augustus. Ovid writes in the *Metamorphoses* about Julius Caesar's death and the comet of 44 BBC:

> No sooner had he spoken when the goddess slipped back into the senate house unseen and took the still-fresh soul from Caesar's body, which she would not let vanish in the air, and carried it up to the stars in heaven; and as she did so, she could see it glowing and feel it start to kindle in her bosom: she let it go; and as it flew through space trailing fire, it flickered like a star.[212]

---

212 Ovid, *Metamorphoses*, XV; 1060.

THE BEST ANSWER IS IN CHINESE

Some historians have questioned what this object was. But, according to David Hughes, what the object was not debatable: "There seems to be insufficient evidence available to enable us to decide whether the 5 BCE event was a comet or a nova and there is therefore no reason to doubt the statement in the Han-shu that the object was a comet."[213]

The observation date of March/April coincides with the Talmud's assertion that the great Jewish prophets, like Isaiah, were born during the Passover month of Nissan. Perhaps if the Magi had been aware of the Torah and Babylonian Talmud they would have taken notice of a new star or comet appearing during Passover.

Not mentioned elsewhere, but something else to consider is the total lunar eclipse that occurred during the Passover Moon on March 23, 5 BCE. If the Magi were associates of Jews or just experts in religion, they would have known that the Jewish Passover is always on the first Full-Moon following the spring equinox.

Lunar eclipses can be viewed anywhere on Earth that is on the night side of the Earth, although, as shown in Figure 6.7 on the next page, some places are better than others.[214] The year is dated as 4 BCE but is actually 5 BCE, because

---

213 David Hughes, *The Star of Bethlehem: An Astronomer's Confirmation* (New York: Walker and Company, 1979), 151.

214 Definitions for Figure 6.5: Total indicates that the Moon was completely eclipsed by the umbra of the earth; Saros 61 is the Saros series number of the eclipse (each eclipse in a Saros is separated by an interval of 18 years,11.3 days; TD is the Dynamical time of Greatest Eclipse, or the instant when the distance between the center of Moon and the axis of the Earth's umbral shadow cone reaches a minimum; Tot. = 102m is the duration of total phase of the lunar eclipse; Par + 222m is the duration of partial phase of the lunar eclipse, or the time interval between first and last contact of the Moon with the umbral shadow.

Chapter 6

there is a zero year in most computer-generated data for scientific research, unlike Gregorian or Julian calendars. One can tell from the figure that the eclipse was very visible in Parthia, and a little less in Judea, and was not seen in the Americas. The top icon within the image shows that the eclipse was a total one, as the Moon was completely in the shadow of the Earth. Therefore, if weather conditions were normal, the Magi in Parthia would have witnessed the eclipse. The eclipse lasted 01h 42m, a very long lunar eclipse; the longest, in 1859, lasted 01h 46m. Interestingly, during the April 4, 6 BCE Passover, only one year earlier, a partial lunar eclipse occurred (Figure 6.7). Two consecutive Passover lunar eclipses most likely concerned some Jews as a sign for change.

Figure 6.7

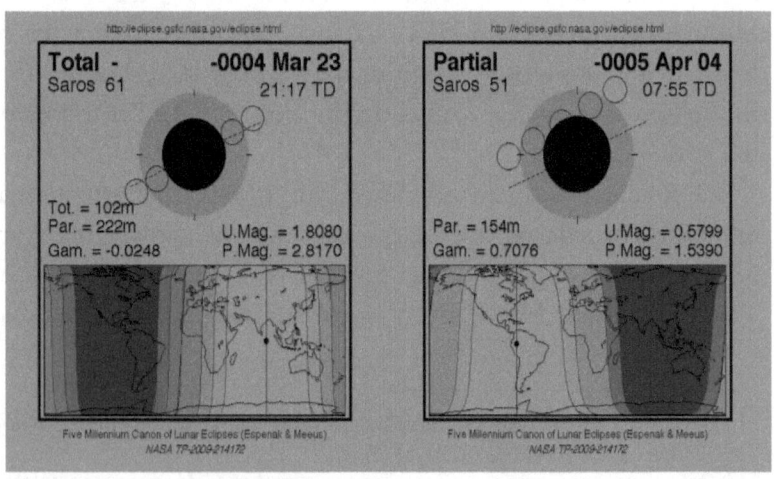

The Magi interpreted each eclipse based on its own individual aspects. Each one was different, and there was no set formula for interpretation. According to scholar Herman Hunger, it is difficult to use Babylonian text to imitate the

Magi. Each tablet containing an omen was filled with contradictions and ambiguities. He notes,

> The aspects of a lunar eclipse which are considered in the proteases are the following:
> A. Date of the eclipse (month, day);
> B. Time and duration
> C. Appearance of eclipse (magnitude, direction of motion of the eclipse shadow, color);
> D. Phenomena associated with the eclipse (wind, weather, earthquakes etc.; stars and planets visible).[215]

For Jews, any eclipse was an ominous sign, but they were infrequent during a Passover Moon, and that likely was upsetting to some, and a harbinger of great change for others. The Babylonian Talmud Sukkah Tract 29a states,

> The rabbis taught: An eclipse of the sun is an ill omen to the whole world. What does this resemble? A human king making a banquet for his servants, and placing a great lantern before them, when he gets angry he says to his servant: Take away the light, let them sit in the dark. We have learned in a Boraitha: R. Meir said: When the sun and the Moon are eclipsed, it is a bad sign to the enemies of the Israelites (meaning, the Israelites themselves), because they are used to troubles: it is equal to the teacher's coming to the school with his whip in his hand. Who is more afraid? The child used to being beaten.[216]

---

215 Herman Hunger and David Pingree, *Astral Sciences in Mesopotamia*, (Leiden, NL.: Brill, 1999), 15.
216 Rodkinson, *New Edition of the Babylonian Talmud*, 2054.

Chapter 6

Many historians agree with 5 BCE for the date of the Nativity based on the consensus view that Herod died in 4 BCE and Jesus was born shortly before. Appendix 1 (back of the book) shows several possible years that the Nativity may have occurred during the Passover Moons. Five BCE is the best choice for several reasons. I have listed them here in the hopes of defending my thesis more easily. Passover in 5 BCE started on March 23 with the Full-Moon phase. The Church Fathers indicated in several different sources that Jesus was born around March 25. This would be the third day of Passover. Of all the years listed in the Appendix, 5 BCE is the only one that Passover could have occurred in on March 25. In keeping with Talmudic tradition, it's the only year that Jesus could have been born near March 25 and at the same time during Passover.

Evidence for a March 25, 5 BCE Passover Nativity

1. The Conception would have occurred around the Jewish fast of Tzom Tammuz on July 3, 5 BCE. This was a fast commemorating the breaching of the walls of Jerusalem before the destruction of the Second Temple. In John 2:19 Jesus said, "Destroy this temple, and I will raise it again in three days."
2. Chinese records indicate that a comet was observed in March of 5 BCE. This is the only evidence of any ancient celestial object in the heavens anywhere else from this time period. It must be remembered that the Chinese were very meticulous in their data. They did not note any other celestial candidates for the Star of Bethlehem. The only other candidates are occultations and conjunctions, mentioned only by recent scholars, which no ancients mention in any

source. The Chinese, not being Christians, also have no bias or reason to falsify the reporting of the comet to correlate with prophecy.
3. A lunar eclipse occurred during the March 23 Passover of 5 BCE. The Talmud states that lunar eclipses are not a good omen for Israel. This would most likely have interested the Magi.
4. A partial lunar eclipse occurred during the April 4, 6 BCE Passover. Was this a prelude to the March 23, 5 BCE total eclipse?
5. A penumbral lunar eclipse occurred during the Passover of April 16, 7 BCE, only two years before the March 23, Passover total eclipse. This was viewable in eastern Asia, but not Israel or Persia. A penumbral lunar eclipse is when the Moon traverses the Earth's penumbral shadow, but misses the Earth's umbral shadow. The result is the Moon appears darker. Was this a prelude to the next two Passover lunar eclipses in 6 BCE and 5 BCE?
6. The 5 BCE Passover eclipse and the Chinese comet were in the sky at the same time. This would have most likely interested the Magi.
7. The *De Pascha Computus*, from the third century, attributed to St. Cyprian, accepts March 28 (the fourth day of creation/Passover and the formation of the Sun) as the birth of Jesus. In 5 BCE the spring equinox in the Jewish calendar was on March 25. It must be remembered that Passover sometimes begins the day before the Full-Moon and sometimes after.
8. Herod died in 4 BCE; therefore, the story of the slaughter of the innocents and the exodus of Joseph, Mary, and Jesus to Egypt fit chronologically.

Chapter 6

9. Hippolytus's statue, of the third century CE, indicates that Jesus was born and died during Passover. Notes on the statue list 2 BCE (three years late) as the birth and 32 CE (two years late) as the death of Jesus.
10. St. Augustine in the fourth century wrote in the *De Trinitate* that Jesus was conceived on March 25. This would fit with Church doctrine that established the birth of Jesus on December 25.
11. March 25, 5 BCE, was the third day of Passover and a Saturday, the day of Jewish worship. Jesus was resurrected on the third day of Passover, a Sunday, the day for Christian worship. Exodus 31:12–13 states: "Then the Lord said to Moses, "Say to the Israelites, 'You must observe my Sabbaths. This will be a sign between me and you for generations to come, so you may know that I am the Lord, who makes you holy.'"
12. The Talmud mentions that Isaac, the son of Abraham, was born and died during the Jewish month of Nissan on Passover. Jesus is often compared to Isaac, and if born on March 25, 5 BCE, would have been born on a Passover.
13. Luke 2:41 states, "Every year his parents went to Jerusalem for the Feast of the Passover." Jesus was born in Bethlehem, about six miles from Jerusalem, even though he was raised in Nazareth.
14. The 5 BCE Chinese comet was observed first near the constellation of Capricorn. Also known as the goatfish. The goat, along with the lamb, were viewed as animals important for sacrifices to God. Capricorn was also the zodiac of Augustus, a sign for pagan Rome that a great change was coming.

CONCLUSION

A Passover eclipse, with a comet near the constellation of Capricorn occurring at the same time, would most likely have warned the Magi or nearby Jews of coming change. Because the eclipse occurred during Passover, they may have linked it to the Jews and believed a great change was about to occur in their leadership politically and religiously. Historically, the great Jewish political leaders were also religious figures (Abraham, Moses, David, and Solomon).

Chinese astronomers maintained careful dates for comets and other celestial events, which have been preserved to this day. They listed two comets between 20 BCE and 10 CE. One of them is recognized to have been Halley's comet in 12 BCE, the other (a comet with its tail in the constellation Capricorn), in 5 BCE. The 5 BCE comet is intriguing. Other astronomers have strongly suggested it was the best candidate for the Star of Bethlehem (Humphreys, 1991), because it fits the timeframe between the death of Herod in 4 BCE and the mention in the Gospels that Jesus was around 30 when his ministry began.[217] Since the comet has not been identified with a known object, it must have an orbit period of greater than about 2,000 years.

Many astronomers dismiss the notion that the Star of Bethlehem was a comet because of the negative messages they bring with them. Throughout history, comets were thought to be harbingers of disaster and were often believed to signal the demise of a king rather than the arrival of a new king. Humphreys further adds that they were associated with sweeping the past away:

---

217 Colin Humphreys, "Star of Bethlehem," *Science and Christian Belief*, 5 (1995), 83–101.

Chapter 6

The Chinese called comets "broom stars" on account of their tails, and at least two ancient Chinese references make a pun of the word "broom." A Chinese description of a comet of 524 BCE saw it as a "new broom" to sweep away traditions and the old order of things (Davidson 1985), and Tsochhiu (ca. 300 BCE) stated that "a comet is like a broom, it signals the sweeping away of evil."[218]

The Chinese star reported during Nissan 5 BCE was viewed in the constellation of Capricorn. Constellations are just groups of stars; there are 88 of them, of which, as I have noted, the 12 of the zodiac are the most popular, each an arrangement that resembles an image (Aries, Taurus, Gemini, etc.). These images have appeared in the sky every year at the same time for thousands of years. Even though each of the 12 represents a time of the year (for example, people born from June 22 to July 22 are considered Cancers), as noted earlier, the constellations are not always most visible during the time named for them. Cancer, even though it represents June/July is a winter constellation best viewed in the sky during February.

The fact that the comet was observed near the constellation of Capricorn may have had additional religious significance. Keep in mind that zodiacs are also constellations, but not all constellations are zodiacs. Zodiac constellations are the specific 12 constellations that pass by the Sun once a year. According to Robin Kerrod, zodiac constellations, meaning "circle of animals," because most constellations are named after animals, are also the constellations that we assign to people according to their birthdate.[219] The Earth makes one

---

218 Ibid, 395.
219 Robin Kerrod, *The Book of Constellations: Discover the Secrets in the Stars*

The Star of Bethlehem

complete orbit around the Sun every 365 ½ days, or one year. But from our viewpoint on Earth, it appears that the Sun is revolving around the Earth, not the other way around. The path the Sun follows stays the same every year and remains constant against the backdrop of the stars. When the Sun "passes through" each Zodiac, the people born during that time consider that Zodiac their sign. Astrology deals with the art of predicting how the Sun will influence the lives of the humans who were born at that time of the year. Most people know their zodiac sign but are not aware that the Sun, because of precession (the slight gyration of the Earth's axis in space) now passes through the constellations a month earlier than it did in Roman times. Thus, you might think you are a Capricorn but were really born while the Sun was in Sagittarius. According to *Time,* many astrologers are not adjusting their readings:

> People who had been reading the Virgo horoscopes might actually be Leos. Plus, there was more—a whole new astrological sign. Anyone born between Nov. 29 and Dec. 17 was now paired up with a new sign, Ophiuchus.[220]

If the Magi observed the same star as the Chinese, they might have been very interested. As mentioned earlier, A. J. Morehouse theorized that the ample celestial activity around 5 BCE put the Magi on alert for something of grander proportions to occur.[221] That may have been the appearance of

---

(London: Quarto Inc., 2002), 22.
220 Melissa Locker, "NASA Addresses Astronomy Zodiac Shift with Science Facts," Time, September 26, 2016, http://time.com/4507672/nasa-on-zodiac-signs/.
221 Morehouse, "The Christmas Star as a Supernova in Aquila," 65–6.

Chapter 6

a guest star in the form of a nova or a comet being observed around the time of Passover. If the Magi needed more evidence to inspire them to prepare for a desert crossing, then the location of the star may have enticed them. The new object observed by the Chinese was in the constellation of Capricorn. The standard image for Capricorn is the goat-fish.

In Roman astrology, the zodiac Capricorn had great significance. Augustus struck coins stamped with Capricorn, his birth sign. Barton points out,

> Suetonius mentioned that Augustus had Capricorn put on his coins... It carried a number of connotations, mainly associated with the idea of a new era, as Capricorn was the sign in which the Sun began to rise again after the winter solstice. Thus, the zodiac sign became the sign of a new age of peace after the civil wars.[222]

Jesus is sometimes compared to the goat, which was pure, that was sacrificed to cleanse the sins of the Jewish people. But, the Chinese comet in Capricorn may have had other importance to the Magi. The comet was first observed near Capricorn (Caesar Augustus' zodiac). The Magi, who may have been from Parthia, could have taken this as an omen for Augustus. The eclipse of the Passover Moon at the same time may have indicated that it was a future Jew who would defeat the Roman Empire. They more than likely pursued the advice of Jewish rabbis. The rabbis would have informed them of the future messiah told in the Old Testament. In 380 CE, the defeat of pagan Rome occurred when Theodosius I proclaimed Christianity the Empire's sole authorized religion.

---

222 Barton, *Ancient Astrology*, 40.

PART III

THE PASSOVER DEATH

Chapter 7

CHAPTER 7
THE CRUCIFIXION

*F*ather Raymond E. Brown was among the first Catholic scholars to apply historical-critical analysis to interpreting the Bible. During the nineteenth century biblical criticism developed. Initially, the Catholic Church opposed this scholarship and essentially forbade it in 1893. In 1943, the Church reversed the decision and issued the encyclical *Divino Affiante Spirtu,* which authorized Catholic scholars to investigate the Bible historically. This included the life of Jesus. According to Brown, any discussion of dating the Crucifixion will produce a sensible solution only if we first assume that the minimal chronological references that all the evangelists supply are reliable—namely, that Jesus was

The Crucifixion

crucified in Jerusalem on a day before the Sabbath on a Passover celebration during the prefecture of Pontius Pilate.

To find the day of the week and date of the month of the Crucifixion by evaluating the evidence that the traditional canonical books provide, this thesis practices the recommendations of Brown by not only examining the written accounts of the evangelists but also any available scientific data. For example, NASA has calculations that can be used in determining dates of the events in the New Testament that can then be situated in the historiography of the Crucifixion. The Bible states that Jesus was crucified during the time of Passover, an ancient Jewish holiday that has not changed much over history. For believers in Jesus and prophecy, the Talmud may provide some helpful answers.

The Talmud, which informed us that the patriarchs were born and died during Nissan, also provides an interesting verse about the destruction of the Temple by the Romans in 70 CE. The Babylonian Talmud Yoma Tract 39b, states the following:

> The rabbis taught: Forty years before the Temple was destroyed, the lot never came into the right hand, the red wool did not become white, the western light did not burn, and the gates of the Temple opened of themselves, till the time that R. Johanan b. Zakkai rebuked them, saying; "Temple, Temple, why alarmist thou us? We know that thou art destined to be destroyed. For of thee hath prophesied Zechariah ben Iddo [Zech. Xi. 1]; 'Open thy doors, O Lebanon, and the fire shall eat thy cedars.'"[223]

---

223 Rodkinson, *New Edition of the Babylonian Talmud,* 1541.

Chapter 7

Thus, before the destruction of the Temple, there were 40 years of unusual events. The random choosing of the "lot" that was cast on the Day of Atonement (Yom Kippur) came up black 40 years in a row during the last 40 years of the Temple. The lot chosen determined which of two goats would be "for the Lord" and which goat would be the *Azazel* or "scapegoat." During the two hundred years before 30 CE, when the high priest picked one of two stones, again this selection was governed by chance, and each year the priest would select a black stone as often as a white one. But for 40 years in a row, beginning in 30 CE, the high priest always picked the black stone. The odds against this happening are astronomical (2 to the 40th power). In other words, the chances of this occurring are about 5.5 billion to one. But, that is not the only unusual event to occur during the last 40 years of the Temple.

The Rabbis also told us of the crimson strip or cloth tied to the Azazel goat. A portion of this red cloth was also removed from the goat and tied to the Temple door. Each year, the red cloth on the Temple door turned white as if to signify the atonement of another Yom Kippur was acceptable to the Lord. This annual event happened until 30 CE when the cloth then remained crimson each year up to the time of the Temple's destruction. This undoubtedly caused much concern and anxiety among the Jews. This traditional practice is linked to Israel confessing its sins and ceremonially placing this nation's sin upon the Azazel goat. The sin was then removed by this goat's death. Sin was represented by the red color of the cloth (the color of blood). But the cloth remained crimson—that is, Israel's sins were not being pardoned and "made white."

For Jews, the number 40 was significant; the Jews remained lost in the wilderness 40 years, and it rained for 40

The Crucifixion

days and 40 nights in Genesis. Historic evidence informs us that the Romans destroyed the Temple of Herod in 70 CE, fulfilling the burning of the Temple's pillars made of cedar stated in Yoma Tract 39b. However, for Christians the number 40 was important: the devil tempted Jesus in the wilderness for 40 days. Some theologians even use Yoma Tract 39b as evidence that Jesus died in 30 CE, because that year would be the first of the 40 years during which the Temple miracles began to occur. Michael Brown writes of the relationship of the negative signs around the sacrifice and the Crucifixion of Jesus:

> According to b. Yoma 39b, God did not accept the sacrifices that were offered on the Day of Atonement *for the last forty years before the destruction of the [Second] Temple* (this was known to the people by means of a series of special signs, all of which turned up negative for those forty years ... What great event happened in year 30? Jesus was rejected and nailed to a cross! Is it possible that God no longer accepted the atonement sacrifices because the Messiah had offered himself as the perfect, final sacrifice?[224]

Therefore, if the Romans destroyed the Temple in 70 CE, something led God 40 years before to not forgive the sins of the Jews. If that event was the Crucifixion of Jesus, then it occurred in 30 CE. Although Jews may interpret this as not being forgiven, but that their sacrifices in the Temple were no longer necessary. Jews would have to find other ways to fine atonement. Although the Temple was gone, the need for atonement was still important.

---

224 Michael Brown, *Answering Jewish Objections to Jesus: General and Historical Objections* (Grand Rapids, MI.: Baker Books, 2005), 74.

Chapter 7

THE DAY OF ATONEMENT

After the destruction of the Temple, the sacrifices ended. This was symbolic because, without the sacrifices, the people were not cleansed of their sins. Leviticus 16:11–34 tells the story of atonement: In it, Aaron is to offer a bull to make atonement for himself and his household. Then he is to take two goats and present them before the Lord at the entrance to the Tent of Meeting, and cast lots to tell which goat was to be sacrificed. The goat chosen by lot as the scapegoat shall be presented alive before the Lord to be used for making atonement by sending it into the desert. Jesus is often compared to the scapegoat.

The concept of atonement, or reconciliation with God, is important in the Judeo-Christian religion. God created the world for humans out of love, and allowed humans a certain amount of freedom in their choices. If the Jews made bad choices, Israel was punished. Sacrifices to God were required in order to obtain atonement. It must be remembered that in Genesis God destroyed the world over human's poor decisions. Many non-Christians, and even Christians, have a difficult time comprehending this concept. They question why a loving God required the blood of innocent animals, or the death of Jesus in order for humans to attain atonement? But, it is also necessary in the order of things. God is holy. For humans, who are not holy, atonement is important so they can be pure enough to have a relationship with God.

Likewise important in the Judeo-Christian religion is the concept of law and order. God gave Moses the Ten Commandments, and later the Oral Law, or what was to become part of the Talmud. Humans must be held responsible for their consequences when they break these laws. Part of this is forgiveness, and at times punishment. Atonement becomes a

The Crucifixion

way for humans to receive mercy from God. Punishment is essential when humans commit harm to one another. Without punishment libel, murder, and theft would be permitted.

The Crucifixion was necessary because Christians can gain atonement when they accept Jesus and ask God for forgiveness. This is told in John 3:16– For God so loved the world that he gave his one and only Son, that whoever believes in him shall not perish but have eternal life. All of this is part of God's perfect plan, including the lifespan of Jesus.

THE CRUCIFIXION ACCORDING TO MATTHEW

Matthew begins with a genealogy of Jesus from Abraham down to Jesus' earthly father Joseph. After the narrative of the Nativity of Jesus, Matthew describes his baptism and temptation and then his healing, preaching, and teaching. Matthew finishes by recalling with ample detail Jesus' final journey from Galilee to Jerusalem, including the Crucifixion.

In the Book of Matthew, Jesus predicts his death and resurrection from the grave on several occasions. Matthew 16:21 states that, "from that time on Jesus began to explain to his disciples that he must go to Jerusalem and suffer many things at the hands of the elders, chief priests and teachers of the law, and that he must be killed and on the third day be raised to life." Matthew 17:23 states, "They will kill him, and on the third day he will be raised to life." And the disciples were filled with grief." Finally, Matthew 20:19 states, "On the third day, he will be raised to life.'" Note that three times the third day is mentioned.

Matthew informs us the authorities were fearful of the disciples stealing the body of Jesus in order to give the appearance that the prophecy was fulfilled. Critics of Jesus might claim this event was invented by overzealous followers

Chapter 7

to give the impression the body of Jesus could not be removed, in an attempt to create the illusion Jesus rose from the dead. Matthew 27:62–65 states the following: The next day, the one after preparation day, the chief priests and the Pharisees went to Pilate. "Sir," they said, "we remember what while he was still alive that deceiver said, "After three days I will rise again." So, give the order for the tomb to be made secure until the third day. Otherwise, his disciples may come and steal the body and tell the people that he has been raised from the dead. This last deception will be worse than the first.

Matthew 28:1–8 confirms the prophecy when Mary Magdalene and the other Mary find the tomb empty after a violent earthquake. If sources for this earthquake were available, it would be easier to find the year the Crucifixion occurred. But, at this time no primary sources are available.

THE CRUCIFIXION ACCORDING TO MARK

According to Mark, the Last Supper was, in fact, a Passover meal partaken on the eve of the 15th of Nisan. Mark 14:12 states, "On the first day of the Feast of Unleavened Bread, when it was customary to sacrifice the Passover lamb, Jesus' disciples asked him, 'Where do you want us to go and make preparations for you to eat the Passover?'" Mark mentions the sacrificial lambs in this verse as if to predict a similar fate for Jesus later the next day.

Mark does present a contradiction on the topic of the Passover. In Mark 14:1–2 it is stated, "Now the Passover and Feast of Unleavened Bread were only two days away, and the chief priests and the teachers of the law were looking for some sly way to arrest Jesus and kill him. . . . "But not during the Feast," they said, "or the people may riot."

According to Mark, the arrest and trial of Jesus, in fact,

did proceed later that night of the Passover despite the earlier concerns of the enemies of Jesus. Critics of the Gospels indicate the trial of Jesus could not have occurred on the night of Passover because it was, in fact, the most significant festival of Judaism and a time of prayer intended to be observed with family. Mark informs us Jesus predicted his own death and Resurrection after the third day more than once. Mark 9:31 states, "And he said to them, The Son of Man is going to be betrayed into the hands of men. They will kill him, and after three days he will rise." Mark 10:34 states, "Who will mock him and spit on him, flog him and kill him. Three days later he will rise."

Later, Mark notifies us Jesus was resurrected on a Sunday. Mark 16:9 states, "When Jesus rose early on the first day of the week, he appeared first to Mary Magdalene, out of whom he had driven seven demons." However, caution must be applied when using this verse, because the earliest manuscripts and some other ancient witnesses do not have Mark 16:9–20. Some Bible scholars argue this section was added at a later date. This is something that Origen, and more recently Ehrman complain about, or the addition of verses to the Bible. Finding the original text would be invaluable.

Nevertheless, although Mark mentions nothing about the Nativity, the account of Jesus being crucified on a Passover Friday and resurrecting from the grave three days later does confirm what the other Synoptics state. Luke confirms with Mark and also indicates that Jesus was crucified on a Friday shortly before Passover began at sunset.

THE CRUCIFIXION ACCORDING TO LUKE

Luke writes in great detail of the events leading up to the Crucifixion. In Luke 22:1–38, he tells of the Last Supper, a

Chapter 7

Passover feast, occurring on the Jewish date of Nissan 15. Luke 22:7–10 informs us that Jesus had sent Peter and John to prepare for the Passover. Luke clearly indicates that Jesus' last meal was a Passover meal when, in verse 22:15–16, Jesus states, "And he said to them, 'I have eagerly desired to eat this Passover with you before I suffer. For I tell you, I will not eat it again until it finds fulfillment in the kingdom of God.'"

Luke indicates the day after Jesus' Crucifixion and burial was the day before Sabbath. Luke 23:50–56 tells of the burial of Jesus on the preparation day for the Sabbath, or Friday morning, while Luke 24:1 informs us on the first day of the week, or Sunday, the women went to the tomb and found it empty. The resurrection-on-the-third-day theme parallels several verses from the Jewish scriptures, including Exodus 19:11, which states, "and be ready by the third day, because on that day the Lord will come down on Mount Sinai in the sight of all the people." Even though Matthew, Mark, and Luke agree chronologically, the author of John throws the whole equation out of sequence.

THE CRUCIFIXION ACCORDING TO JOHN

John can lead readers to believe that perhaps John was a direct witness to many of the miracles of and Crucifixion of Jesus, during which Jesus asked the disciple he loved to take care of Mary, his mother (John 19:25–27). This also implies that John knew what year Jesus was crucified. However, there is no historical evidence for this. The New Testament also informs us that John was a friend to Simon Peter; Jesus sent the two of them together to prepare for the Passover Meal (Luke 22:7–13), and both ran together to the tomb of Jesus when Mary Magdalene told them Jesus was missing (John 20:1–9). Both were early disciples of Jesus and shared the common vocation of fishermen.

Scholars have intensely debated that the Gospel of John, as we know it in modern times, had an original unknown source, perhaps John himself, or was a collaboration of several of John's followers known as the Johannine community. Most scholars agree that the source known as *Q* was not a source for John. Whoever the true author or authors of John were, they provide an ample amount of historical information that can be used in an attempt to date the Crucifixion. John 13:1 informs us that the Last Supper was before the Passover feast:

> It states, "It was just before the Passover Feast. Jesus knew that the time had come for him to leave this world and go to the Father. Having loved his own who were in the world, he now showed them the full extent of his love.

Unlike the other canonical Gospels, this places the date of the Last Supper as Nisan 14, or one day before the actual Passover meal on Nisan 15. John 19:31 further confirms this when John is narrating the aftermath of Jesus' death:

> Now it was the day of Preparation, and the next day was to be a special Sabbath. Because the Jews did not want the bodies left on the crosses during the Sabbath, they asked Pilate to have the legs broken and the bodies taken down.

As in Matthew, Mark, and Luke, in John it is a Friday, but instead of Nissan 15 like the others, it is Nissan 14, the day of Passover preparation. Therefore, the Jews asked that the three crucified men be removed before sunset, the start of the preparation meal. Because the other two men were alive, the

Chapter 7

Roman soldiers broke their legs to hasten their deaths. Jesus was dead, so his legs were not broken; instead, one of the soldiers pierced his side, from which came blood and water, to prove he was dead. John 19:36 notes these events: "These things happened so that the scripture would be fulfilled: Not one of his bones will be broken," and another scripture says, "They will look on the one they have pierced." John confirms that Jesus was crucified on the Passover preparation day, but also that the next day was not only a Sabbath but a special day or perhaps a day that fell on two holy days. Thus, John marks Friday morning as the time of Jesus' death, and later that night the start of both the Passover and the Sabbath.

John 20:1 later recounts that Jesus was resurrected on the first day of the week, or Sunday. It states, 'Early on the first day of the week, while it was still dark, Mary Magdalene went to the tomb and saw that the stone had been removed from the entrance." It can be gathered from the four canonical Gospels that Jesus was crucified on a Friday, then was buried before Friday sunset, or the beginning of Sabbath. He was resurrected on Sunday. This theme becomes the most significant concept in all the canonical Gospels, and the belief that Jesus died for the sins of human beings becomes the cornerstone of the Christian faith. Historians can use these temporal milestones as a starting point in the attempt to date the Crucifixion of Jesus.

THE SYNOPTICS VS. JOHN

Raymond E. Brown asserts in *The Death of the Messiah: From Gethsemane to the Grave*, that the Synoptic canons never clearly disclose that the Last Supper of Christ was a Passover meal. He argues. "Yet even if that refers to 'the feast' of Passover (as I think), it is not definitive as to which day is

The Crucifixion

meant before or during the eight-day festal period of Passover/Unleavened Bread."[225] This dilemma may appear to be trivial on the surface, but its existence has driven the scholars of the history of Jesus senseless since humans first set out to date the Passion of Christ after it was forgotten.

Two exceedingly fascinating Passovers 29 and 30 CE, have all the right elements to fit the Crucifixion date mentioned by Clement: The Passover of 29 fits in perfectly with the canon of John because the Full-Moon phase falls on an early Sunday. This allows for a Friday-night Passover and fits the three-day rule of Jesus being crucified on a Friday and rising on a Sunday. However, the Passover of 30, with a Full-Moon phase of Thursday, fits nicely with the Synoptic canons' belief that the Last Supper was a Passover meal and that Jesus was crucified the following Friday, before sunset. Perhaps the best source, a primary source, is that of Paul's account in the canon of 1 Corinthians 11:23–26:

> For I received from the Lord what I also passed on to you: The Lord Jesus, on the night he was betrayed, took bread, and when he had given thanks, he broke it and said, "This is my body, which is for you; do this in remembrance of me." In the same way, after supper he took the cup saying. "This cup is the new covenant in my blood; do this, whenever you drink it, in remembrance of me." For whenever you eat his bread and drink this cup, you proclaim the Lord's death until he comes.

Absent from this account is any mention of a Passover night or Passover meal. However, Paul was not Jewish, and

---

225 Brown, *The Death of the Messiah*, 1354.

Chapter 7

may not have believed it was important enough or was too self-evident to point out. It must be remembered that the authors of the Gospels were most likely not primary sources for their accounts of the Last Supper, which were written several years after the fact. If this is the case, then human error could slightly have altered the true facts of the story by changing it each time it was retold. Nevertheless, even though John is different, the Gospels still have a common theme—a Passover celebration that calls for a Friday-night Full-Moon. The day difference is only a minor problem since the Jews did not use precise astrological observation. Therefore, only a one-day difference is not enough to cause error.

Figure 7.1

Nissan 15*	Weekday of Nissan 15	Full Moon Phase**
April 14, 2014	Monday	April 15 07:42
April 03, 2015	Friday	April 04 12:06
April 22, 2016	Friday	April 22 05:24
April 10, 2017	Monday	April 11 06:08
March 30, 2018	Friday	March 31 12:37
April 19, 2019	Friday	April 19 11:12
April 08, 2020	Wednesday	April 08 02:35
March 27, 2021	Saturday	March 28 18:48
April 15, 2022	Friday	April 16 18:55
April 5, 2023	Wednesday	April 06 04:35
April 22, 2024	Monday	April 23 23:49

"Moon Phases Table courtesy of Fred Espenak, www.Astropixels.com"
* Holiday begins at Sundown
** Moon phases are in Greenwich Time

The Crucifixion

THE FIRST DAY OF PASSOVER

Matthew, Mark, and Luke inform us that Jesus was executed before Passover on a Friday, although John suggests it was the day of Passover preparation. It is necessary to find out more about when Passover began, and whether it began on a Friday after sunset. Once again, the Jewish holiday of Passover begins on the Full-Moon in the Jewish month of Nissan. Timing the exact beginning of the phases of the Moon with the Jewish calendar is by no means a perfect science. As you can see from Figure 7.1, based on NASA's Moon phases from the NASA website,[226] the United States Navy's Julian Date Converter,[227] and modern Passover festivals, there is no set pattern to the calculation to the start of the Passover date based on a solar calendar. This is due to the fact that a Full-Moon phase does not always start at the same time as a solar day and because of complex calculations of the 19-year Moon cycles used by Hillel II to mark the beginning of Passover. Figure 7.1 shows the different days Passover begins in the modern era. It appears that no one day has had preference over another, only that the Moon phase is full.

The only knowledge for certain that can be gained by this chart is that Passover almost never starts the day after the complete Full-Moon phase peak. Most of the time, Passover begins on the same day as or the day before the peak. For certain, we can determine by studying Passover dates that it begins either the day of a Full-Moon phase, the day prior, or sometimes closely after. The day of the week for the beginning of Passover is not relevant in the Jewish tradition. It has

---

226 NASA.gov, s.v. "Moon Phases,"
http://sunearth.gsfc.nasa.gov/eclipse/phase/phasecat.html.
227 Navy.mil, s.v. "Julian Date Converter,"
http://aa.usno.navy.mil/data/docs/JulianDate.html.

Chapter 7

occurred on every day of the week at some point in history.

Unlike the early Church Fathers, modern historians have computers and vast Internet resources that make the task of calculating the time and day of the week for Full-Moon phases around the death of Jesus not only a possibility but extremely accurate. The canonical books of the Bible agree that Jesus was crucified on a Friday and rose from the tomb on a Sunday. It is then important to establish a Passover date, or Full-Moon phase, that occurred close to a weekend sometime around 30 CE. This is where the importance of the United States Naval Julian Date Converter is significant. However, historians will most likely first question how reliable the converter is, and then test it against the annals of the past.

In 1849, the U.S. Congress established the Nautical Almanac Office to prepare and publish an official national almanac. Before that time, American scientists and sailors depended on foreign almanacs, particularly British ones. Over the years, some of the world's best astronomers, mathematicians, and later computer scientists have worked for the Nautical Almanac Office. Today, it is a valuable resource for historians. However, its reliability should still be tested against authentic historic sources.

The best way to test the certainty of this system is to analyze some of the writings that primary sources have left behind that mention both a Julian date along with the day of the week. Julian dates, or dates before 1582, are a critical test because they date from before the adaptation of the Gregorian calendar and are therefore more likely to contain error. Also significant is that the Julian calendar was in use by the ancient Roman Church. These dates also test the accuracy of the Julian Date Converter in calculating from the Julian calendar, which is a less precise solar calendar than the modern Gregorian calendar.

The Crucifixion

In 49 BCE, Julius Caesar was elected "dictator in perpetuity" of Rome. He quickly undertook several reforms that were sorely needed, including producing a new calendar, today known as the Julian calendar. In order to accomplish this monumental task, he summoned a renowned Alexandrian astronomer named Sosigenes to Rome. Sosigenes advised Caesar to adapt a solar calendar, abandoning all pretense to a lunar one. Sosigenes suggested that the new calendar be divided into 12 months, with no relationship to the cycles of the Moon, and that a single intercalary day be introduced every four years at the end of February, giving an average of 365¼ days in those years. Caesar welcomed his advice and also augmented the number of days in 46 BCE in order to bring the start of the year back into synchronization with the vernal equinox. This resulted in 46 BCE having 445 days, earning it the title "year of confusion." Nevertheless, Caesar's reforms were to last for the next 1600 years.

However, the Julian calendar had several defects in its design. The average number of days in a Julian year was 365¼. But, the true length of the tropical year is 365.24219 days. This small discrepancy caused important annual events, such as the vernal equinox, to fall earlier each year at a rate of about one day for every 128 years. This also affected the date of Easter, a spring holiday that was now occurring earlier and earlier, and would eventually occur during winter.

By the time of the pontiff of Pope Gregory XIII, in the late sixth century, the difference was ten days. This meant that the equinox of 1582 occurred on March 11. His 1582 reforms included adding ten days to the calendar. This changed the day after Thursday, October 4, to become Friday, October 15. It was also decreed that years with a date ending in two zeros would not become leap years unless the first two digits were divisible by four. Under the Julian calendar, the years 1600,

Chapter 7

1700, 1800, 1900, 2000 ... etc., would be leap years. After the new reforms, the years 1700, 1800, and 1900 were no longer leap years, but 1600 and 2000 remained so, thus eliminating three days every four hundred years and keeping the equinoxes on the same date. However, even this system is not perfect. It produces a calendar that is 0.0003 days longer than the solar year, meaning that in 3000 to 4000 years, calendar corrections may be needed.

TESTING THE U.S. NAVAL CONVERTER

In order to test how accurate the Naval Julian Converter is, one needs only to study accounts from historical archives. One example of a Julian date, that is, a date from before 1582, is from Bernal Diaz del Castillo's (1495–1584) book, *The Discovery and Conquest of Mexico,* about his adventures as a conquistador. He shows an excellent memory, with an overabundance of dates and facts. He describes Hernando Cortes's mass mobilization against the final assault on the Aztec capital Tenochtitlan. Shortly before the battle, Diaz del Castillo writes, "On the morning of Friday the 5th April, 1521, after hearing Mass we set out for Tlamanalco, where we were well received, and slept there."[228] This passage verifies the Julian Date Converter's calculations, which also places the 5th of April 1521 as a Friday. Figure 7.2 was adapted from the website of the Julian Date Converter of the United States Navy.

One can clearly see that April 5, 1521 was on a Friday indicating that either Castillo and the US Navy are both right or happened have the same weekday wrong. Since there is a one-in-seven chance that the right day of the week will come

---

228 Bernal Diaz del Castillo, *The Discovery and Conquest of Mexico* (New York: Da Capa Press, 1996), 368.

The Crucifixion

up by chance, it is better to test more dates from even older dates to make sure history did not loss a day somewhere.

Figure 7.2

> The Julian date for CE 1521 April 5
> 00:00:00.0 UT is
> JD 2276697.500000
>
> JD 2276697.500000 is
> CE 1521 April 05 00:00:00.0 UT Friday

Figure 7.3

> The Julian date for CE 1087 March 21
> 00:00:00.0 UT is
> JD 2118163.500000
>
> JD 2118163.500000 is
> CE 1087 March 21 00:00:00.0 UT Sunday

Another example from history, with an even earlier date, is the date on which Abbot Desiderius was canonically elected pope at Capua on Palm Sunday, March 21, 1087, taking the name Victor III in the process.[229] Although Pope Victor III reigned, belatedly, only from May 9 to May 24, 1087, the date of his election to the papacy informs us not only of the date of the month but also the day of the week. When this is verified against the Julian Date Converter, the primary source matches

---

229 Richard P. McBrien, *Lives of The Popes* (San Francisco: Harper Collins, 1997), 189.

Chapter 7

the converter. Figure 7.3 is from the Julian Date Converter. One again the source is verified as correct by agreeing with the naval converter. March 21, 1087, was, in fact, a Sunday.

An even older example from history that supports the Julian Date Converter is from the Anglo-Saxon Chronicles. Originally the chronicles were a number of separate manuscripts that were compiled under the order of King Alfred the Great of Wessex around 890. It was subsequently maintained and carefully added to by generations of anonymous scribes until the middle of the 12th Century. It was from this source that historians know much pertaining to the Norse raids on the British Isles during the late 8th to 12th century.

In this source, it is noted in the year of 832 the following occurred, "In this year archbishop Wulfred passed away, and abbot Feologild was elected to succeed him in the archiepiscopal see on 25 April. He was consecrated on Sunday, 9 June, but he died on 30 August."[230] When assessed against the converter, June 9th is confirmed as a Sunday. The *Anglo-Saxon Chronicle* also lists a number of lunar eclipses that can be tested against NASA's Moon phases catalog. Figure 7.4 proves that the Julian date of June 9, 832, was also a Sunday.

Figure 7.4

> The Julian date for CE 832 June 9
> 00:00:00.0 UT is
> JD 2025105.500000
>
> JD 2025105.500000 is
> CE 832 June 09 00:00:00.0 UT Sunday

---

230 G.N. Garmonsway, *The Anglo-Saxon Chronicle*, (London: J.M. Dent & Sons, 1954), 63.

The Crucifixion

The Chronicle also tells of a lunar eclipse that occurred in 828. It states, "In this year there was an eclipse of the Moon on Christmas morning."[231] When compared to the NASA Moon-phase catalog from the website, the date for an eclipse on Christmas morning of 828 parallels the NASA calculations for the same Christmas morning. This supports both the work of NASA and the painstaking engagement of the abbots from medieval England. Figure 7.5 was produced from information on the NASA Moon Phases website. The lower-case t after December 25 02:20 indicates that a full (umbral) lunar eclipse occurred on that date, thus matching the astronomical data presented in the Saxon Chronicles. This technique was used throughout the process of writing this book to verify what date Passover Full-Moons fell on.

Figure 7.5

Year	New Moon	First Quarter	Full Moon	Last Quarter
0828			Jan 6 02:59 t	Jan 13 23:56
	Jan 20 15:32 P	Jan 27 16:25	Feb 4 21:44	Feb 12 09:59
	Feb 19 02:19	Feb 26 11:08	Mar 5 13:39	Mar 12 17:22
	Mar 19 13:10	Mar 27 06:31	Apr 4 02:14	Apr 10 23:11
	Apr 18 00:37	Apr 26 01:01	May 3 12:04	May 10 04:37
	May 17 13:19	May 25 17:23	Jun 1 20:06	Jun 8 10:54
	Jun 16 03:34 P	Jun 24 07:06	Jul 1 03:19 t	Jul 7 19:16
	Jul 15 19:02 P	Jul 23 18:18	Jul 30 10:36	Aug 6 06:49
	Aug 14 10:59	Aug 22 03:34	Aug 28 18:43	Sep 4 22:14
	Sep 13 02:33	Sep 20 11:35	Sep 27 04:33	Oct 4 17:17
	Oct 12 17:18	Oct 19 19:03	Oct 26 16:55	Nov 3 14:34
	Nov 11 07:06	Nov 18 02:50	Nov 25 08:19	Dec 3 11:57
	Dec 10 19:53 T	Dec 17 11:49	**Dec 25 02:20 t**	

"Moon Phases Table courtesy of Fred Espenak, www.Astropixels.com"

Traveling even farther back, a German monk named Einhard, who was both a member of the court and a biograp-

---

231 Ibid, 61.

Chapter 7

her of Charlemagne, informs us that the emperor celebrated Easter, April 2, 769,[232] at Rouen. The date of April 2 is, in fact, a Sunday, as indicated by Figure 7.6, which is displayed below, and was developed from the Julian Date Converter. This proves that April 2, 769, was, in fact, Sunday, the seven-day week was unbroken all the way to 769, and Einhard was at least able to read a calendar and record dates without error. But this is still a long way from 30 CE, and it would be better to have even earlier sources to test.

Figure 7.6

> The Julian date for CE 769 April 2
> 00:00:00.0 UT is
> JD 2002026.500000
>
> JD 2002026.500000 is
> CE 769 April 02 00:00:00.0 UT Sunday

When assessed against actual historic dates from primary documents and manuscripts, the naval converter is reliable to the point that when it does not match the documents or manuscripts, the primary sources must be scrutinized. In the task of developing this thesis, the Naval Converter was the most significant instrument employed for discovering the best possible year for an integral calculation. In its absence, the task of discovering days of the week for relevant dates would be difficult and time consuming.

Finally, it is important to establish the fact that the seven-day week has been continuous since ancient times. By examining some of the historical sources and the dated days of

---

[232] Allen Cabaniss, *Charlemagne* (New York: Twayne Publishers, Inc., 1972), 9.

The Crucifixion

the week that these sources claimed for significant events in their writings, it can be established that the seven-day week was unaltered both before and after April 3, 397 CE. On that date, St. Ambrose of Milan lay on his deathbed close to his final breath. St. Ambrose's historian, Angelo Paredi, describes the scene:

> "On Good Friday, April 3, 397, he (Ambrose) entered into his agony. At five o'clock in the evening he stretched his arms out in the form of a cross and thus, moving his lips in prayer, he reminded until the end ... he breathed his last. It was the dawn of Holy Saturday."[233]

When assessed against the Julian Date Converter, this source is verified. Figure 7.7 is from the Julian Date Converter utility, proving that April 3 was, in fact, a Friday. This table and the previous ones are excellent evidence that the seven-day week cycle has stayed intact from 397 CE until the present. However, even earlier sources that list both the date and day of week would be more helpful in helping scholars place a date on the Crucifixion.

Figure 7.7

```
The Julian date for CE  397 April  3 00:00:00.0
UT is
JD 1866154.500000

JD 1866154.500000 is
CE  397 April 03 00:00:00.0 UT  Friday
```

---

233 Angelo Paredi, *Saint Ambrose: His Life and Times* (Notre Dame: University of Notre Dame Press, 1964), 375.

Chapter 7

DATES FROM THE GOSPELS

As stated earlier, the date for the Crucifixion occurs between the years 29 CE and 33 CE. The canonical books do leave historians two important verses that have tantalized Bible historians for centuries in their pursuit of dating the Crucifixion. The first is Luke 3:1–21:

> In the fifteenth year of the reign of Tiberius Caesar—when Pontius Pilate was governor of Judea, Herod (Antipas) Tetrarch of Galilee, his brother Philip Tetrarch of Iturea and Tracontitis, and Lysanias Tetrach of Abilennee—during the high priesthood of Annas and Caiaphas, the word of God came to John son of Zechariah in the Desert. He went into all the country around the Jordan, preaching a baptism of repentance for the forgiveness of sins etc. . . . When all the people were being baptized, Jesus was baptized too.

Tiberius became emperor of the Roman Empire after the death of his stepfather Augustus Caesar on August 19, 14 CE. If this is the first year of his reign, then 29 CE could be considered his fifteenth year as emperor. This places the baptism of Jesus by John the Baptist in the year 29 CE. The first three canonical books indicate that the ministry of Jesus lasted for one year. That places the Crucifixion of Jesus in the year 30 CE. However, the Gospel of John appears to disagree with the other canonical books by mentioning three Passover celebrations that occurred during the ministry of Jesus. But as explained earlier, it is possible that the three Passovers mentioned in the Gospel of John are different narratives of the same celebration.

The Crucifixion

According to Bart Ehrman, the author of the Gospel of John had sources for his narrative of the life of Jesus:

> It is possible, though, that John actually produced several different versions of his Gospel. Readers have long noted, for example, that chapter 21 seems to come to an end in 20:30–31; and the events of chapter 21 seem to be a kind of afterthought, possibly added to fill out the stories of Jesus' resurrection appearances and to explain that when the "beloved disciple" responsible for narrating the traditions in the Gospel had died, this was not unforeseen (cf. 21:22–23).[234]

If this is the case, then it is quite possible that the three Passovers mentioned in John were one and the same, which parallels the other canonical books. It could also be possible that the authors of John intended passages from the book to be read every day, as the Jewish scriptures are read. If this is true, then the three daily readings that mentioned a Passover may have been confused as three Passovers. This may explain why some scholars date Jesus' ministry as three years. It may also be that the period of Jesus' ministry included two Passovers within the same calendar year.

Perhaps the best defense for the three-in-one Passover theory for the Gospel of John is that crimes against the Jewish religion were considered the worst in the eyes of the law. According to Henri Daniel-Rops in *Daily Life in the Time of Jesus*, rebelling against God was high treason. Breaking the Sabbath was a crime worthy of death, while failing to celebrate Passover could result in the guilty being outlawed.[235] John

---

[234] Ehrman, *Misquoting Jesus*, 61.
[235] Henri Daniel-Rops, *Daily Life in the Time of Jesus* (New York: Hawthorn

Chapter 7

mentions three Passovers. The first is John 2:13–3:25, in which Jesus clears the Temple of sellers and money changers and proclaims himself in authority. This event alone was enough for Jewish leaders to consider Jesus worthy of death or banishment. But John mentions two more Passovers. John 6:1–70 tells of the feeding of five thousand right before Passover, and John 13:1–19:42 tells of Jesus' final days. It is possible that John was composed of several narratives that were combined into one book. This may explain the differences between John and the other Gospels. Despite the confusion, John does leave an important clue about when this event happened. John 2:13–22 states,

> When it was almost time for the Jewish Passover. Jesus went up to Jerusalem. In the temple courts, he found men selling cattle, sheep, and doves, and others sitting at tables exchanging money. So he made a whip out of cords, and drove all from the temple area, both sheep and cattle; he scattered the coins of the money changers and overturned their tables. To those who sold doves he said, "Get these out of here! How dare you turn my Father's house into a market!" His disciples remembered that it is written: "Zeal for your house will consume me." Then the Jews demanded of Him "What miraculous sign can you show us to prove your authority to do all this?" Jesus answered them, "Destroy this temple, and I will rise it again in three days." The Jews replied, "It had taken forty-six years to build this temple, and you are going to raise it in three?" But the temple he had spoken of was his body.

Books, 1962), 201.

The Crucifixion

John informs the reader in this verse that Jesus was in Jerusalem during his ministry shortly before Passover 46 years after the construction of the Temple of Jerusalem commenced. According to Graetz in the History of the Jews, "In the eighteenth year of the Herod's reign (19 BCE) the building was begun, and in one year and a half (17 BCE) the inner part of the Temple was finished."[236] This places Jesus' cleansing of the Temple to around 29 or 30 CE. If Jesus' ministry lasted one year, this also places the Crucifixion from 29 to 30 CE.

This brings to the forefront the question of which year, 28, 29, or 30 CE is the better fit for what the writers of Gospels had in mind when they were calculating the date for the Crucifixion. Appendix 2 (in the back of the book) shows when the Passover Full-Moon occurred during each year. We can run the dates of the Full-Moon phases of Passover for the years 29 and 30 CE through the Naval Converter in order to learn whether either Passover in those two years occurred on a Friday night. Passover always occurs on the first Full-Moon after the vernal equinox. According to NASA's vernal equinox time and date converter,[237] the vernal equinox for 28 CE, 29 CE, and 30 CE occurred on March 20. The first Full-Moon after March 20, 28 CE, was March 29 03:22 Greenwich Time; the first Full-Moon after March 20, 29 CE, was on April 17, 02:45 Greenwich Time, while the first Moon after March 20, 30 CE, was on April 6, 19:42 Greenwich Time.

The Gospels provide some evidence in the matter. Mark begins its narrative of Jesus telling of the prophecy written in Isaiah about the coming of John the Baptist before Jesus, but he leaves out any information on the Nativity or childhood of Jesus. Nevertheless, Luke tells of the virgin birth by Mary, and

---

236 Graetz, *History of the Jews*, 109.
237 NASA.gov, s.v. "Time and Date of Vernal Equinox," http://aom.giss.nasa.gov/srver4x3.html.

Chapter 7

describe Jesus at the age of 12 asking the Temple teachers questions, but neither says anything about the Star of Bethlehem or the Magi mentioned in Matthew. John also omits any information of the two. It must be remembered that each Gospel was intended for a different audience, with different purposes.

Figure 7.8

Jewish Day*	Julian Day
Wed., Nissan 13 Nissan 14	April 5, 30 CE
Thr., Nissan 14 Nissan 15	April 6, 30 CE Full Moon
Fri., Nissan 15 Nissan 16	April 7, 30 CE
Sat., Nissan 16 Nissan 17	April 8, 30 CE
Sun., Nissan 17 Nissan 18	April 9, 30 CE
Mon., Nissan 18 Nissan 19	April 10, 30 CE

"Moon Phases Table courtesy of Fred Espenak, www.Astropixels.com"
*It is not known for certain when Passover (Nissan 15) commenced, sometime around the Full-Moon.
** Jewish dates began after sundown, so Nissan 14 and Nissan 15 occur in on the same Julian Day.

THE DIFFERENCE A DAY MAKES

Of the years in which the Crucifixion could have taken place, the year 30 CE is the favorable date for a Passover

The Crucifixion

occurring on Friday night because the preceding Thursday marked the beginning of the Full-Moon. A Sunday or Monday Full-Moon peak is not compatible enough for a Friday night prior to the Full-Moon as the commencing of the Jewish Passover holiday. Also, a Sunday or Monday morning Full-Moon phase is probably too far from the next Friday night to parallel the narrative in the canonical Gospel of John that tells of Jesus' Crucifixion occurring on a Friday, the same day as Passover.

The other canonical Gospels, which tell of Thursday being the Passover night, are even further from the Monday Full-Moon phase to the point of its being a highly inconceivable occurrence. Thus, of the two years that are possible for the Crucifixion date, 30 CE is by far the superior choice. If these calculations are correct, it would be highly possible that April 7, 30 CE, a Friday, was the date of the Crucifixion, and Jesus' Resurrection then occurred on April 9, a Sunday.

OTHER POSSIBLE CRUCIFIXION DATES

The same United States government website test that was performed on the dates of 29 CE and 30 CE can be used to calculate other possible Passover dates. In this case, all of the first Full-Moon phases that occurred after the ten vernal equinoxes during Pilate's prefecture in Judea can be compared in order to view on which other dates the Crucifixion might have occurred on. Figure 7.9 (next page) provides the dates for the first Full-Moon phases after the spring equinoxes (Passover). Figure 7.10 shows the day of the week in the year that each Full-Moon occurred for possible years of the Crucifixion. Passover likely started either on the day of the Full-Moon or the day before or after to keep it close to the Full- Moon.

Chapter 7

Figure 7.9

Year	New Moon	First Quarter	Full Moon	Last Quarter
27	Mar 26 17:57	Apr 2 14:19	Apr 9 16:27	Apr 17 16:34
28	Mar 15 00:26	Mar 22 11:34	Mar 29 03:22	Apr 5 12:55
29	Apr 2 17:29	Apr 10 12:37	Apr 17 02:45	Apr 24 04:45
30	Mar 22 17:46	Mar 30 22:18	Apr 6 19:42	Apr 13 11:34
31	Mar 11 22:19	Mar 19 21:41	Mar 27 10:55	Apr 3 04:30
32	Mar 29 20:00 P	Apr 6 11:58	Apr 14 09:00 t	Apr 21 06:57
33	Mar 19 10:38 T	Mar 26 10:33	Apr 3 14:51 p	Apr 11 03:45
34	Apr 7 11:42	Apr 14 05:18	Apr 22 07:39	Apr 30 03:35

"Moon Phases Table courtesy of Fred Espenak, www.Astropixels.com"

Figure 7.10

Date of Full Moon	Day of the Week
April 9, 27 CE	Wednesday
March 29, 28 CE	Monday
April 17, 29 CE	Sunday
April 6, 30 CE	Thursday
March 27, 31 CE	Tuesday
April 14, 32 CE	Monday
April 3, 33 CE	Friday
April 22, 34 CE	Thursday

"Moon Phases Table courtesy of Fred Espenak, www.Astropixels.com"

Figure 7.10 shows the weekday each Full-Moon occurred on for possible years of the Crucifixion. Therefore, Passover likely started either on the day of the Full-Moon or either the day before or after. Although it is possible for a Passover to occur two days before or after a Full-Moon, it is most likely that the Jews did not error that much. They wanted to keep Passover on the Full-Moon.

CONCLUSION

Figure 7.10 shows that April 6, 30 CE was a Full-Moon and a Thursday. As stated earlier this could be close enough for a Passover. According to the data that was gathered and displayed in Figure 7.9, other years that are highly possible for the Crucifixion are 33 and 34. While we do not know for sure which is correct, our method has arrived at two possible years that Jesus may have died in and eliminated years that are highly unlikely. Some astronomers attribute the darkness at the Crucifixion (Matthew 27:45) to an eclipse. One did occur in 33 CE on Passover, but according to Easton's Bible Dictionary, it is argued that the great intensity of darkness caused by an eclipse never lasts for more than six minutes, and this darkness lasted for three hours.

In the modern era, we have computers to calculate Moon phases and days of the week. But in the first century, they did not. Thus, there were many theories of the day and month that Jesus was crucified, even though they date from around a hundred years after Jesus. While the Church Fathers at times provide conflicting theories and do not always provide us with all the correct answers, we can still learn much about how Christians lived during a time period close to that of Jesus' lifetime. The evidence they have left us does prove that, even in his time, the date of the Crucifixion was of some significance to Christians and was also in debate. However, using contemporary techniques, April 7, 30 CE is the dominant choice for the day that the Crucifixion occurred.

Chapter 7

Evidence for a 30, CE Passover Crucifixion

1. The Talmud states that for 40 years before the destruction of Herod's Temple several ominous miracles occurred before the Roman attack and following Temple destruction in 70 CE—meaning something unusual occurred in 30 CE.
2. Of the Passover dates from around this period, only 30 and 33 CE have a Full-Moon that are close to the time of Jesus' Friday death. The 30 CE date is on a Thursday and the 33 date is on a Friday, so these would fit with the Friday Crucifixion and Sunday Resurrection.
3. John 2:20 states, The Jews replied, "It has taken forty-six years to build this temple, and you are going to raise it in three days? The reconstruction of the Temple by Herod was begun in 19 BCE, with the inner Temple finished in 17 BCE. Forty-six years later would be around 29 CE. This is close enough to fit with the one-year ministry suggested in Matthew, Mark, and Luke to allow for a 30 CE Crucifixion.
4. Luke 3:1–23 informs us that Jesus was baptized by John the Baptist in the fifteenth year of the reign of Tiberius, and his ministry lasted one year. Tiberius's reign began in 14 CE; therefore, the fifteenth year would have been 29 CE, the start of Jesus' one-year ministry. The following year, 30 CE, Jesus was crucified.
5. Clement wrote in the third century of the followers of Basilides, "Making a precise calculation, there are some who place his Passion in the sixteenth year of Tiberius Caesar on the twenty-fifth of Phamenoth." The sixteenth year of Tiberius was 30 CE. But, the 25

The Crucifixion

of Phamenoth, the spring equinox, was on March 21, which is far from the April 6 start of Passover.[238]

One of the stranger connections between March 25 and April 6 are the deeper meanings the two dates have in the celebrations of Christmas. As stated earlier in the book, by 336 CE the Roman Catholic Church was celebrating Christmas on December 25, based on the concept that the Immaculate Conception occurred on March 25, nine months earlier, during Passover. But, churches outside of Rome had a different perspective, according to the *Salem Press Encyclopedia*:

> By the fourth century, Christians throughout most of the East celebrated the Feast of the Epiphany in a multiple sense as the anniversary of the physical birth of Jesus Christ, of the adoration of the Magi, of Christ's baptism, and of the miracle at Cana. From the East, the feast entered Europe sometime in the fourth century in Gaul, Spain, and northern Italy, it was observed primarily as the commemoration of Christ's birth.[239]

Sometime between 380 and 430, the Eastern Church followed Rome and also accepted December 25 as the date of the Nativity, but in Armenia, January 6 is still celebrated as the combined festival for the birth and baptism of Jesus because of the differences in the Gregorian and Julian calendars. This is interesting because January 6 would be exactly nine months

---

238 Based on the Alexandrian calendar date of Phamenoth 25, 30 CE, from Robert Harry van Gent's Almagest Ephemeris Calculator, www.staff.science.uu.nl/~gent0113/astro/almagestephemeris.htm.
239 "Feast of the Epiphany," *Salem Press Encyclopedia* (January 2016): *Research Starters*, EBSCO*host*.

Chapter 7

from the April 6 Gregorian date for the 30 CE Passover. It is my contention that Christians preferred the idea that Jesus was born or conceived during Passover; however, the differences between the Gregorian calendar, the calendar of choice for Gentiles, and the Jewish lunar calendar meant that the dates do not match. This and the lack of computers made a difficult task nearly impossible. This is one of the reasons Easter is sometimes in March and sometimes April.

I expect much debate and reproach over this matter. Surprisingly, the Star of Bethlehem crowd can be very critical about everything. I will let the evidence speak for itself. It will be asked how much I believe in these chosen dates. As for the 5 BCE date as a Nativity, I believe that for some reason the early Church was fixed on a March 25 date for the Nativity. This date becomes a recurring one for something of importance. Augustine leads us to believe that later this was changed to a Conception date in order to make way for a December 25 birthdate so that the Roman Church could compete with pagan holidays around the winter equinox. I believe the Nativity could not have occurred after 4 BCE, the accepted date for the death of Herod, and before 6 BCE Jesus would have been too old to start his ministry in 29 CE to be around the age of 30. As for the Crucifixion date, 30 CE makes the most sense, but in the tradition of the integral idea, it does not matter. We know Jesus was crucified during Passover. Therefore 33 CE would also make a valid date because that Full-Moon was on a Friday and it matches the gospels.

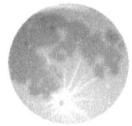

CHAPTER 8
THE RESURRECTION

We are told by the Gospel of John that Jesus received a message that Lazarus was ill. Jesus reassured the Apostles that Lazarus's sickness will not result in death, and prepares to visit him in Bethany. But the Apostles are afraid of returning to Judea, and Jesus delays his departure by two days. Then Jesus receives word that Lazarus is dead, and he decides to take the opportunity to raise Lazarus from the dead so that the Apostles will believe in the power of Jesus. John 11:38–43 states:

> Jesus, once more deeply moved, came to the tomb. It was a cave with a stone laid across the entrance. "Take away the stone," he said. "But, Lord," said Martha, the sister of the dead man, "by this time there is a bad odor, for he has been there four days."

Chapter 8

> Then Jesus said, "Did I not tell you that if you believed, you would see the glory of God?" So they took away the stone. Then Jesus looked up and said, "Father, I thank you that you have heard me. I knew that you always hear me, but I said this for the benefit of the people of the people standing here, that they may believe that you sent me." When he had said this, Jesus called in a load voice, "Lazarus, come out!" The dead man came out, his hands and feet wrapped with strips of linen, and a cloth around his face. Jesus said to them, "Take off the grave cloths and let him go."

This event occurred shortly before the death of Jesus. In fact, this miracle worried the Pharisees, who believed that the Romans would come and "take away" their place and nation. This proves that some of the Pharisees did not believe Jesus had the qualities they desired for a Messiah. Mainly to defeat the Romans once and for all, the high priest of that year, Caiaphas, suggested that it was best for Jesus to die instead of Judea. It appears that Caiaphas was not impressed with Jesus' ability to perform miracles. This may have been because resurrection was not an everyday occurrence, though it took place several times in the Old Testament.

In 1 Kings 17:17–24, the great prophet Elijah prayed to God and resurrected the dead son of the widow of Zarephath. In 2 Kings 13:21, some men were burying a dead man when some bandits appeared. They then threw the dead body into Elijah's tomb. When the dead man's body touched Elijah's bones, the dead man was resurrected. In Matthew 27:51–53, an earthquake occurred after Jesus died, and the tombs of many holy people were opened, and they appeared to many

The Resurrection

people in Jerusalem after Jesus' resurrection.[240] In Mark 5:35–43, Jesus resurrected the daughter of Jairus, the synagogue ruler. In Luke 7:11–17, Jesus resurrects a widow's only son in the town of Nain. Finally, two resurrections occur in Acts. The first is in Acts 9:36–41, when Peter prayed to God and ordered a dead woman named Tabitha to "get up," and the second, in Acts 20:7–12, was done when Paul put his arms around Eutychus, who had fallen from a three-story building and died, and claimed him alive.

The difference in Jesus' resurrection was that he was not only alive but now the chosen Messiah. In the other cases, we are not told much about what happened afterward to the risen people. In most cases, before death, they lived important lives. For example, the widow's only son was much needed in her life. It must be remembered that even today it is not unusual for people to come back to life after death—although it generally occurs only a few minutes after death, after which the lack of oxygen causes too much damage. In Jesus' case, the effects afterward are profound. After his Resurrection, for his believers, there was no doubt that Jesus was the chosen one, and the work of God was at hand.

Elsewhere in the ancient world, the idea of resurrection was by no means unique. For example, in the ancient Egyptian religion, there is a god who represents life triumphing over death. Osiris is the god of the afterlife, the underworld, and the dead. Originally, he was a god of nature who symbolized the cycle of vegetation. At birth, he was proclaimed the "Universal Lord" and became pharaoh of Egypt when his father Geb retired. Apparently, he was a tall, handsome deity who also possessed great charisma. He built towns and wrote laws that helped to civilize Egypt. But his brother Seth was

---

240 It must be noted that we are not sure if the holy people were resurrected in the form of a human body or more in the form of a ghost, or spirit.

jealous and had him killed. In some versions, Seth was directly responsible, in others he was only an observer. Nevertheless, Osiris's wife and sister, Isis, was overcome with grief, and when Osiris's body was discovered, she performed a magic ritual that restored Osiris to life. Alive again, he was now so disillusioned with the behavior of his brother that he decided to retire from life and reign over the judgment of the dead in the underworld. For Egyptians, the dead were in fact known as the living, and Osiris is also called king of the living.

When it comes to Jesus' Resurrection, each of the Gospels has a narrative for it.

THE RESURRECTION ACCORDING TO MATTHEW

Matthew 27:45–66 tells of the time Jesus was on the cross shortly before his death and preceding burial. According to this passage, his last words were, "My God, my God, why have you forsaken me?" Shortly afterward, he died and the curtain of the Temple was torn in two from top to bottom. This was followed by an earthquake and the resurrection of the Holy. The earthquake was enough to terrify the Roman centurion and guards who exclaimed, "Surely he was the Son of God!"

It was Joseph of Arimathea who provided Jesus with a new tomb cut out of rock. His body was placed in the tomb and a large stone rolled in front of it. The following day, the Pharisees began to worry that the apostles would steal the body of Jesus to give the appearance that he rose after the third day, similar to what he had earlier prophesied. Because of this, they went to Pilate to ask for guards for the tomb for three days. Matthew 28:1–18 does not give any details about the actual Resurrection, just that Mary Magdalene and the other Mary went to the tomb on Sunday only to find it empty.

The Resurrection

It was then they were told by an angel to gather the apostles and go to Galilee to meet Jesus.

According to Matthew, when news spread that Jesus was missing from the tomb, the chief priest and elders bribed the soldiers with money to report that the disciples took the body at night. This became the main defense against Jesus' Resurrection, and it became important for the authorities to produce a body in order to halt the spread of any further worship of Jesus. It did not work of course, and in time Jesus' followers would found a new religion. Immediately, though, the disciples went to Galilee, and there, just as they were told, they saw Jesus. Some still doubted him, but his last words to them were these:

> All authority in heaven and Earth had been given to me. Therefore go and make disciples of all nations, baptizing them in the name of the Father and of the Son and of the Holy Spirit, and teaching them to obey everything I have commanded you. And surely I am with you always to the very end of the age.

Matthew does not tell of Jesus' Ascension into heaven, a very important part of Church doctrine. Jesus' final instructions to the disciples, although vague, indicate that he had faith in them to make the right decisions.

THE RESURRECTION ACCORDING TO MARK

Similar to Matthew's account, Mark 16:1–19 tells of Mary Magdalene, Mary the mother of Jesus, and Salome finding Jesus' tomb empty when they went there on Sunday to anoint the body with spices. There, they saw a young man dressed in a white robe who told them to tell the disciples that they

Chapter 8

would see Jesus at Galilee. According to the New International Version of the Bible, some of the earlier manuscripts did not include Mark 16:9–20. In those verses, Jesus said to them,

> Go into all the world and preach the good news to all creation. Whoever believes and is baptized will be saved, but whoever does not believe will be condemned. And these signs will accompany those who believe: In my name they will drive out demons; they will speak in new tongues; they will pick up snakes with their hands; and when they drink deadly poison, it will not hurt them at all; they will place their hands on sick people, and they will get well.

Jesus was ascended into heaven, where he sat at the right hand of God, and the apostles went out and preached everywhere. It is very interesting that Matthew left this out. Perhaps, it was common knowledge, or perhaps Matthew wanted to make the point that Jesus was still with us.

THE RESURRECTION ACCORDING TO LUKE

Luke 24:1–53 informs us of both the Resurrection and Ascension. This episode in Jesus' life becomes one of the most significant themes of the New Testament: The most important event, after Jesus dying for mankind, is that he rose from the tomb on the third day.

There are several events that led to the Crucifixion. Earlier in Luke, Jesus foresees his own death and Resurrection in several different verses. In Luke 9:22, Jesus predicts, "And he said, 'The Son of Man must suffer many things and be rejected by the elders, chief priest and teachers of the law, and he must be killed and on the third day be raised to life.'" Luke

18:33 predicts, "On the third day he will rise again." Luke 24:7 states, "The Son of Man must be delivered into the hands of sinful men, be crucified and on the third day be raised again."

As in Matthew and Mark, Luke recounts that women whom he later names as Mary Magdalene, Joanna, and Mary, the mother of Jesus—and others, how many or who they were we do not know—go to the tomb with fresh spices. It would make sense for several to go, since removing the stone would require many people. It was there they saw in the tomb "two men in cloths that gleamed like lightning." They were told that Jesus had risen. Luke 24:9–12, unlike Matthew and Mark, informs us that Peter, not believing the women, went to the tomb. Once there, he finds the strips of linen and wonders what has just happened.

According to Luke 24:13–27, Jesus, in disguise, on the road to Emmaus. appears before two of his followers, pretending not to know what had happened. When asked, they appeared very disappointed that he did not redeem Israel. Jesus responds to them, "How foolish you are, and how slow of heart to believe all that the prophets have spoken! Did not the Christ have to suffer these things and then enter his glory?" Jesus stays with them until they recognize him after he breaks bread with them and then disappears.

Once back in Jerusalem, they meet up with the eleven disciples and told them they saw Jesus alive. During this time Jesus appeared before the men, showed them his wounds, and ate a fish in their presence. Therefore, Jesus was not a ghost, but alive. Similar to Matthew and Mark, he tells them, "This is what is written: The Christ will suffer and rise from the dead on the third day, and repentance and forgiveness of sins will be preached in his name to all nations, beginning at Jerusalem. You are witnesses of these things. I am going to send you what my father has promised; but stay in the city until you

Chapter 8

have been clothed with power from on high." He then led them to Bethany, blessed them one final time, and ascended to heaven.

THE RESURRECTION ACCORDING TO JOHN

John 20:1–31, similar to the synoptic gospels, has Mary Magdalene go to the tomb on Sunday, before sunrise, to find an empty tomb. Unlike the account in the other Gospels, in John there was no angel in the tomb. Mary then left and told Peter what she saw. The disciples, despite what Jesus told them, did not understand what happened and left, believing the body was stolen. It was only when the others left and Mary was outside the tomb crying that the two angels appeared. They asked her why she was crying, and she responded that she did not know where they took the body. When she turned around, Jesus was there, but she did not recognize him. She then went and told the other disciples.

Jesus later visited the disciples, minus Thomas, and said, "Peace be with you. "After this he showed them his wounds, and again said, "Peace be with you. Receive the Holy Spirit. If you forgive anyone his sins, they are forgiven; if you don't forgive them, they are not forgiven." Afterward, the others told Thomas they had seen Jesus, and Thomas, the famous doubter, told them he did not believe them. It was only when Jesus came to him later that he believed.

Jesus appeared for the third and last time to the disciples while they were fishing in the Sea of Tiberias. After they failed to catch anything, Jesus appeared along the coast, but they did not recognize him. He told them, "Throw your net on the right side of the boat and you will find some." When they did this, there were so many fish in the net that they could not haul it in. Then Peter realized it was the Lord. Later at breakfast, Jesus told them to take care of his followers and predicts Peter's death by suggesting he would be led where he did not want to go. Afterward, Peter asks about the disciple Jesus loved, and Jesus said, "If I want him to remain alive until I return, what is that to you? You must follow me." But Jesus said nothing about his death. John 21:24–25 ends by stating,

> This is the disciple who testifies to these things and who wrote them down. We know that his testimony is true. Jesus did many other things as well. If every one of them were written down, I suppose that even the whole world would not have room for the books that would be written.

Thus, John does not tell of the Ascension and ends with much unsaid. While each of the four Gospels is different in some of the details, they are all vague about what happened during the Resurrection of Jesus, and what it was like, and therefore, we do not know. But there is one piece of evidence that might could provide some clues.

THE SHROUD OF TURIN

The Bible records no witnesses to the Resurrection, which is kind of surprising, and Jesus does not provide any details about the process. The only evidence, and its legitimacy has been widely debated, is the Shroud of Turin. I wanted to avoid linking the Shroud into the debate of the integral idea. But, it, because of its unexplainable image, provides evidence that the integral idea is more than just being same birthday and day of death on the calendar. It is a miracle from God. Many of the Shroud's critics point to a so called lack of evidence before the 1350s. But, Ian Wilson, in his book *The Blood and the*

Chapter 8

Shroud, provides several passages that at least validate the existence of something that reassembled the Shroud being housed in Edessa, Turkey soon after the death of Jesus in 30 CE. He states, "As a result of which, instead of there being absolutely no record of our Shroud before the 1350s, as is so often contended, we have been able historically to trace an object that sounds and looks most uncannily like it, almost all the way back to the very time of Jesus himself."[241]

Tristan Casabianca, in an article entitled "The Shroud of Turin: A Historical Approach," believes that the shroud, referred to here as "TS," should be allowed as part of the history of Jesus:

> He states, "A consequence of our historiographical approach is that the probability of this linen sheet being the real shroud of Jesus of Nazareth is very high. Historians and natural theologians should therefore treat the TS seriously, if ever cautiously, when the life and death of Jesus comes up for discussion.[242]

The shroud remains the only evidence to the Resurrection, and if true, could help explain what happened to Jesus' body during this period. This is important because it would help explain the importance of the integral idea and further prove the God is perfect. In July of 2015, the BBC posted an article for its magazine online titled "How did the Turin Shroud Get Its Image?" In it, they suggested several possible explanations for the shroud's existence. In 1978, an

---

241 Ian Wilson, *The Blood and the Shroud: New Evidence that the World's Most Sacred Relic is Real* (New York: The Free Press, 1998), 174.
242 Tristan Casabianca, "The Shroud of Turin: A Historiographical Approach," *Heythrop Journal* 54 (May 2013): 414. *Complementary Index*, EBSCOhost.

international team of experts known as the Shroud of Turin Research Project (STURP) conducted the first comprehensive research on the shroud. They found that the image on the shroud is not painted. There is no evidence of pigments or dyes on the linen cloth and no brush strokes. It was not until 1898 that the image could be viewed as a negative image of a photograph. This gave the Shroud the artistic qualities of a photograph 1800 years before the invention of the camera. The BBC concludes as follows:

> The STURP group asserted that the image is the real form of a "scourged, crucified man ... not the product of an artist. There are genuine bloodstains on the cloth, and we even know the blood group (AB, if you're interested). There are traces of human DNA too, although it is badly degraded."[243]

Perhaps the best explanation comes from Giulio Fanti of the University of Padua. He theorizes that the image was burned into the upper layers of the linen cloth by a burst of "radiant energy." This may have been a bright light, ultraviolet light, X-rays, or streams of fundamental particles that emanated during the process of Resurrection. The New Testament may offer some helpful explanation here.[244] Luke 9:29–30 states, "As he was praying, the appearance of his face changed, and his clothes became as bright as a flash of lighting. Two men, Moses and Elijah, appeared in glorious splendor, talking with Jesus. They spoke about his departure, which he was about to bring to fulfillment at Jerusalem." Therefore, Jesus had a history of giving off a powerful aura.

---

243 "How Did the Turin Shroud Get Its Image?" *BBC News*, June 19, 2015, www.bbc.com/news/magazine-33164668.
244 Ibid.

Chapter 8

The Shroud has become the subject of one of most heated arguments in Christendom between the believers and the proponents of a scientific approach. True believers will never disagree with the authenticity of the shroud, and scientists will always find something to doubt about. In 1989, three teams of independent scientists carbon-dated the Shroud to between 1260 and 1390. This should have ended some of the hype, but the believers never gave up hope. Objections include that the shroud's carbon was tainted due to being exposed to several fires; in addition, they believed the process of Resurrection itself would be difficult to carbon date. Also questioned was whether the part of the shroud that was tested was not part of the original but rather part of a restoration patch. This led to Fanti conducting nonstandard dating methods involving spectroscopy, the absorption of light of different colors, which he claims dates the shroud to between 300 BCE and 400 CE. However, even this dating is a wide range, and should be used cautiously when used to prove the Shroud dates from 30 CE.

If the Shroud is an image created by some form of light energy, this might explain the image, but what about the healing of Jesus' body? I believe I owe the readers of this book some sort of answer. The best explanation to date, although just a theory at the present, and one that may be omitted, updated, or made more persuasive in later editions should more information come to light, is the possible link between Resurrection and meditation. In meditation, one thinks deeply or focuses the mind for a period of time in silence, or with the aid of chanting for religious or spiritual purposes, or as a method of relaxation. In recent years, scientists have studied the effects of meditation on the body and found some interesting results.

The Resurrection

By comparing blood samples of long-term meditators and a control group, the scientists found that the meditators had 2209 genes that were differently expressed (switched on or off). Specifically, 1275 were up-regulated (their activity increased) and 934 were down-regulated (their activity decreased. Additionally, it was found that there were 1561 genes that expressed differently between a group of novice meditators who did eight weeks of meditation training and the control group. Specifically, 874 genes were up-regulated and 687 were down-regulated. The research team concluded the following:

> The RR (relaxation response) is clinically effective for ameliorating symptoms in a variety of stress-related disorders including cardiovascular, autoimmune, and other inflammatory conditions and pain. We hypothesize that RR elicitation is associated with systemic gene expression changes in cellular metabolism, oxidative phosphorylation/generation of reactive oxygen species and response to oxidative stress and that these changes to some degree serve to ameliorate the negative impact of stress.[245]

In short, they concluded that meditation changes your genes, and the more experience one has in meditation the more gene changes are possible. Some nurses even suggest meditation practice to ease patient suffering. Mary Grace Umlauf, PhD, RN, wrote a book titled *Healing Meditation* that explores this subject and suggests that nurses use meditation

---

245 Jeffery Dusek, et al., "Genomic Counter-Stress Changes Induced by the Relaxation Response," *Plos ONE* 3, no. 7 (July 2008): 1–8. *Academic Search Premier*, EBSCO*host*.

Chapter 8

as part of their nursing practice.[246]

Buddhists and Hindus have been practicing meditation for thousands of years. In the oldest texts from India, it is used to calm the mind. There are several different ways to achieve this. It can be done through breathing techniques, concentrating on an object, or by chants. Sometimes people have experienced parts of their body vibrating during the process. Once the body is calm, the mind can investigate how things really are. This will lead to what Buddhist call insight. The ultimate form of insight is enlightenment.

CONCLUSION

Not mentioned, but something else to consider, is that Jesus' body may have been predetermined for Resurrection after three days through prayer. I am not suggesting by this that anyone could resurrect himself from the dead. This would understandably require a person who was special and had the will of God. Jesus was after all unique.

Jesus was surely different from Osiris, who was murdered by the deception of his brother. Jesus knew beforehand he was destined to die a long and miserable death. According to Thomas Torrance, in *Space, Time and Resurrection*,

> To sum up, then, the ascension of Christ in this sense is his exaltation from humiliation to royal majesty, but through Crucifixion and sacrifice, for the power and glory of the Royal Priest are bond up with his self-offering in death and resurrection.[247]

---

246 Mary Grace Umlauf, *Healing Meditation* (Albany (NY): Delmar, 1997), 9.
247 Thomas Torrance, Space, Time and Resurrection (Edinburgh: The Handsel Press, 1976), 111.

The Resurrection

The reason that Jesus became the foundation of a new religion and Osiris is regulated to annals of mythology is that Jesus' Resurrection had a purpose. He went from the son of a carpenter to the King of Kings in the matter of a weekend Passover. He was willing to die for the world. Osiris was never given that choice. Like Osiris, however, Jesus left the world of the living to prepare a place for his followers in the afterlife. This becomes a pivotal moment for the apostles. They were now leaderless, but Jesus knew that his presence would only endanger the others because Herod and Pilate will order their deaths. The significance of Caiaphas is also relevant at this point. Although it was the Romans who crucified Jesus, it is the Pharisees who broke the commandment of bearing false witness in order to have Jesus killed.

In Matthew and John, Caiaphas is important in the final verdict of death for Jesus. But Mark does not mention him by name, and Luke 3:2 notes only that he was high priest. Over time, many have criticized the differing accounts in the four Gospels, but it must be remembered that each was written at least thirty-years after the Resurrection, and each was based on different witnesses. Although each witness had a slightly different story, the important facts remain: Jesus' tomb was found empty on the third day, he appeared to several witnesses, and he established his wish that they spread the word not only throughout Judea but the world that he was the way to salvation for those who believed in him.

Many question why Jesus left the disciples? If he did not leave, he could have created a perfect world. Instead, Jesus told them to preach the Word to everyone, and to do it everywhere. If Jesus stayed, there would have been a major conflict between him and Pilate, and we know that Jesus did not want conflict.

Chapter 9

CHAPTER 9
PERFECTION IN NATURE

If the Nativity occurred sometime during the Passover of 5 BCE, and Jesus' Resurrection occurred on Sunday, Nissan 17 (April 7, 30 CE), then he would have been 34 years old, based on the Jewish calendar, when he died or was reborn. One must ask the question why the number 34 is so important, and what that number has to do with his perfect life. Simply put, the number 34 is a perfect number. Thirty-four is a number within the Fibonacci sequence. Based on the Golden Ratio, the Fibonacci sequence is not only in mathematics but within nature and the heavens.

THE GOLDEN RATIO

The mathematical proportion branded the Golden Ratio, also called the Golden Section, or Golden number, has always

Perfection in Nature

existed in the physical universe. Since buildings can last much longer than paper, we can see evidence of the Golden Ratio from the ancient world in Egyptian and Greek architecture. It has been theorized that both used pi and phi in the design of some the world's best-known structures, including the Great Pyramids and the Parthenon.[248] Today, the Greeks seem to get more credit than their neighbors to the south of the Mediterranean Sea. Phidias (500 BCE–432 BCE), a Greek sculptor and mathematician, was thought to have studied phi and applied it in the construction of the Parthenon.

Plato, based on his stances on natural science and cosmology written in the *Timaeus*, considered the Golden Section to be the important link to all mathematics and physics. But, it was Euclid of Alexandria (365 BCE–300 BCE), also a Greek, who in *Elements* referred to the Golden Ratio. This occurs when a line is divided into two parts to create the extreme and mean ratio, so that the sum of the whole length of the line, when divided by the longest part, is the same as the sum of longest line divided by the shortest line. In nature, this is the most perfect number: 1.61803399 (although on the surface, this number may seem very imperfect; this will be explained more in depth later).

Figure 8.1

The Golden Ratio is displayed in Figure 8.1. By examining the figure, we can see that segment *AC* is longer than segment *AB*, and at the same time, *AB* is longer than *BC*.

---

248 Phi and pi are ratios defined by geometric constructions. Pi is the ratio of the circumference of a circle to its diameter, while Phi is the ratio of the line segments that result when a line is divided in a particular way.

Chapter 9

If the ratio of AB to that of BC is the same as AC to AB, then the line has been divided into the extreme and mean ratio or Golden Ratio, a never-ending number beginning 1.618... Such ratios intrigued the ancients because they are neither whole numbers or numbers that could be put into a fraction. If that wasn't intriguing enough, another great mathematician, this time an Italian, came along during the thirteenth century CE and further proved the greatness of the Golden Ratio.

LEONARDO FIBONACCI

The man we know today as Fibonacci, literally meaning son of Bonaccio, was born Leonardo Pisano in 1175, most likely in the city of Pisa, Italy. He was the son of Guglielmo Bonaccio, a medieval customs official who was secretary to the Republic of Pisa. When he was born, his father wanted him to become a merchant. Guglielmo was soon assigned work at a Pisan trading colony in Algeria, bringing Leonardo along with him to learn the trade.

It was in Algeria that Fibonacci was tutored in calculation with the hopes of learning how to become a successful merchant. During this time Leonardo learned how to use an abacus and was taught how to count using Hindu-Arabic numerals. Since his teachers were Muslims, he was learning the mathematical techniques of the Arab world at a time when most Europeans were still counting with Roman numerals. It was in his travels around the Mediterranean that he learned algebra, compared several numerical systems, and learned to use the abacus quickly and accurately when calculating numbers.

According to Bunny Crumpacker, Fibonacci was not well received at first. She states in *Perfect Figures: The Lore of Numbers and How We Learned to Count*, that

Perfection in Nature

"Pisans called him *Bigollne*—a sort of blockhead, a man of no importance. He was supposedly often seen walking around the city, stopping frequently to stand lost in thought for a moment and then scribbling Arabic numerals on the nearest wall with the pieces of chalk that were always in one pocket or another."[249]

Fibonacci best known book was *Liber Abaci,* in which he elegantly explained how to translate Roman numerals into Hindu-Arabic numerals. In his book, he presents the world with the following mathematical riddle about the numbers of offspring of an isolated pair of rabbits after a year's time:

A certain man put a pair of rabbits in a place surrounded on all sides by a wall. How many pairs of rabbits can be produced from that pair in a year if it is supposed that every month each pair begets a new pair which from the second month on becomes productive?[250]

The resulting sequence is 1, 1, 2, 3, 5, 8, 13, 21, 34, 55, 89, 144 ... This sequence, in which each number is the sum of the two preceding numbers is found everywhere throughout nature. The Fibonacci sequence is found in many varieties of flowers when the petals are counted; three (lily, iris), five (buttercup, columbine), eight (cosmo, rue anemone), 13 (yellow daisy, marigold), 21 (English daisy, aster) 34 (oxeye daisy), and 55 (Coral Gerber daisy). Fibonacci sequences are

---

249 Bunny Crumpacker, *Perfect Figures: The Lore of Numbers and How We Learned to Count* (New York: Thomas Dunne Books, 2007), 126.
250 Leonardo Fibonacci. *Liber Abbaci*, 283–4., 1202.

Chapter 9

found in the bracts of pine cones, which spiral in different directions of rows of eight and 13, while the scales of pineapples spiral in different directions of rows of 8, 13, and 21. Other things in nature with the sequence include apples, chilies, lemons, sand dollars, starfish, and pussy willows. Most plants on Earth use the Fibonacci sequence when generating new shoots or buds. Figure 8.2 is the oxeye daisy. The Fibonacci number 34 is represented by the spiral of seeds.

Figure 8.2 Daisy

Image Credit: Oxeye Daisy (Pixabay)

Figure 8.3 Nautilus and Half Cut Shell

Image Credits: Nautilus and Shell (Pixabay)

Perfection in Nature

The Fibonacci sequence is also found in many types of spirals of nature including nautilus shells (Figure 8.3), hurricanes (Figure 8.4), and spiral galaxies (Figure 8.5) in space. However, it is not fully understood why this mathematical concept is connected with objects of nature.

Figure 8.4 Cyclone or Hurricane

Image Credit : Tropical Cyclone Catarina (Pixabay)

Figure 8.5 Spiral Galaxy

Image Credit: NASA, ESA, and the Hubble Heritage

Chapter 9

Of further interest, when numbers in the Fibonacci sequence are divided by the ones just before them, the answers are close to the ratio of 1.6180339 to 1, the Golden Ratio, also known by the Greek symbol Φ (phi). For example, 1÷1 =1; 2 ÷ 1 = 2; 3 ÷ 2 = 1.5; 5 ÷ 3 = 1.666; 8 ÷ 5 = 1.6; 13 ÷ 8 = 1.625; 21 ÷ 13 =1.615; 34 ÷ 21 =1.619 ... The size of the object does not matter. This ratio is the mathematical basis for many things in nature from the smallest snails (Figure 8.3) to the largest spiral galaxies (Figure 8.4). To the ancient Greeks, the Golden Ratio was magical. They proclaimed it the divine proportion, a gift from the gods. The symbol Φ, used to represent the Golden Ratio, was chosen because it was the first Greek letter in Pheidias's (ca. 480–430 BCE) name. It is believed that he used the Golden Ratio in the proportions of his sculptures, as well as in the architecture of his most renowned building, the Parthenon, which sits on the Acropolis in Athens. It has also been suggested that Leonardo da Vici used the Golden Ratio in his drawings and paintings, including the Mona Lisa, but there is no documentation to prove this. However, it is known that Salvador Dali (1904–1989) and Piet Mondrian (1872–1944) used the technique in some of their modern paintings.

If Jesus was meant by God to live a perfect life based on the Fibonacci number 34, then there should be some evidence that would back up the importance of this number. Accordingly, the number 34 is the largest number of measurement in a DNA structure (Figure 8.5). DNA is measured in units known as ångströms. This is a unit of length equal to one hundred-millionth of a centimeter, or 10^{-10} meters. It is used mainly to express wavelengths and interatomic distances. DNA is made up of molecules called nucleotides. Each nucleotide is composed of a phosphate group, a sugar group, and a nitrogen base. There are four types

Perfection in Nature

of nitrogen bases adenine (A), thymine (T), guanine (G), and cytosine (C). The sequence of the bases is what makes up the genetic code.

In the DNA molecule, the sugar and phosphate groups provide the backbone of the structure, forming a helix. The helix twists much like a spiral staircase, or a stack of dominos, with each one twisted a little more than the last. This twisting effect, caused by the torsional stress of the DNA helix (similar to a rubber band being twisted), also forms grooves, with the longest ones measuring 34 ångströms in length and around 21 ångströms in width, thus the Fibonacci sequence. The relationship between DNA and Fibonacci numbers is just being explored. There is a small amount of scientific research on the way in which the crystallographic structure of DNA relates to the Golden Ratio, but ample Internet blogs with unreliable sources, or no sources, on the topic. Perhaps updated versions of this book will be able to supply more information on DNA—or might have none, depending on the findings of future research.

Figure 8.5 DNA Module

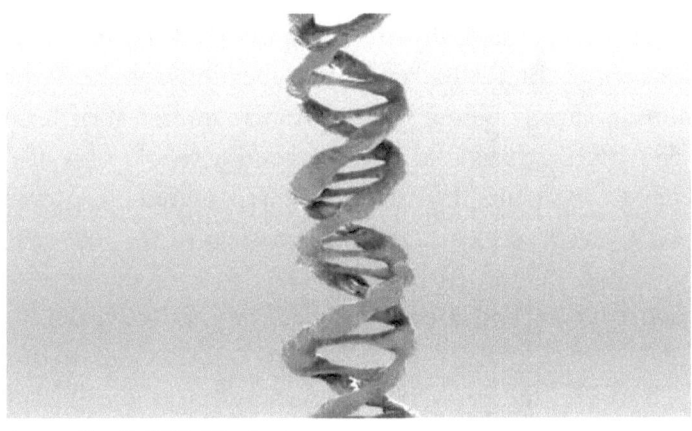

Image Credit: DNA (Pixabay)

Chapter 9

FIBONACCI NUMBERS IN THE BIBLE

Fibonacci numbers are found throughout the Bible. But some caution should be used because many different numbers are found throughout it in one place or another. For example, the numbers 10 and 40, not Fibonacci numbers, are very popular throughout the Bible. Nevertheless, some of the most important objects God commanded men to create in the Bible have Fibonacci proportions. For example, in Exodus 25:10–11, God commands Moses to build the Ark of the Covenant to hold the Ten Commandments. God says to Moses, "Then have them make a chest of acacia wood—two and a half cubits long, a cubit and a half wide, and a cubit and a half high. Overlay it with pure gold, both inside and out, and make a gold molding around it."

Although Fibonacci numbers are not present in fractions, the ratio of 2.5 cubits by 1.5 cubits is still phi or the same as the ration of 5 to 3, which is 1.666. In Exodus 27: 1–2, God further commands Moses to, "Build an altar of acacia wood, three cubits high; it is to be square, five cubits long and five cubits wide."

The whereabouts of the Ark of the Covenant have been a mystery since the Babylonian captivity of Jerusalem in the sixth-century BCE. Its last known location was the Temple of Solomon shortly before the Babylonian conquest of Jerusalem in 587 BCE. It was said to have been a visible sign of God's covenant with the Jews and displayed incredible powers. At times it was used to vanquish the enemies of the Jews.

The Book of Joshua 3:14–17 tells of an amazing experience when the Israelites crossed the Joran River.

> So when the people broke camp to cross the Jordan, the priests carrying the ark of the covenant went

Perfection in Nature

ahead of them. Now the Jordan is at flood stage all during harvest. Yet as soon as the priests who carried the ark reached the Jordan and their feet touched the water's edge, the water from upstream stopped flowing... So the people crossed over opposite Jericho. The priest who carried the ark of the covenant of the Lord stood firm on dry ground in the middle of the Jordan, while all Israel passed by until the whole nation had completed the crossing on dry ground.

Later, at the Battle of Jericho, the ark was carried by a procession around the walls of the city for seven days followed by the army and trumpet blowers. After the seventh day, the walls fell. The ark eventually was captured by the Philistines, but it was not the trophy they desired. Plague broke out in whatever city it was taken to. Eventually, it was given back to the Israelites. This was not the only holy relic that was constructed using Fibonacci numbers.

A ratio of 5 to 3 was also used in the construction of Noah's Ark. In Genesis 6:15, from the New International Version of the Bible, God commands Noah to build an ark saying, "This is how you are to build it: The ark is to be 450 feet long. 75 feet wide and 45 feet high." The Hebrew version, in cubits, is 300 cubits long, 50 cubits wide, and 30 cubits high (3 to 5). But in both versions, the ratio is the same, 75 to 45 or 50 to 30, which comes out to 1.666. If God is truly perfect, then everything he created must have order and reason, including the Golden Ratio and the amount of time Jesus, a perfect being, spent on a not so perfect Earth. I do not know if the 34 Passovers spent by Jesus from the Nativity to the Resurrection have a greater meaning. The final decision of Jesus' dying was God's. But the time, in a chronological sense,

Chapter 9

was important to the Church Fathers. They believed that Jesus was meant to be alive on Earth for a certain amount of time.

CONCLUSION

The length of time that each of us lives on Earth, measured in days or years, can't be compared to Jesus' time here. He was the Son of God, and perfect. We are not, but what we do with our time on Earth and how we interact with our fellow humans is important. The early Church Fathers had a unique interpretation of time. According to Glenn Chesnut in *The First Christian Histories: Eusebius, Socrates, Sozomen, Theodoret, and Evagrius*,

> For Eusebius, following Origen, the "Garden" of Eden had been a realm outside this present space-time continuum, and "Adam" had been the totality of humankind. All our souls preexisted before this Earth was ever created. An act of disobedience on the part of some of those unembodied noetic beings caused God to cast them into human bodies and imprison them on Earth for a period of discipline, assailed by death and corruption.[251]

We may not be here as prisoners, as Eusebius believed, but the actions we take while alive on Earth may make the difference between finding salvation in the afterlife or not. Some early Christians even believed that if we did not learn the lessons intended to be learned by God, we would be

---

251 Glenn Chesnut, *The First Christian Histories: Eusebius, Socrates, Sozomen, Theodoret, and Evagrius* (Macon, GA: Mercer University Press, 1986), 69.

Perfection in Nature

doomed to repeat the lessons of life again through reincarnation. Other early Christians, the same as today, imagined an even darker punishment—spending eternity in hell.

Jesus' time on Earth may have other implications. We consider God as perfect, and he sent his son to die for us as proof of his love for us. Perhaps there are more answers we should take from the time, in years, that Jesus was on this Earth.

The future will include some controversy over the self-assembly of DNA. Currently, scientists are debating what would be the most efficient way to complete this process. One known chemical process is spiral-step assembly. According to Mel Mendelson, in this process, "a spiral step of atoms occurs due to line defects in solids, which are called screw dislocations . . . As the crystal grows, the step winds around a central core like a rotating screw."[252] The interesting part is that the path of the spiral increases its length by the same size ratio of squares as a Fibonacci number sequence. Thus, as found throughout nature, the new structure seems to self-assemble itself into a geometrical pattern. Perhaps God is reminding humans that if you are going to create or replicate atoms, it is best to use the same mathematical processes that he does. Jesus' integral existence may provide the answers to many more problems or solutions, if one believes.

---

252 Mel Mendelson, *Learning Bio-Micro-Nanotechnology* (Boca Raton, FL: CRC Press, 2013) 506.

Epilogue

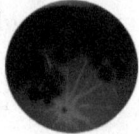

EPILOGUE
▪▪▪▪▪▪▪▪▪▪▪▪▪▪

During the creation of this book, there were many times that I went in a completely new direction and altered my thesis. Sometimes this happened because of a calculation using a different calendar—for example the dates for St. Clement's Basilidians celebrations for Christmas at one time played a greater role in the main thesis. These dates required more exploration of the Egyptian Alexandrian calendar and its conversion into the Gregorian calendar. Then, I had an epiphany, not in the sense of the manifestation of spiritual presence, but more of an intuitive perception. The epiphany was that one calendar was the most significant, the Jewish lunar calendar. Following this, the research was much easier, and everything began to connect. I believe that the researchers before me erred by not considering the Jewish calendar more

Epilogue

prominently in their calculations. As any historian should do, I saved several earlier drafts of the book just in case they were needed later, and at times sources that did not work earlier took on greater roles as the book developed. I further believe that many scholars who tried to write about some of this subject matter erred in creating their thesis first, and then trying to find the evidence that fit with it. In my research, I have come across this more than once. Theories should be based on thorough observation, and not the opposite. Unfortunately, for some scholars, the appearance of good research is more important than the actual research, which when more closely examined only disproves the scholar.

When reflecting back on previous versions, I realized that the finished product went in a completely different direction than previously intended, and perhaps the detour was required to come to the final conclusion. At some point, I asked myself what my agenda was for spending ample amounts of time researching and writing this book. At that point, I created the one thing that any scholar should have, a set of envisioned outcomes. These are important and should be thought out carefully. They assisted me by reminding me to stay on task.

When developing the final theory for this book, I discovered that the simplest solution was the best. Instead of focusing on an extremely complicated text—for example, some scholars analyze the Book of Revelations in order to find hidden meanings within the interpretations—I believe it better to avoid overcomplicating theories. Therefore, after reading my book I ask readers to keep three things in mind. By doing this, you will have a greater insight into my interpretations of the subject. The first is very easy to understand. Jesus was Jewish. He celebrated Passover, was distraught over the conditions at the Temple in Jerusalem, such as the moneychangers, visited synagogues, and was well versed in the

Epilogue

Old Testament. The reader needs to think of Jesus as a Jewish prophet first. This will help us understand how his life fulfilled Jewish prophecy in the Talmud—for example, that great prophets are born and die during the Jewish month of Nissan. Second, it is helpful to think of time in the Jewish sense of it. Their calendar was lunar, not solar, and Passover accordingly, has always been a lunar holiday, occurring on the first Full-Moon after the spring equinox. Knowing this makes it easier to calculate Jesus' birth and death dates. Third, it is better to under- rather than overestimate the astrological skills of the Magi or Jewish authorities involved. My theory works just as well if the people involved could acknowledge only simple phenomena like a Full-Moon or comet instead of complicated astrological signs. A comet is something we may consider just a temporary celestial object, but the ancients considered it to have greater meanings.

In closing, I would like to address Christians. Try not to forget that, Jesus was Jewish, and observed Jewish holidays that most Christians today do not. I will leave it up to readers to decide to what extent to follow Jesus on this. I would hope that Christians would be more proactive on certain controversial issues, and ask themselves to reason what is the best solution based on the fact that Jesus was Jewish. History has not been kind to the Jews, and they have taken much of the blame for the Crucifixion. But the final sentence came down from Roman authority under Pontius Pilate. Jesus also went willingly to his death, because he knew he was predestined to die for the sins of mankind. If this was the case, his death would also cleanse the sins and forgive those who were responsible for it. Luke 23:31 states that Jesus said on the cross, "Father, forgive them, for they do not know what they are doing." In the end, as in all things, the final decision was God's

Appendix

APPENDIX A

Passover dates for 1 BCE to 7 BCE (highlighted)
"Moon Phases Tables courtesy of Fred Espenak, www.Astropixels.com"

Possible Passover Day for 1 BCE.

Year	New Moon	First Quarter	Full Moon	Last Quarter
0000		Jan 3 07:43	Jan 9 23:05 t	Jan 17 05:49
	Jan 25 09:46	Feb 1 16:18	Feb 8 10:57	Feb 16 01:54
	Feb 24 00:27	Mar 1 23:01	Mar 8 23:16	Mar 16 21:37
	Mar 24 11:48	Mar 31 05:04	Apr 7 12:16	Apr 15 15:25
	Apr 22 20:31	Apr 29 11:36	May 7 02:13	May 15 06:16
	May 22 03:45	May 28 19:36	Jun 5 17:09	Jun 13 17:58
	Jun 20 10:35 P	Jun 27 05:59	Jul 5 08:36 t	Jul 13 03:00
	Jul 19 17:58 P	Jul 26 19:30	Aug 3 23:48	Aug 11 10:19
	Aug 18 02:44	Aug 25 12:28	Sep 2 14:06	Sep 9 16:59
	Sep 16 13:36	Sep 24 08:20	Oct 2 03:18	Oct 9 00:03
	Oct 16 03:16	Oct 24 05:28	Oct 31 15:39	Nov 7 08:28
	Nov 14 20:02	Nov 23 01:41	Nov 30 03:24	Dec 6 19:01
	Dec 14 15:11 A	Dec 22 19:11	Dec 29 14:35 p	

Possible Passover Day for 2 BCE.

Year	New Moon	First Quarter	Full Moon	Last Quarter
-0001	Jan 6 11:54	Jan 13 12:07	Jan 20 11:41 p	Jan 28 10:28
	Feb 5 01:30 A	Feb 11 19:18	Feb 19 02:50	Feb 27 05:55
	Mar 6 12:18	Mar 13 02:55	Mar 20 18:36	Mar 28 22:17
	Apr 4 20:44	Apr 11 11:58	Apr 19 10:19	Apr 27 11:02
	May 4 03:44	May 10 23:04	May 19 01:29	May 26 20:19
	Jun 2 10:28	Jun 9 12:28	Jun 17 15:48	Jun 25 02:54
	Jul 1 18:10	Jul 9 04:08	Jul 17 05:03 p	Jul 24 08:03
	Jul 31 03:48 H	Aug 7 21:47	Aug 15 17:07	Aug 22 13:14
	Aug 29 16:04	Sep 6 16:44	Sep 14 04:07	Sep 20 19:59
	Sep 28 07:10	Oct 6 11:49	Oct 13 14:31	Oct 20 05:33
	Oct 28 00:54	Nov 5 05:26	Nov 12 00:54	Nov 18 18:35
	Nov 26 20:22	Dec 4 20:14	Dec 11 11:42	Dec 18 10:57
	Dec 26 15:58 P			

Possible Passover Day for 3 BCE.

Year	New Moon	First Quarter	Full Moon	Last Quarter
-0002			Jan 1 13:58	Jan 9 18:01
	Jan 17 00:32	Jan 23 16:25	Jan 31 07:23 n	Feb 8 12:12
	Feb 15 11:01 T	Feb 22 02:42	Mar 2 01:20 n	Mar 10 02:22
	Mar 16 19:57	Mar 23 14:50	Mar 31 18:17	Apr 8 12:41
	Apr 15 03:49	Apr 22 05:02	Apr 30 09:12	May 7 19:53
	May 14 11:29	May 21 21:03	May 29 21:52	Jun 6 01:04
	Jun 12 20:08	Jun 20 14:13	Jun 28 08:44	Jul 5 05:32
	Jul 12 06:53	Jul 20 07:40	Jul 27 18:28 n	Aug 3 10:43
	Aug 10 20:26 A	Aug 19 00:36	Aug 26 03:42 n	Sep 1 18:11
	Sep 9 12:45	Sep 17 16:24	Sep 24 12:58	Oct 1 05:16
	Oct 9 06:57	Oct 17 06:31	Oct 23 22:46	Oct 30 20:37
	Nov 8 01:43	Nov 15 18:29	Nov 22 09:34	Nov 29 15:47
	Dec 7 19:44	Dec 15 04:11	Dec 21 21:50	Dec 29 13:07

Possible Passover Day for 4 BCE.

Year	New Moon	First Quarter	Full Moon	Last Quarter
-0003		Jan 4 14:45	Jan 12 12:54	Jan 20 15:37
	Jan 27 08:53	Feb 3 04:34	Feb 11 07:41	Feb 19 03:39
	Feb 25 18:33 T	Mar 4 20:16	Mar 13 00:46 p	Mar 20 11:56
	Mar 27 03:59	Apr 3 13:17	Apr 11 15:01	Apr 18 17:41
	Apr 25 13:38	May 3 06:57	May 11 02:16	May 17 22:20
	May 25 00:12	Jun 2 00:21	Jun 9 11:12	Jun 16 03:18
	Jun 23 12:26	Jul 1 16:32	Jul 8 18:56	Jul 15 09:52
	Jul 23 02:52	Jul 31 06:50	Aug 7 02:38	Aug 13 19:14
	Aug 21 19:22 A	Aug 29 19:04	Sep 5 11:09 p	Sep 12 08:19
	Sep 20 12:58	Sep 28 05:31	Oct 4 21:02	Oct 12 01:34
	Oct 20 06:17	Oct 27 14:39	Nov 3 08:38	Nov 10 22:20
	Nov 18 22:13	Nov 25 23:04	Dec 2 22:14	Dec 10 20:41
	Dec 18 12:18	Dec 25 07:26		

Possible Passover Day for 5 BCE.

Year	New Moon	First Quarter	Full Moon	Last Quarter
-0004			Jan 24 13:07	Jan 2 15:43
	Jan 9 06:56	Jan 16 08:22		Feb 1 02:04
	Feb 7 17:33	Feb 15 03:28	Feb 23 05:10	Mar 1 09:24
	Mar 8 04:45 P	Mar 15 22:46	Mar 23 18:17 t	Mar 30 14:55
	Apr 6 16:51 P	Apr 14 16:58	Apr 22 04:32	Apr 28 20:08
	May 6 05:58	May 14 09:16	May 21 12:30	May 28 02:30
	Jun 4 20:01	Jun 12 23:12	Jun 19 19:14	Jun 26 11:14
	Jul 4 10:56	Jul 12 10:35	Jul 19 01:59	Jul 25 23:06
	Aug 3 02:29	Aug 10 19:41	Aug 17 09:57	Aug 24 14:27
	Sep 1 18:10 P	Sep 9 03:12	Sep 15 20:06 t	Sep 23 09:03
	Oct 1 09:16 P	Oct 8 10:11	Oct 15 08:55	Oct 23 05:59
	Oct 30 23:09	Nov 6 17:50	Nov 14 00:22	Nov 22 03:29
	Nov 29 11:33	Dec 6 03:10	Dec 13 18:00	Dec 21 23:20
	Dec 28 22:40			

Possible Passover Day for 6 BCE.

Year	New Moon	First Quarter	Full Moon	Last Quarter
-0005			Jan 5 17:07	Jan 12 22:02
	Jan 19 17:43	Jan 27 11:27	Feb 4 07:36	Feb 11 05:28
	Feb 18 07:00	Feb 26 07:56	Mar 5 19:21	Mar 12 12:15
	Mar 19 21:28	Mar 28 01:43	Apr 4 04:47 p	Apr 10 19:28
	Apr 18 12:50 A	Apr 26 16:06	May 3 12:32	May 10 04:14
	May 18 04:23	May 26 03:11	Jun 1 19:22	Jun 8 15:29
	Jun 16 19:20	Jun 24 11:38	Jul 1 02:16	Jul 8 05:44
	Jul 16 09:19	Jul 23 18:14	Jul 30 10:25	Aug 6 22:49
	Aug 14 22:21	Aug 22 00:01	Aug 28 21:02	Sep 5 17:54
	Sep 13 10:39	Sep 20 06:11	Sep 27 10:54 p	Oct 5 13:43
	Oct 12 22:26 T	Oct 19 14:04	Oct 27 03:58	Nov 4 08:50
	Nov 11 09:41	Nov 18 00:50	Nov 25 23:09	Dec 4 01:51
	Dec 10 20:27	Dec 17 15:04	Dec 25 18:44	

Possible Passover Day for 7 BCE.

Year	New Moon	First Quarter	Full Moon	Last Quarter
-0006		Jan 8 19:13	Jan 16 08:18	Jan 23 01:08
	Jan 30 10:54	Feb 7 15:22	Feb 14 19:03	Feb 21 10:11
	Mar 1 03:31	Mar 9 07:54	Mar 16 03:57	Mar 22 20:35
	Mar 30 20:16	Apr 7 20:12	Apr 14 11:48 n	Apr 21 08:41
	Apr 29 12:15 A	May 7 04:45	May 13 19:22 n	May 20 22:44
	May 29 02:34	Jun 5 10:44	Jun 12 03:25	Jun 19 14:46
	Jun 27 14:53	Jul 4 15:32	Jul 11 12:49	Jul 19 08:24
	Jul 27 01:29	Aug 2 20:35	Aug 10 00:32	Aug 18 02:42
	Aug 25 11:10	Sep 1 03:11	Sep 8 15:15	Sep 16 20:22
	Sep 23 20:49	Sep 30 12:30	Oct 8 08:57 n	Oct 16 12:19
	Oct 23 07:02 T	Oct 30 01:22	Nov 7 04:28 n	Nov 15 01:55
	Nov 21 17:56	Nov 28 18:07	Dec 6 23:47	Dec 14 13:04
	Dec 21 05:28	Dec 28 14:04		

Eclipse Types

Solar Eclipse	Lunar Eclipse
T - Total	t - Total (Umbral)
A - Annular	p - Partial (Umbral)
H - Hybrid (Annular/Total)	n - Penumbral
P - Partial	

APPENDIX B

Passover dates for 28 CE to 34 CE (highlighted)
"Moon Phases Tables courtesy of Fred Espenak, www.Astropixels.com"

Possible Passover Day for 28 CE.

Year	New Moon	First Quarter	Full Moon	Last Quarter
0028				Jan 7 14:11
	Jan 15 12:59 A	Jan 23 15:04	Jan 30 08:54	Feb 6 03:47
	Feb 14 07:49	Feb 22 03:04	Feb 28 18:24	Mar 6 19:35
	Mar 15 00:27	Mar 22 11:35	**Mar 29 03:23**	Apr 5 12:55
	Apr 13 14:11	Apr 20 17:32	Apr 27 12:42	May 5 06:43
	May 13 01:19	May 19 22:08	May 26 23:21	Jun 3 23:53
	Jun 11 10:34	Jun 18 02:50	Jun 25 12:02 p	Jul 3 15:43
	Jul 10 18:42 T	Jul 17 09:09	Jul 25 02:51	Aug 2 05:54
	Aug 9 02:30	Aug 15 18:33	Aug 23 19:18	Aug 31 18:23
	Sep 7 10:45	Sep 14 08:02	Sep 22 12:30	Sep 30 05:10
	Oct 6 20:16	Oct 14 01:44	Oct 22 05:34	Oct 29 14:24
	Nov 5 07:49	Nov 12 22:36	Nov 20 21:43	Nov 27 22:35
	Dec 4 21:49 P	Dec 12 20:38	Dec 20 12:13 t	Dec 27 06:35

Possible Passover Day for 29 CE.

Year	New Moon	First Quarter	Full Moon	Last Quarter
0029	Jan 3 14:01 P	Jan 11 17:39	Jan 19 00:35	Jan 25 15:26
	Feb 2 07:29	Feb 10 11:53	Feb 17 10:43	Feb 24 01:57
	Mar 4 00:59	Mar 12 02:17	Mar 18 19:09	Mar 25 14:26
	Apr 2 17:30	Apr 10 12:38	**Apr 17 02:46**	Apr 24 04:46
	May 2 08:25	May 9 19:35	May 16 10:39	May 23 20:35
	May 31 21:27 P	Jun 8 00:23	Jun 14 19:45 t	Jun 22 13:27
	Jun 30 08:37	Jul 7 04:37	Jul 14 06:48	Jul 22 06:52
	Jul 29 18:16	Aug 5 09:56	Aug 12 20:16	Aug 21 00:07
	Aug 28 03:07	Sep 3 17:50	Sep 11 12:13	Sep 19 16:14
	Sep 26 12:04	Oct 3 05:20	Oct 11 06:18	Oct 19 06:18
	Oct 25 21:57	Nov 1 20:47	Nov 10 01:24	Nov 17 17:53
	Nov 24 09:13 T	Dec 1 15:42	Dec 9 19:50 p	Dec 17 03:13
	Dec 23 21:52	Dec 31 12:50		

Possible Passover Day for 30 CE.

```
Year      New Moon        First Quarter      Full Moon           Last Quarter

0030                                          Jan  8  11:59      Jan 15  11:08
          Jan 22  11:40   Jan 30  10:18      Feb  7  01:05      Feb 13  18:35
          Feb 21  02:21   Mar  1  06:00      Mar  8  11:24      Mar 15  02:30
          Mar 22  17:47   Mar 30  22:19      Apr  6  19:43      Apr 13  11:35
          Apr 21  09:37   Apr 29  10:41      May  6  03:01 n    May 12  22:27
          May 21  01:13 A May 28  19:34      Jun  4  10:10 p    Jun 11  11:35
          Jun 19  15:46   Jun 27  02:02      Jul  3  18:01      Jul 11  03:19
          Jul 19  04:49   Jul 26  07:24      Aug  2  03:27      Aug  9  21:21
          Aug 17  16:27   Aug 24  12:59      Aug 31  15:22      Sep  8  16:39
          Sep 16  03:14   Sep 22  19:59      Sep 30  06:28      Oct  8  11:39
          Oct 15  13:51   Oct 22  05:30      Oct 30  00:39      Nov  7  04:53
          Nov 14  00:42 T Nov 20  18:15      Nov 28  20:34 n    Dec  6  19:24
          Dec 13  11:45   Dec 20  10:31      Dec 28  16:05
```

Possible Passover Day for 31 CE.

```
Year      New Moon        First Quarter      Full Moon           Last Quarter

0031                                                              Jan  5  06:56
          Jan 11  22:53   Jan 19  05:38      Jan 27  09:21      Feb  3  15:46
          Feb 10  10:15   Feb 18  02:01      Feb 25  23:35      Mar  4  22:37
          Mar 11  22:20   Mar 19  21:42      Mar 27  10:56      Apr  3  04:31
          Apr 10  11:33   Apr 18  15:07      Apr 25  20:00 p    May  2  10:43
          May 10  01:58 A May 18  05:37      May 25  03:31      May 31  18:30
          Jun  8  17:06   Jun 16  17:17      Jun 23  10:18      Jun 30  05:01
          Jul  8  08:20   Jul 16  02:36      Jul 22  17:22      Jul 29  18:59
          Aug  6  23:08   Aug 14  10:13      Aug 21  01:50      Aug 28  12:20
          Sep  5  13:20   Sep 12  16:55      Sep 19  12:48      Sep 27  08:12
          Oct  5  02:52   Oct 11  23:44      Oct 19  03:00 p    Oct 27  05:01
          Nov  3  15:39 H Nov 10  07:53      Nov 17  20:14      Nov 26  01:05
          Dec  3  03:28   Dec  9  18:25      Dec 17  15:20      Dec 25  18:44
```

Possible Passover Day for 32 CE.

```
Year      New Moon        First Quarter      Full Moon           Last Quarter

0032      Jan  1  14:15   Jan  8  07:54      Jan 16  10:37      Jan 24  08:49
          Jan 31  00:13   Feb  7  00:02      Feb 15  04:35      Feb 22  19:03
          Feb 29  09:56   Mar  7  17:48      Mar 15  20:12      Mar 23  02:00
          Mar 29  20:01 P Apr  6  11:59      Apr 14  09:01 t    Apr 21  06:58
          Apr 28  07:01 P May  6  05:38      May 13  19:10      May 20  11:34
          May 27  19:17   Jun  4  22:02      Jun 12  03:15      Jun 18  17:21
          Jun 26  08:58   Jul  4  12:41      Jul 11  10:18      Jul 18  01:39
          Jul 26  00:06   Aug  3  01:14      Aug  9  17:32      Aug 16  13:22
          Aug 24  16:25   Sep  1  11:40      Sep  8  02:04      Sep 15  04:54
          Sep 23  09:15 P Sep 30  20:22      Oct  7  12:43 t    Oct 14  23:57
          Oct 23  01:33 P Oct 30  04:11      Nov  6  01:47      Nov 13  21:25
          Nov 21  16:21   Nov 28  12:09      Dec  5  17:08      Dec 13  19:22
          Dec 21  05:10   Dec 27  21:11
```

Possible Passover Day for 33 CE.

Year	New Moon	First Quarter	Full Moon	Last Quarter
0033			Jan 4 10:15	Jan 12 15:25
	Jan 19 16:10	Jan 26 07:52	Feb 3 04:22	Feb 11 07:43
	Feb 18 01:49	Feb 24 20:21	Mar 4 22:21	Mar 12 19:38
	Mar 19 10:39 T	Mar 26 10:34	Apr 3 14:52 p	Apr 11 03:46
	Apr 17 19:10	Apr 25 02:20	May 3 04:55	May 10 09:21
	May 17 04:00	May 24 19:16	Jun 1 16:20	Jun 8 13:51
	Jun 15 13:58	Jun 23 12:42	Jul 1 01:43	Jul 7 18:42
	Jul 15 01:57	Jul 23 05:39	Jul 30 10:07	Aug 6 01:15
	Aug 13 16:34	Aug 21 21:15	Aug 28 18:35	Sep 4 10:39
	Sep 12 09:43 A	Sep 20 10:58	Sep 27 03:51 p	Oct 3 23:52
	Oct 12 04:17	Oct 19 22:43	Oct 26 14:18	Nov 2 17:14
	Nov 10 22:35	Nov 18 08:45	Nov 25 02:04	Dec 2 14:02
	Dec 10 15:11	Dec 17 17:29	Dec 24 15:20	

Possible Passover Day for 34 CE.

Year	New Moon	First Quarter	Full Moon	Last Quarter
0034				Jan 1 12:15
	Jan 9 05:30	Jan 16 01:31	Jan 23 06:14	Jan 31 09:18
	Feb 7 17:31	Feb 14 09:37	Feb 21 22:33 n	Mar 2 03:13
	Mar 9 03:27 T	Mar 15 18:37	Mar 23 15:25 n	Mar 31 17:14
	Apr 7 11:43	Apr 14 05:19	Apr 22 07:40	Apr 30 03:36
	May 6 18:56	May 13 18:16	May 21 22:24	May 29 11:03
	Jun 5 02:07	Jun 12 09:31	Jun 20 11:25	Jun 27 16:34
	Jul 4 10:28	Jul 12 02:38	Jul 19 23:00	Jul 26 21:24
	Aug 2 21:09	Aug 10 20:45	Aug 18 09:42 n	Aug 25 02:56
	Sep 1 10:57 A	Sep 9 14:54	Sep 16 19:58 n	Sep 23 10:40
	Oct 1 03:46	Oct 9 08:09	Oct 16 06:06	Oct 22 21:51
	Oct 30 22:36	Nov 7 23:32	Nov 14 16:26	Nov 21 13:05
	Nov 29 17:56	Dec 7 12:21	Dec 14 03:18	Dec 21 07:50
	Dec 29 12:16			

Eclipse Types

Solar Eclipse	Lunar Eclipse
T - Total	t - Total (Umbral)
A - Annular	p - Partial (Umbral)
H - Hybrid (Annular/Total)	n - Penumbral
P - Partial	

APPENDIX C
Timeline for the Integral Existence

7-6 BCE
- John the Baptist born.

July 3, 6 BCE
- The Immaculate Conception occurs sometime around July 3 which is the fast of the 17th of Tammuz..

March 10, 5 BCE
- The Chinese observe a comet (the Star of Bethlehem) near Capricorn beginning sometime from March 10 to April 7, and lasting seventy days.
- The Magi leave for Bethlehem.

March 23, 5 BCE
- Passover, Nissan 15, begins on the Full Moon of March 23 with a lunar eclipse.
- Jesus is born on March 25, the third day of Passover.

December 25, 1 CE
- Traditional birth of Jesus.

29 CE
- 15th year of Tiberius, beginning of the one-year ministry of Jesus.

April 6, 30 CE
- Passover begins after sunset. Thursday, April 6, 30 CE
- Crucifixion of Jesus occurs on Friday, April 7, 30 CE.

April 9, 30 CE
- Resurrection occurs Sunday morning, the third day of Passover. Jesus is 34 years old based on the Jewish calendar.

APPENDIX D
Chronology

ca. 1400 BCE	Life of Moses
ca. 1000 BCE	Babylonian astrologers began to watch the skies for omens
	First Temple built by Solomon
ca. 750 BCE	Constellations that will become the zodiacal signs first appear in Babylonian documents.
586 BCE	Babylonians, under Nebuchadnezzar, destroy Solomon's Temple
ca. 536 BCE	Second Temple built by the Persian King Cyrus the Great
ca. 410 BCE	Natal horoscopes make their appearance in Babylonia. The twelve signs of the zodiac are standardized.
ca. 428–347 BCE	Life of Plato
356–323 BCE	Life of Alexander the Great
146 BCE	Rome conquers Greece
44 BCE	Assassination of Julius Caesar
37 BCE	Herod named "King of Judea" by the Roman Senate
27 BCE	Augustus Caesar defeats Marcus Antonius and Cleopatra at Actium

ca. 19–17 BCE	Herod rebuilds the Temple
March 25, 5 BCE	Jesus born on the third-day of Passover
4 BCE	Herod dies
ca. 1 CE	Rome governs Judea
14 CE	Augustus dies and Tiberius becomes emperor
26–39 CE	Pontius Pilate is prefect of Judea
29 CE	Jesus begins his ministry
April 9, 30 CE	Jesus Resurrected on the third-day of Passover
70 CE	Herod's Temple destroyed by the Romans
ca. 70–110 CE	The Gospels are written
ca. 150–ca. 216 CE	Life of Clement of Alexandria
ca. 200–500 CE	The Talmud is transferred from oral tradition into written text
306–337 CE	Reign of Constantine the Great
354–430 CE	Life of St. Augustine of Hippo
380 CE	Emperor Theodosius I makes Christianity the sole authorized religion of the Roman Empire

BIBLIOGRAPHY

Primary Sources

Articles

Dusek, Jeffery A., et al. "Genomic Counter-Stress Changes Induced by the Relaxation Response." *Plos ONE* 3, no. 7 (July 2008): 1–8. *Academic Search Premier*, EBSCO*host*.

Fish, Isaac Stone. "In China, Pushing the Talmud as a Business Guide." *Newsweek*. December 30, 2010. Accessed March 22, 2017. http://www.newsweek.com/china-pushing-talmud-business-guide-69075#most-popular.

Moore, Jack. "Why Do Jewish activists Keep Trying to Sacrifice Goats in Jerusalem's Old City?" *Newsweek*, April 18, 2017, www.newsweek.com/why-do-jewish-activists-keep-trying-sacrifice-goats-jerusalems-old-city-583433.

Staff, Times of Israel (2017). "In Modern First, Passover Sacrifice to Take Place in Old City." The Times of Israel, April 05, 2017. http://www.timesofisrael.com/in-first-passover-sacrifice-to-take-place-in-old-city/5, .

Tucker, Ruth A. "An Evangelist with Chutzpah: At First Reluctant Street Preacher, Moishe Rosen, Founder of Jews for Jesus, Came to Relish Insults and Controversy." *Christianity Today*, 2010, 38, *Academic OneFile*, EBSCO*host*.

Books

SAugustine. *Basic Writings of Saint Augustine, Volume Two*. New York: Random House, 1948.

———. and Philip Schaff. *A Select Library of the Nicene and Post-Nicene Fathers of the Christian Church Vo 3*. Grand Rapids, MI: Eerdmans, 1956.

Castillo, Bernal Diaz del. *The Discovery and Conquest of Mexico*. New York: Da Capa Press, 1996.

Clement. *The Stromata or Miscellanies VI*. Whitefish, MT: Kessinger Pub., 2004.
Eusebius, Pamphili. *Ecclesiastical History, Books 1-5: Fathers of the Church, a New Translation, v. 19*. New York, Fathers of the Church, Inc., 1953.
Fibonacci. Leonardo. *Liber Abbaci*, 1202.
Holy Bible: New International Version. Grand Rapids, MI: Zondervan, 2001.
SIgnatius. *The Ante-Nicene Father, Translations of the Writings of the Fathers down to A.D. 325 Vol 1*. Buffalo: C.L. Pub. Co., 1885.
Josephus, Flavius. *The Complete Works of Flavius Josephus, the Celebrated Jewish Historian*. Philadelphia: John E. Potter, 1870.
Origen. *The Ante-Nicene Father, Translations of the Writings of the Fathers down to A.D. 325 Vol 4*. Buffalo: C.L. Pub. Co., 1885.
_____, and Gary Wayne Barkley. 1990. *Homilies on Leviticus, 1–16*. Washington, D.C.: Catholic University of America Press, 1990. *eBook Academic Collection (EBSCOhost.*
Plato, and Richard Dacre. Archer-Hind, *Platonos Timaios = The Timaeus of Plato*. London: Macmillan & Co., 1888.
Polo, Marco. *The Travels of Marco Polo. With 25 Illus. in Full Color from a Fourteenth-Century Manuscript in the Bibliotheque Nationale, Paris*. New York: Orion Press, 1958.
Roberts, Alexander, et al. *The Ante-Nicene Fathers: Translations of the Writings of the Fathers down to A.D. 325*. Vol III, Grand Rapids (MI): Eerdmans, 1957.
Roberts, Alexander, et al. *The Ante-Nicene Fathers: Translations of the Writings of the Fathers down to A.D. 325*. Vol VI, Grand Rapids (MI): Eerdmans, 1957.
Strabo, *The Geography of Strabo Vol. 7*. Cambridge, MA: Harvard University Press, 1961.

Secondary Sources

Articles

Adair, Aaron Michael. "Science, Scholarship, & Bethlehem's Starry Night." *Sky & Telescope* 114, no. 6 (December 2007): 26, *MasterFILE Complete*, EBSCO*host*.

Arbes, Ross. "How the Talmud Became a Best-Seller in South Korea." *The New Yorker*, June 23, 2015, (accessed March 22, 2017http://www.newyorker.com/books/page-turner/how-the-talmud-became-a-best-seller-in-south-korea).

Casabianca, Tristan. "The Shroud of Turin: A Historiographical Approach."HISTORIOGRAPHICAL APPROACH." *Heythrop Journal* 54, no. 3 (May 2013): 414. *Complementary Index*, EBSCO*host*.

Cohn-Sherbok, Dan. *Messianic Judaism: A Critical Anthology*. London: Continuum, 2000.

Craig, Winston J. "Myrrh: Nature's Ancient Anti-Inflammatory Agent." *Vibrant Life*, 2008, 20, *Academic OneFile*, EBSCO*host*.

Eichenwald, Kurt. 2015. "The Bible; So misunderstood it's a Sin." *Newsweek Global* 164, no 1; 24-41. *Business Source Premier* EBSCO*host*.

"Feast of the Epiphany." *Salem Press Encyclopedia* (January 2016). *Research Starters*, EBSCO*host*.

Fish, Isaac Stone. "In China, Pushing the Talmud as a Business Guide." *Newsweek*, December 30, 2010, www.newsweek.com/china-pushing-talmud-business-guide-69075#most-popular.

Gartenhaus, Solomon, and Arnold Tubis. "The Jewish Calendar—a Mix of Astronomy and Theology." *Shofar* no. 2 (2007): 104. *Literature Resource Center*, EBSCO*host*.

Hildreth, S. P. "The Wise Men from the East," no. 4: Origin of the Magi." *Family Visitor* 3, no. 6 (June 15, 1852): 42. *Agricultural Periodicals from the Southern, Midwestern, and Western U.S., 1800–1878*, EBSCO*host*.

Humphreys, Colin, J. "Star of Bethlehem." *Science and Christian Belief,* October, Vol 5, 1995, 83-101.

―――. ."The Star of Bethlehem—a Comet in 5 BC—and the Date of the Birth of Christ." *Quarterly Journal of the Royal Astronomical Society* 32 (1991): *389–407.*

Hussein, Ramadan B. "A Visit to Denidera." *Calliope* 21, no. 3 (November 2010): 20. *Master FILE Complete,* EBSCO*host.*

Jackson, A. V. Williams "The Magi in Marco Polo and the Cities in Persia from Which They Came to Worship the Infant Christ." *Journal of the American Oriental Society* 26 (1905): 79-83. doi:10.2307/592877.

Jenkins, R. M. "The Star of Bethlehem and the comet of AD 66." *Journal Of The British Astronomical Association* 114, no. 6 (December 2004): 336-342. *Academic Search Premier,* EBSCO*host.*

Kelly, Joseph F. "The Birth of Christmas." *Baylor University.* 14. www.baylor.edu/content/services/document.php/15911 9.pdf.

Morehouse, A. J. "The Christmas Star as a Supernova in Aquila." *Journal of the Royal Astronomical Society of Canada*, vol. 72 (1978): 65–7.

Mueller, Ian. "Chapter 4: Mathematics and the Divine in Plato." *Mathematics and the Divine.* (January 1, 2005): 99–121. *ScienceDirect,* EBSCOhost.

Podro, Joshua. "A 1st-Century Jewish Sage: The Life and Teachings of Rabbi Joshua ben Hananiah." *Commentary Magazine*, March 14, 2017https://www.commentarymagazine.com/articles/a-1st-century-jewish-sagethe-life-and-teachings-of-rabbi-joshua-ben-hananiah/, www.commentarymagazine.com/articles/a-1st-century-jewish-sagethe-life-and-teachings-of-rabbi-joshua-ben-hananiah/.

Sachs, A. J., and C. B. F. Walker. "Kepler's View of the Star of Bethlehem and the Babylonian Almanac for 7/6 B.C." *Iraq* 46, no. 1 (1984): 43–55, doi:10.2307/4200210

Steinmann, Andrew E. "When Did Herod the Great Reign?." *Novum Testamentum* no. 1 (2009), p. 3 : 1. *JSTOR Journals*, EBSCO*host*.

Winlock, H. E. "The Origin of the Ancient Egyptian Calendar." *Proceedings of the American Philosophical Society* 83, no. 3 (1940): 447-64. http://0-www.jstor.org.rosi.unk.edu/stable/985113.

Books

Allen, Lindsay. *The Persian Empire.* Chicago: The University of Chicago Press, 2005.

Asimov, Isaac. *The Exploding Suns: The Secrets of the Supernovas,* New York: Truman Talley Books, 1985.

_____ . *Exploring the Earth and the Cosmos.* New York: Crown Publishers, Inc., 1982.

Avermaete, Rodger. *Rubens and His Times.* South Brunswick (NY): A. S. Barnes and Company, 1968.

Avi-Yonah, Michael, ed. *A History of the Holy Land.* London: Weidenfeld and Nicolson, 1969.

Barton, Tamsyn. *Ancient Astrology. London:* Routledge: 1994.

Benedict XVI, Pope. *The Fathers.* Huntington, IN: Our Sunday Visitor, Inc., 2008.

Boardman, John, Jasper Griffin, and Oswyn Murray, eds. *The Oxford Illustrated History of the Roman World.* Oxford: Oxford University Press, 2001.

Boteach, Shmuel. *Kosher Jesus.* Jerusalem: Gefen Publishing House, 2012.

Brown, Michael. *Answering Jewish Objections to Jesus: General and Historical Objections.* Grand Rapids (MI): Baker Books, 2005.

Brown, Raymond E. *The Death of the Messiah: From Gethsemane to the Grave: A Commentary on the Passion Narratives in the Four Gospels,* vol. *2.* New York: Doubleday, 1994.

Bruce, F. F., *The New Testament Documents: Are They Reliable?.* Grand Rapids (MI): William B. Eerdmans, 1981.

Cabaniss, Allen. *Charlemagne*. New York: Twayne Publishers, Inc., 1972.
Casper, Max. *Kepler*. Translated by C. Doris Hellman. London: Abelard-Schuman, 1959.
Carter, George William. *Zoroastrianism and Judaism*. New York: AMS Press, 1970.
Charlesworth, James H. ed. *Jesus and Temple: Textual and archaeological explorations*. Minneapolis: Fortress Press, 2014.
Chesnut, Glenn. *The First Christian Histories: Eusebius, Socrates, Sozomen, Theodoret, and Evagrius*. Macon (GA), Mercer University Press, 1986.
Chester, Craig. "Star of Bethlehem." *Imprimis* 22(12) (December 1993): 1–7.
Cohn-Sherbok, Lavinia, and Dan Cohn-Sherbok. *A Short Reader in Judaism*. Oxford: Oneworld, 1997.
Crumpacker, Bunny. *Perfect Figures: The Lore of Numbers and How We Learned to Count*. New York: Thomas Dunne Books, 2007.
Daniel-Rops, Henri. *Daily Life in the Time of Jesus*. New York: Hawthorn Books, 1962.
Dhalla, Maneckji, *Zoroastrian Theology*. New York: AMS Press, 1972.
Duchesne, L., and M. L. McClure. *Christian Worship: Its Origin and Evolution: A Study of the Latin Liturgy up to the Time of Charlemagne*. London: Society for Promoting Christian Knowledge, 1910.
Ehrman, Bart D. *Misquoting Jesus*. New York: Harper San Francisco, 2005.
Ferguson, Everett. ed. *Encyclopedia of Early Christianity*. New York: Garland Publications, 1990.
Ferguson, John. *Clement of Alexandria*. New York: Twayne, 1974.
France, R. T. *The Gospel of Matthew*. Grand Rapids (MI), Wm. B. Eerdmans, 2007.
Fraser, Peter. *Ptolemaic Alexandria*. Oxford: Oxford University Press, 1972.

Fruchtenbaum, Arnold. *Hebrew Christianity: Its Theology, History, and Philosophy.* Washington, DC: Canon Press, 1974.

Gager, John G. *Reinventing Paul.* New York: Oxford University Press, 2002.

Garmonsway, G. N. *The Anglo-Saxon Chronicle.* London: J.M. Dent & Sons, 1954.

Glatzer, Nahum N. *Hillel the Elder: The Emergence of Classical Judaism.* New York: Schocken Books, 1966.

Graetz, Heinrich. *History of The Jews, Volume II.* Philadelphia: The Jewish Publication Society of America, 1956.

Grant, Robert. *Augustus to Constantine: The Thrust of the Christian Movement into the Roman World.* New York: Harper & Row, 1970.

_____. *Eusebius As Church historian.* Oxford: Clarendon Press, 1980.

Grayzel, Solomon. *A History of the Jews: From the Babylonian Exile to the Present.* Philadelphia: The Jewish Publication Society of America, 1968.

Hastings, James, *Encyclopedia of Religion and Ethics. Vol 3: Burial-Confessions.* Edinburgh: T. & T. Clark, 1910.

Helms, Randel. *Who Wrote the Gospels?* Altadena (CA): Millennium Press, 1997.

Herbermann, Charles G., and Edward A. Pace. *The Catholic Encyclopedia: An International Work of Reference on the Constitution, Doctrine, Discipline and History of the Catholic Church: in Fifteen Volumes.* New York: Appleton, 1907.

Hughes, David. *The Star of Bethlehem: An Astronomer's Confirmation.* New York: Walker and Company, 1979.

Hunger, Herman and David Pingree. *Astral Sciences in Mesopotamia.* Leiden, NL.: Brill, 1999.

Illyricus, Matthias Flacius. *Magdeburg Centuries.*

Johnson, Paul. *A History of the Jews.* New York: Harper & Row, 1987.

Kerrod, Robin. *The Book of Constellations: Discover the Secrets in the Stars.* London: Quarto Inc., 2002.

Kidger, Mark. *The Star of Bethlehem: An Astronomer's View*. Princeton: Princeton University Press, 1999.

Klein, Mordell. *Passover*. New York: Leon Amiel Publisher, 1973.

Livio, Mario. *Is God a Mathematician?* New York: Simon & Schuster, 2009.

Loomis, Louise Ropes. *The Book of the Popes (Liber Pontificalis)*. New York: Columbia University Press, 1916.

Love, David. *Kepler and the Universe: How One Man Revolutionized Astronomy*. Amherst (NY): Prometheus Books, 2015.

Lukefahr, Oscar, C.M., *The Catholic Catechism Handbook*. Perryville (MO): Wehmeyer Printing Co., 1996.

MacCulloch, Diarmaid. *Christianity: The First Three Thousand Years*. New York: Penguin Books, 2009.

McBrien, Richard P. *Lives of The Popes*. San Francisco: Harper Collins, 1997.

McIntosh, Jane R. *Ancient Mesopotamia: New Perspective*. Santa Barbara, CA: ABC-CLIO, 2005.

McNamer, Elizabeth Mary., and Bargil Pixner. *Jesus and First-Century Christianity in Jerusalem*. New York: Paulist Press, 2008.

Mears C. Henrietta, *What the Bible Is All About*. Ventura (CA): Regal Books, 1999.

Mendelson, Mel I. *Learning Bio-Micro-Nanotechnology*. Boca Raton (FL): CRC Press, 2013.

Molnar, Michael. *The Star of Bethlehem: The Legacy of the Magi*. New Brunswick: Rutgers University Press, 2000.

Morris, Adler, *The World of the Talmud*. New York: Schocken Books, 1963.

Mosshammer, Alden. *The Easter Computus and the Origins of the Christian Era*. New York: Oxford University Press, 2008.

Mott, Nevill, Sir. *Cosmos, Bios, Theos: Scientists Reflect on Science, God, and the Origins of the Universe, Life, and Homo Sapiens*. Edited by Henry Margenau and Roy Abraham. Varghese. La Salle (IL): Open Court, 1992.

Nietzsche, F. W. *The Antichrist*. New York: Alfred A. Knopf, I1924.

Packer, J. I., Merrill C. Tenney, and William White, eds. *Nelson's Illustrated Encyclopedia of Bible Facts*. Nashville: T. Nelson, 1995.

Parkes, James. *The Conflict of the Church and the Synagogue: A Study in the Origins of Antisemitism*. Cleveland: Meridian Books, 1964.

Paredi, Angelo. *Saint Ambrose: His Life and Times*. Notre Dame: University of Norte Dame Press, 1964.

Pullapilly, Cyriac, *Caesar Baronius: Counter-Reformation Historian*. Notre Dame: University of Notre Dame Press, 1975.

Quasten, Johannes *Patrology Vol 2: The Ante-Nicene Literature After Irenaeus*. Allen (TX): Christian Classics, 1983.

Rodkinson, Michael L., and Isaac M. Wise. *New Edition of the Babylonian Talmud*. Boston: Boston New Talmud Society, 1918.

Roll, Susan K. *Toward the Origins of Christmas*. Kampen, The Netherlands: Kok Pharos, 1995.

Steinsaltz, Adin. *The Essential Talmud*. New York: Basic Books, Inc., 1976.

Tasker, R. V. G. *The Gospel According to St. John: An Introduction and Commentary*. Grand Rapids (MI): Wm. B. Eerdmans, 1965.

Tillich, Paul. *A History of Christian Thought*. New York: Harper and Row, 1968.

Torrance, Thomas. *Space, Time and Resurrection*. Edinburgh: The Handsel Press, 1976.

Trexler, Richard. *The Journey of the Magi: Meanings in History of a Christian Story*. Princeton, Princeton: University Press, 1997.

Umlauf, Mary Grace. *Healing Meditation.* Albany (NY): Delmar Publishers, 1997.

Walker, Williston, *A History of the Christian Church.* New York: Charles Scribner's Sons, 1970.

Walsh, William S. *Curiosities of Popular Customs: Rites, Ceremonies, Observances, and Miscellaneous Antiquities.* Philadelphia, PA: J.B. Lippincott, 1897.

Warren, Nathan Boughton. *The Christmas Book: Christmas in he Olden Time, Its Customs and Their Origin: the Holly and Ivy, Sports of the Eve, Yule Log, Boar's Head, the Dinner, Mummers, Lord of Misrule, Saturnalia, Carols, Mysteries and Plays, Boxes, &c. &c.* London: James Pattie, 1859.

Westcott, Brooke. *A General Survey of the History of the Canon of the New Testament. 7th ed.* London: Macmillan, 1896.

Williamson, G. M. *The World of Josephus.* Boston: Little, Brown and Company, 1964.

Wilson, Ian. *The Blood and the Shroud: New Evidence That the Most Sacred Relic is Real.* New York: The Free Press, 1998

Witty, Abraham and Racheal Witty. *Exploring Jewish Tradition: A Transliterated Guide to Everyday Practice and Observance.* New York, Doubleday, 2001.

Wolfson, Harry Austryn. *The Philosophy of the Church Fathers: Volume I.* Cambridge: Harvard University Press, 1970.

Wood, Michael. *In Search of the Trojan War.* New York: Facts on File Publications, 1985.

Wordsworth, Christopher. *St. Hippolytus and the Church of Rome* London: Rivingtons, 1880.

Zolar. *The History of Astrology.* New York: Arco Publishing Company, Inc, 1972.

Electronic Resources

Larson, Rick. *The Star of Bethlehem*, DVD, Stephan Vidano, Stephen Vidano Films, Mpower Pictures. 2009.

Websites

Crockett, Christopher. "What Is Retrograde Motion?" EarthSky. earthsky.org/space/what-is-retrograde-motion

Gilad, Elon. "Why Jews Stopped Sacrificing Lambs and Baby Goats for Passover." Haaretz.com. April 24, 2016.

How did the Turin Shroud get its image?" *BBC News*. June 19, 2015, www.bbc.com/news/magazine-33164

Holweck, Frederick. "The Feast of the Annunciation." The Catholic Encyclopedia. Vol. 1. New York: Robert Appleton Co, www.newadvent.org/cathen/01542a.htm.

"How did the Turin Shroud get its image?" *BBC News*. June 19, 2015. www.bbc.com/news/magazine-33164668.

"*JewishEncyclopedia.com*." RABBI—*JewishEncyclopedia.com*, Ahttp://www.jewishencyclopedia.com/articles/12494-rabbiwww.jewishencyclopedia.com/articles/12494-rabbi.

Kirsch, Johann. "St. Hippolytus of Rome." *The Catholic Encyclopedia. Vol. 7*. New York: Robert Appleton Company, 1910. 11 Jul. 2014. www.newadvent.org/cathen/07360c.htm.

Larson, Fredrick A. "Setting the Stage," The Star of Bethlehem, n.d., www.bethlehemstar.net/stage/stage.htm.

Lawrence, Natan "View of the Torah-Law." Hoshanarabbah.org. www.hoshanarabbah.org/pdfs/paul_vw.pdf

Locker, Melissa. "NASA Addresses Astronomy Zodiac Shift With Science Facts." Time. September 26, 2016. ttime.com/4507672/nasa-on-zodiac-signs/.

NASA.gov, s.v. "Moon Phases" sunearth.gsfc.nasa.gov/eclipse/phase/phasecat.html

NASA.gov, s.v. "Time and Date of Vernal Equinox" aom.giss.nasa.gov/srver4x3.html

Navy.mil, s.v. "Julian Date Converter" aa.usno.navy.mil/data/docs/JulianDate.html

Nicene and Post-Nicene Fathers, First Series, Vol. 3. Translated by Arthur West-Haddan. Edited by Philip Schaff. (Buffalo, NY: Christian Literature Publishing Co., 1887.) Revised and edited for New Advent by Kevin Knight. www.newadvent.org/fathers/130104

Pingree, David "Astrology and Astronomy in Iran," *Encyclopædia Iranica*, Vol II/8, p. 858-871; www.iranicaonline.org/articles/abul-hasan-ahwazi-astronomer-fl

Van Gent, Robert Harry. "Almagest Ephemeris Calculator." www.staff.science.uu.nl/~gent0113/astro/almagest

GENERAL INDEX

A
Aaron (biblical), 222
Adair, Arron, 184
Adler, Morris, 17, 53
Albumassar, 180
Alexander the Great, 75, 90–94, 164
Alexandria (Egypt), 75
    Basilidians in, 22, 31, 49, 50
    as capital of Egypt, 75
    as center of knowledge, 34, 73, 75
    Christianity in, 73, 79
    as economic and religious center, 75
    religious tolerance in, 26, 49, 75–76
    school of, 29, 57, 70–71
Alexandrian Egyptian calendar, 31, 34, 113-4, 278
Alfred the Great (king of England), 236-37
Allen, Lindsay, 171
Ambrose of Milan (saint), 240
Anglo-Saxon Chronicles, 236–37
Anna (biblical), 147
Annunciation, 40–41, 126
Antichrist, The (Nietzsche), 69–71
Antiochus IV, 94, 97
Antipas. *See* Herod Antipas
Antipater, 96, 191
Antiquities of the Jews (Josephus), 179
archaeology, 9
Archelaus. *See* Herod Archelaus
architecture, and the Golden Ratio, 270
Aristotelianism, 98
Aristotle, 23, 24, 164, 197
Ark of the Covenant, 129, 274-75
Armenia, celebration of the birth and baptism of Jesus, 250
Ascension, 255, 256, 258.. *See also* Resurrection of Jesus

Asimov, Isaac, 196, 197, 203, 294
astrology
    in the Arab world, 180
    vs. astronomy, 179–80
    Augustine's campaign against, 166
    biblical contradictions on, 161–60
    Chinese, 203–04
    consultation by Catholic rulers and popes, 180
    decline in popularity of, 180
    Egyptian, 34, 164
    Hellenistic, 115
    Jewish, 161–62, 230
    Korean, 204, 205
    Persian (Iranian), 155–156, 159
    popularity of, 101, 160
    Ptolemaic and Greek, 163–65
    Roman, 165–167, 214
    and the Star of Bethlehem, 193–195
    used by the Magi, 169, 183, 193, 205, 280
    and the Zodiac, 213–15
    Zoroastrian, 157
astronomy
    Alexandrian, 233
    Arabic, 109
    vs. astrology, 179–82
    Babylonian, 150, 155–156, 160–61, 164-65
    and the calendar, 109, 110, 112-13
    Chaldean, 150, 159–60
    Chinese, 203–207, 210, 211-12
    Egyptian, 163–64
    European, 109
    Hillel's use of, 110
    Japanese, 204
    Jewish, 105
    Korean, 204

Mesopotamian, 161
Persian (Iranian), 150, 159
used by the Magi, 155–56, 159, 169
Western, 198, 204
Augustine of Hippo
background and family, 89
on chastity, 89
condemnation of the Jews, 130–31
on date of Jesus' Conception, 21–22, 39, 91, 100–06, 210, 250
De Trinitate, 5, 90, 100, 210
influence of, 99–100
on just war, 90, 90n96
on the Magi, 168
on mathematical perfection, 90–91
objections to astrology, 166, 186
on Original Sin, 50, 90, 90n96
Augustus Caesar, 96, 127, 166, 192, 214, 240
Avi-Yonah, Michael, 93-94
Azazel goat, 220

B

Baade, Walter, 196
Babylonian astronomers (Chaldeans), 150–51, 159–160
Babylonian Jews, 19–20, 110
Balaam, 157
baptism, 90n96
bar Gioras, Simon, 27
Bar-Kokhba, Simon, 60
Bar-Kokhba revolt, 60
Barnes, Timothy, 43–44
Baronius, Caesar, 77
Barton, Tamsyn, 165–66
Basilides, 22, 31–32
Basilidian celebrations, 31–34, 248–49, 278
Basilidians, 22, 31–32, 33–34, 49–50, 101, 248–49
Battle of Jericho, 275
Benedict XVI (pope), 72–73, 79
Bethlehem, 126, 129

Bible
inaccuracies in transcription, 133–34
interpretation of, 5
translation into Greek, 76, 93
See also Gospel of John; Gospel of Luke; Gospel of Mark; Gospel of Matthew; Gospels; **Index of Scriptural References**; New Testament; Old Testament
birth of Jesus. *See* Christmas; Nativity
birthdays
celebration of, 102
Origen's stance on, 81–82
Boteach, Shmuley, 54
Brahe, Tycho, 198-99
Brown, Raymond E., 103–04, 218–19, 228
Bruce, F. F., 140–41

C

Caiaphas, 240, 252, 265
calendars
Alexandrian Egyptian, 31, 34, 113–14, 278
CE and BCE designations, 35n24
Chinese, 204
computer programs for, 5
A.D. and B.C. designations, 35n24
of Dionysius Exiduus, 35
Gregorian, 34, 110, 117–19, 208, 232–233, 250, 278
Hillel's, 110
Julian, 22, 114–5, 208, 232–34, 244, 250
lunar, 39, 104–5, 114, 115, 118–19, 198, 250, 280
Roman, 35, 115, 116, 121
solar, 39, 113, 115, 118, 119, 121, 231, 231–33
See also Jewish calendar
Capricorn (zodiac), 185, 204–05, 211, 212–215

coins stamped with, 187–89, 216
Carter, George, 152–53, 157–58
Casabianca, Tristan, 260
Catholic Catechism handbook (Lukefahr), 61
Catholic Church. *See* Christianity
Chaldaeans, 150–51, 159–60
Charlesworth, James, 129
Chesnut, Glenn, 276
Chester, Craig, 188–89
Children of Abraham, 67
China
   astrology in, 203
   astronomical observations, 203–206, 209, 211, 212
   calendar, 204
   comets, 211
Christ. *See* Jesus
Christian Worship: Its Origin and Evolution (Duchesne), 90–96, 130
Christianity
   under Constantine, 98–99
   conversion of Gentiles to, 65, 66
   conversion of Jews to, 64–65, 66, 67, 67–68
   and the Gnostics, 33
   as official religion, 116
   in Rome, 99
   schism of 1054, 99
   similarities with Judaism, 51–52
   See also Christians
Christianity: The First Three Thousand Years, 136
Christians
   Gentile, 29, 65, 66
   Hebrew, 27–28
   Jewish antagonism toward, 49
   persecution by Rome, 42, 58, 63–64, 76, 116
   See also Christianity
Christmas
   Basilidian celebrations of, 278
   celebration of, 2
   date of, 1, 16, 46, 250
   historiography of, 130–33
   intended as replacement for pagan festival, 91, 131
   and papal authority, 132–35
   See also Nativity
Church Fathers, 6–7, 47
   Apostle Paul, 66–71
   belief that Conception/Nativity/Passion occurred on the same date, 130
   on calendar dating of the Nativity and Passion, 34
   on the date of the Nativity, 209
   on the divinity of Jesus, 36
   Hippolytus of Rome, 80–83
   Ignatius of Antioch, 72–73
   James, the Lord's brother, 62–66
   Origen of Alexandria, 78–80, 101
   See also Augustine of Hippo; Clement of Alexandria
circumcision, 59, 65, 66, 94
City of God (Augustine), 89–90
Clement of Alexandria
   allegorical interpretation of scripture, 57–58, 134
   on Basilides and his followers, 30–31, 34, 49, 248–44, 278
   chronology of Christian history, 26, 30, 36, 38, 58, 132
   dating of the Nativity, 30, 34, 36, 50, 75, 92
   dating of the Passion, 22, 30, 34, 58, 75, 90, 114, 229
   and the Egyptian calendar, 113
   on Greek philosophy, 26, 29, 30, 98
   ideas from Philo of Alexandria, 57
   influence on Hippolytus, 81
   and the integral idea, 7–8, 22, 73–74
   and Jewish philosophy, 100–01
   ministry of, 76–78
   Philo's influence on, 57–58
   Stromata, 5, 101
Clement VIII (pope), 77

Cohn-Sherbok, Dan, 67
coins, with zodiac symbols, 185–86, 214

comets
   200–206, 209, 211, 212–3, 280
   in Chinese tradition, 210
   negative connotations of, 206
Commentary on Daniel (Hippolytus), 38–39, 80
Conception
   date of, 21, 39, 46, 92, 100, 190, 193, 209, 249–50
   during Passover, 16, 50
   on same date as Crucifixion, 125
Confessions (Augustine), 83
conjunctions (planetary), 187–194, 198
Constantine the Great, 42–47
   and the calendar, 115–19
   and the codification of scripture, 46–47
   Jesus' appearance to, 43–44
Constantius II, 167
Copernicus, Nicholas, 181, 198
Corpus Hermeticum, 33
Counter-Reformation, 77
Craig, Winston, 170
Crassus, 95–96, 151
Creation, date of, 41, 58
Crucifixion, 5, 7, 120
   beliefs of the Basilidians, 101
   Clement's date of, 58, 75
   date of, 21, 46, 103–04, 115, 116, 218, 221, 239–40, 243, 244–45, 250
   evidence for 30, CE Passover date, 248–50
   historiography of, 218
   during Passover, 14, 50
   possible dates for, 245–47
   on same date as Conception, 131
   See also Passion
Crumpackder, Bunny, 268–69
Curiosities of Popular Customs (Walsh), 82

Cyprian of Carthage, 85-86
Cyrus (Persian king), 127, 158

D

Daily Life in the Time of Jesus (Daniel-Rops), 241
Dali, Salvador, 272
Daniel-Rops, Henri, 241
Day of Atonement (Yom Kippur), 115, 119, 220, 220–23
De Pascha Computus (Pseudo-Cyprian), 85, 100, 213
De Trinitate (Augustine of Hippo), 5, 89–90, 91, 100, 210
death of Jesus, 1, 3, 9, 14, 219, 280
   date of, 30
   during Passover, 20
   See also Crucifixion
Death of the Messiah, The: From Gethsemane to the Grave (Brown), 228
Dhalla, Maneckji Nusservanji, 157–58
Diocletian, 42, 116
Dionysius Exiguus, 35
DNA molecules, 272–73, 277
Dositheus, 75
Duchesne, Louis Marie Olivier, 91, 130

E

Easter, 1, 2, 8. *See also* Resurrection of Jesus
Eastern (Orthodox) Church, 62, 99, 249
Ecclesiastical History (Eusebius), 139
eclipses, 190–92, 206–07, 210, 211, 236–37
   Jewish beliefs regarding, 208
   and Passover dates, 281–83, 284–86
Edict of Milan, 116
Egypt
   Holy Family's flight to, 200, 210
   proximity to Israel, 163–64

ten plagues of, 106
Ehrman, Bart, 133–34
Eichenwald, Kurt, 93
Einhard (German monk), 237–238
Elements (Euclid), 267
Elijah (biblical), 261
Encyclopedia of Religion and Ethics, 38–39
Enlightenment, 30, 70, 181
Epicureanism, 98
Epiphany, 249. *See also* Magi
Epitome (Kepler), 2–3
Euclid of Alexandria, 267
Eusebius, 47, 58, 63, 79, 139, 276

F
Fanti, Giulio, 261
Fathers, The (Benedict XVI), 72–73
Feast of the Annunciation of the Blessed Virgin Mary. *See* Annunciation
Feast of the Epiphany, 249. *See also* Magi
Feast of the Nativity, 38, 81. *See also* Nativity
Feast of the Weeks, 130
Ferguson, John, 76
Festival of the Booths, 130
Fibonacci, Leonardo, 268–69
Fibonacci sequence, 266, 269–73, 275–77
    in the Bible, 274–76
    and the DNA molecule, 272–73, 277
    and the Golden Ratio, 272
    in nature, 269–71
First Christian Histories, The: Eusebius, Socrates, Sozomen, Theodoret, and Evagrius (Chesnut), 276
forms (Platonic), 26
Foucquet, Jean-François, 194
France, R. T., 137
frankincense, as symbolic gift, 170
Fraser, Peter, 75–76
Fruchtenbaum, Arnold, 27

G
Gager, John, 71
Gamaliel II, 110
Gemarah. *See* Talmud

Gentiles, conversion to Christianity, 29, 65, 66
Glatzer, Nahu, 56
Glaucias, 32
Gnosticism, 22, 32–34, 32n23
gold, as symbolic gift, 170
Golden Ratio, 266–268, 272
Gospel of John, 33, 114, 121, 245, 251
    authorship of, 142, 227
    on the Crucifixion, 226–228, 229
    on Passover celebrations, 240–42
    perspective of, 135
    on the Resurrection, 258–59
    sources for, 143
    See also Gospels
Gospel of Luke, 33, 114, 121, 130
    on the age of Jesus, 134
    authorship of, 140–41
    on the birth of Jesus, 126–29
    on the Crucifixion, 225–26
    events unique to, 146
    on Jesus in the Temple, 244
    on the Nativity, 244
    perspective of, 135
    on the Resurrection, 256–57
    similarities with Matthew, 144–45
    sources for, 140–41
    on the Transfiguration, 261
    See also Gospels
Gospel of Mark, 33, 114, 121
    authorship of, 138–40
    on the Crucifixion, 224–25
    dating of, 138
    perspective of, 135
    on prophecy from Isaiah, 243
    on the Resurrection, 255–56
    as source for Gospel of Matthew, 137
    See also Gospels

Gospel of Matthew, 28, 33, 114, 121, 126, 130
   authorship of, 137–38
   on the birth of Jesus, 126
   on the Crucifixion, 223–25, 244

(Gospel of Matthew)
   on the Crucifixion and Resurrection, 223
   dating of, 136–37
   events unique to, 145
   on Jesus' ministry, 223
   on the Magi, 168, 170
   on the Magi and Star of Bethlehem, 149–50
   on the Nativity, 178, 223, 244
   perspective of, 135
   on the Resurrection, 254–55
   similarities with Luke, 144–45
   Two-Source theory, 138
   See also Gospels
Gospel of Thomas, 33, 138
Gospels, 14, 20, 47, 50, 103–04, 108, 114–15, 121
   accounts of the Resurrection, 265
   apocryphal, 33
   on the birth of Jesus, 126
   canonical, 114, 245
   on the Crucifixion, 14, 20, 50, 103
   dates from, 240–44
   on the life of Jesus, 135
   on the Passion, 265
   Passion narratives, 245, 250
   perspective of, 135–136, 143–45, 243–44
   purpose of, 125
   on the Resurrection, 254–259
   synoptic, 114, 135, 258
   Two-Source Theory, 138
   See also Gospel of John; Gospel of Luke; Gospel of Mark; Gospel of Matthew
Graetz, Heinrich, 49
Grant, Robert, 46–47, 58
Greek culture, 93–95
   clashes with Roman culture, 98–99
   influence on Jewish culture, 98
Gregorian calendar, 34, 110, 115–17, 208, 232–33, 250, 278
Gregory XIII (pope), 233

H

Halley's Comet, 178, 211
Harris, William, 133
Hasmoneans, 94–95, 96
Hastings, James, 38–39
Healing Meditation (Umlauf), 263
Hebrew Bible, Septuagint translation of, 18, 93
Hebrew Christians, 27–28
Helms, Randel, 137–38
Herod Agrippa I, 64
Herod Antipas 192, 240
Herod Archelaus, 192, 203
Herod the Great, 90–91, 169
   death of, 190–91, 201–02, 208, 210
   massacre of the infants, 203, 210
   visit of the Magi to, 158–59, 170
Hildreth, S. P., 152
Hillel II, 110
Hillel the Elder, 6, 55–57, 99
Hillel the Elder (Glatzer), 56
Hipparchus, 109
Hippolytus of Rome, 7, 21, 36–40, 50, 80–81, 102, 131, 208
History of Astrology (Zolar), 160
History of the Jews, A (Johnson), 151
Holford-Strevens, Leofranc, 115
Holy Family, flight to Egypt, 202, 210
Homer (poet), 175–76
Homilies on Leviticus (Origen), 81–82
Hughes, David, 206
Humphreys, Colin, 194, 202
Hussein, Ramaden, 163
Hyrcanus II, 169

I

Ignatius of Antioch, 71–73
Iliad (Homer), 175–76
Immaculate Conception, 46. *See also* Conception
In Search of the Trojan War (Wood), 176
integral age, of Jewish prophets, 13
integral existence, 3, 4, 6, 7, 16, 22, 30, 100, 244, 277
    and the Church Fathers, 42
    establishing proof for, 120–22
    origins of idea, 49
    timeline, 287
Iran, Marco Polo's travels through, 153–54
Is God a Mathematician? (Livio), 23
Isaac (biblical)
    birth and death of, 211
    birth date of, 14
Islam, 51–52
Israel, as "Lion of Judah," 193

J

Jack, Lindsay, 160
Jackson, A. V. Williams, 153
James (apostle), 64
James, the Lord's brother, 62–66
    death of, 66
Jenkins, R. M., 178
Jerusalem
    Babylonian conquest of, 274
    Christians in, 63–65, 68
    civil war in, 26–27
    destruction of the Temple, 26, 58, 127, 137, 209
    Jesus' birth near, 211
    Jesus' crucifixion in, 104, 140, 219, 223, 261
    Jesus' disciples in, 257
    Muslim conquest of, 127
    Passover celebration in, 108, 111, 129, 211, 244, 279
    persecution of Jews in, 44, 94
    rebuilding of the Temple in, 158
    Roman conquest of, 95
    travels of the Magi to, 149, 156, 158, 164, 187
    visibility of the occultation in, 184
Jesus
    age of, 203
    appearance to Constantine, 43
    appearance to disciples, 255, 256, 257, 258
    Ascension of, 255, 256
    baptism of, 31, 32
    biblical prophecy and fulfillment, 177
    brought to the T7mple as an infant, 146–41
    cleansing of the Temple, 242–43, 279
    connection to Adam and Moses, 26
    divinity of, 36
    feeding of the five thousand, 242
    genealogy of, 223
    gift given to the Magi, 154–55
    historical information regarding, 35–36
    as Jewish prophet, 29, 50–51, 279
    last days of, 242
    life span of, 39–40
    links to Isaac, 14
    mathematically perfect life of, 90–91
    mentioned in the Talmud, 28–29
    as Messiah, 39, 51
    as Paschal lamb, 65, 130–31, 224
    as Passover sacrifice, 108, 109, 114
    perfect life of, 266, 275–76
    perfection of, 12–13
    as practicing Jew, 280
    prophecies regarding, 145–46
    prophecy of birth by Balaam, 157
    as prophet or rabbi, 6

resurrection of Lazarus, 251–52
sacrifice of, 13
as Son of God, 30, 39
as Sun, 39, 41, 46
in the Temple, 243
See also Conception;
Crucifixion; Messiah;
Nativity; Passion;
Resurrection of Jesus
Jesus and Temple: Textual and Archaeological Explorations (Charlesworth), 129
Jewish calendar, 7, 21, 35, 39, 102, 104–106, 113, 221, 231, 243, 250, 278, 280. *See also* calendars; Nissan (month)
   in days, 116, 117–18
   days of the week, 114–19
   lunar basis of, 112–14
   in months, 104–05, 119–20
   and the Passover celebration, 103–106, 120–22
Jewish exegesis, 57
Jewish prophets, 7, 14–15
   birth and death of, 48, 122, 206
   integral age of, 13
   messages from, 15
Jews
   Augustine's condemnation of, 130–31
   Babylonian, 18–22
   Greek influence on, 98
   in Palestine, 19
   persecution by Constantine, 44
   persecution by Rome, 18, 19, 76, 94
   persecution in Babylon, 20
   practice of ritual sacrifice, 20
   rejection of Jesus by, 169
   relationship with Christians, 28
Jews for Jesus, 68
Joanna (at the tomb of Jesus), 257
Johannine community, 143
John, identity of, 142
John the Baptist, 240, 243
Johnson, Paul, 151
Joseph of Arimathea, 107, 254

Josephus, Titus Flavius, 40, 108, 176, 190, 192
   on the Magi, 179
Journey of the Magi (Trexler), 168
Judaism
   classical, 56
   Jesus' connections to, 3
   normative, 56

   similarities with Christianity, 49–50
   and Zoroastrianism, 152–53
Judea
   Alexander the Great's conquest of, 93
   Christians in, 163
   clashes with Rome, 27, 151
   Greek influence in, 93
   under the Hasmoneans, 94–95
   under Herod the Great, 179
   Jesus' birth in, 149
   Jesus' ministry in, 251
   Jesus' teachings in, 135
   Jewish return from Babylon to, 19
   persecution of Christians in, 64
   under Pontius Pilate, 240
   prophecy of Jesus' birth in, 183, 185
   under Roman rule, 64, 95–97
   travels of the Magi to, 183, 189, 199, 204
Julian calendar, 22, 114, 208, 233–34, 244, 250
Julius Africanus, 85-6, 100
Julius Caesar, 96, 166, 233
just war, 89–90, 90n86
Justinian I, 47–48
Justinian's Code, 48

K

Kepler, Johannes, 2–3, 181–82, 194, 199
   Star of 1604, 196
Kerrod, Robin, 213
Kidger, Mark, 156, 183–84, 199–200, 204
Kirsch, Johann, 81

Klein, Mordell, 105, 107
Koine Greek language, 76, 92–93
Koran (Quran), 51–52
Korea, astrological observations from, 204–205
kosher dietary habits, 19, 66
Kosher Jesus (Boteach), 54

L

Larson, Rick, 189–90, 193
Last Supper
    Gospel accounts of, 230
(Last Supper)
    as Passover meal, 114, 121, 224, 225, 226, 227, 228–30
    as Passover preparation meal, 114, 227
Lazarus, resurrection of, 251–52
Leonardo da Vinci, 272
Liber Abaci (Fibonacci), 269
Liber Pontificalis, 132
Libo Drusus, Marcus Sribonius, 166
Livio, Mario, 23
London Society for Promoting Christianity Amongst the Jews (LSPC), 67
Loomis, Louise, 132
Love, David, 181–82
Lukefahr, Oscar, 61
lunar calendar, 113–19
Lysanias tetrarch, 240

M

Maccabeus, Simon, 94
MacCulloch, Diarmaid, 136
Magi
    as astrologers, 162
    as Chaldeans, 159–60
    distance traveled, 156
    gift received from Jesus, 154–55
    gifts brought by, 172–73
    journey to Bethlehem, 168–69
    Matthew's account of, 149–50
    names of, 154
    observations of, 214
    origin of, 167
    political motives of, 172
    reasons for journey, 7–8, 158, 169, 170
    reasons for worshipping Jesus, 171
    visit to Herod, 158–59, 170
    as Zoroastrians, 152–53, 156, 171
Marcus Antonius, 96, 166, 169
Marcus Aurelius, 98, 166
Marshack, Alexander, 160
martyrdom
    of the apostles, 70
    celebration of, 101
    of Hippolytus and Pontianus, 80
    of Ignatius, 73
    of saints, 88–89, 101
    of Stephen, 63
Mary (the "other" Mary), 224, 254
Mary Magdalene, 143, 224, 225, 227, 228, 254, 255, 256, 258
Mary the mother of Christ, 40, 126–27, 129, 137, 142, 142–146, 147, 150, 193, 210, 226, 244
    Jesus' birth announced to, 40–41, 126
    at the tomb of Jesus, 254, 255, 256–58
mathematics, and philosophy, 23, 25
Mathematics and the Divine (Mueller), 24–25
Mattathias (Jewish priest), 88
Matthias the Apostle, 32
McNamer, Elizabeth, 63–64
Mears, Henrietta C., 14, 135
meditation, 260–62
Melito of Sardis, 65
Mendelson, Mel, 277
Messiah
    anticipated birth during Passover, 20
    belief by Jews, 20
    in Christian belief, 51–52
    Jesus as, 39, 51
    Jewish concept of, 51–52
    prediction by prophets, 15
    See also Jesus

Messianic Judaism: A Critical Anthology (Cohn-Sherbok), 67
Milky Way, 196
Mishnah, 16
Misquoting Jesus (Ehrman), 133
Mithras (sun god), 91, 131
Molnar, Michael, 8, 183–84, 193
Mondrian, Piet, 272
moon phases, 117–18
Moore, Jack, 111
Morehouse, A. J., 205, 214
Morgan, G. Campbell, 15
Moses (biblical), 17–18, 54, 57, 106, 261, 274
Mosshammer, Alden, 37
Mott, Nevill F., 3
Mueller, Ian, 24–26
Muhammad, 52
myrrh, as symbolic gift, 170–71

N
Nag Hammadi library, 33
Nativity, 2, 3, 5, 7, 14
    beliefs of the Basilidians, 101, 278
    calculation of date, 21, 34
    celebration of, 96, 278
    census as explanation for traveling, 127
    Clement's date of, 74
    date of, 16, 31, 32, 35, 38, 42, 51, 81, 92, 100–01, 148, 208, 249, 250
    evidence for March 25, 5 BCE Passover date, 209–11
    Hippolytus's date of, 38
    Justinian's codification of, 48
    lack of rooms suggesting Passover, 126–27, 129
    Luke's account of, 126
    Matthew's account of, 126
    popular conception of, 126
    presence of shepherds suggesting spring, 126
    on same day as Passion, 91
    See also Christmas
Nautical Almanac Office, 232
Neoplatonism, 78n75

New Testament, 33, 47, 51, 61, 107
    Book of Revelations, 279
    Koine Greek language of, 93
    translation into Hebrew, 67
    See also Bible; Gospels
Newton, Isaac, 184
Nicodemus, 107
Nietzsche, Friedrich, 69–71
Nissan (month), 6, 14, 50, 53, 58, 105, 121–22, 127, 183, 206, 211, 226, 227, 230, 231, 280
    See also Jewish calendar
Noah's ark, 275
novas, 204

O
occultations, 180–85
Old Testament, 51, 161
    Book of Exodus, 105–106
    Book of Genesis, 26, 29
    Koine Greek translation of, 93
    See also Bible
On the Trinity (Augustine), 5, 89, 91, 100, 210
Onias IV, 75
Oral Law, 62, 66
Oral Torah, 106
Origen of Alexandria, 5, 40, 78–80, 101–02, 202
    on the Star of Bethlehem, 200–01
original sin, 50, 89, 90n86
Orthodox (Eastern) Church, 62, 99, 249

P
pagans, 44–45, 46, 49
    holidays celebrated by, 91
Palestine
    Magi's arrival at, 158
    prophecy of Jesus' birth in, 183
    Roman influence in, 95
    Roman rule in, 19
papal authority, and Christmas, 132–33
Papias (bishop of Hierapolis), 139
Paredi, Angelo, 239
Parkes, James, 28, 28–29

Parthians, 20, 97n93, 151, 159, 169, 171
    wars with Rome, 59, 96–97, 151
Paschal Sermons (Melito of Sardis), 65
Paschal Table, 37
Passion
    calculation of date, 34
    Clement's date of, 74–75
    date of, 3, 31, 35, 39, 90
    dating of, 22
    on same day as Nativity, 91
    See also Crucifixion
Passover, 6, 7, 13, 14
    ancient celebrations of, 106–109
    celebration of, 105–106
    celebration of by Christians, 64–65
    as Conception of Jesus, 16, 50
    dates for 1 BC to 7 BC, 281–83
    dates for 28 CE to 34 CE, 284–86
    dates of, 231–32
    first day of, 225–27
    Jesus' birth during, 16, 36–37, 42
    Jesus' Crucifixion during, 14, 50, 229
    and the Jewish calendar, 103–106, 120–22
    modern celebrations of, 109–12
    moon phase tables, 246
    pregnant women involved in celebration, 127–29
    ritual sacrifice, 107–8, 111–12, 230
Patrology Vol 2 (Quasten), 38
patterns (Platonic), 26
Paul the Apostle, 66–72, 98
    conversion of, 68–69
    on freedom from Jewish law, 66–67
    Nietzsche's critique of, 69–71
Pentateuch. *See* Torah
Pentecost (Shavuot), 119, 130
Perfect Figures: The Lore of Numbers and How We Learned to Count (Crumpacker), 268
Peter (saint), 63–64, 65
Peter Chrysologus, 82
Phasael, 90
phases of the moon, calculation of, 117–18
Pheidias, 272
Phidias, 267
Philip the Tetrarch, 192, 240
Philo of Alexandria, 57–58
Philometor, 75
philosophy
    of Aristotle, 23, 24, 98, 165, 197
    of Pythagoras, 22–23
    schools of, 98
    of Socrates, 24
    Stoic, 57, 98
    See also Plato
Philosophy of the Church Fathers: Volume I (Wolfson), 62
Phipps, William, 178
Pingree, David, 159
Pixner, Bargil, 63–64
planetary conjunctions, 186–194 196
Plato, 22, 34, 164, 267
    founding of the Academy, 30
    philosophy of, 24–26
Platonism, 98
Polo, Marco, 153–55, 167
Pompey, 95
Pontianus (Bishop), 80
Pontius Pilate, 240, 245, 280
Porphyry, 78
prophets. *See* Jewish prophets
Ptolemy III, 113
Ptolemy of Alexandria, 109
Pythagoras, 22–23
Pythagorean arithmetic, 90

Q

quadrivium, 25
Quasten, Johannes, 38, 81
Quran (Koran), 51–52

R

rabbis. *See* Talmudic rabbis

[314]

Reinventing Paul (Gager), 71
Renaissance, 180
Republic (Plato), 34
resurrection
    in the ancient world, 253–54
    in the Bible, 252–53
    Resurrection of Jesus, 1, 7
        52, 253, 263–65
    date of, 245
    John's account of, 226–228,
        258–59
    (Resurrection of Jesus)
    Luke's account of, 225–26,
        256–57
    Mark's account of, 224–25,
        255–56
    Matthew's account of, 223–24,
        252–53
    Shroud of Turin as evidence of,
        259–63
    synoptic Gospels compared to
        John, 228–30
retrograde motion, 187–189, 193
Roll, Susan, 42
Roman Civil War, 27
Rome
    Bar Kokhba revolt, 60
    Battle of Milvian Bridge, 43
    as center of the church, 99
    civil wars in 27, 43, 95
    Flavian dynasty, 27
    Greek influence on, 94–96
    Jewish opposition to, 26
    Jewish Wars with, 76
    Judea as province of, 64
    observance of Christ's birthday
        in, 46
    persecution of Christians by, 76
    persecution of Jews by, 42, 58,
        64, 76
    rise of Christianity in, 99
    Triumvirate, 95–96
    victory over Syracuse, 95
    wars with Parthians, 59, 96–97,
        145
Rosen, Moishe, 68
Rosh Hashanah, 114
Rosh HaShanah Tractate, 13, 122

Rudolphine Tables (Kepler), 182

S

Sachs, A. J., 197
saints, as martyrs, 88, 101
Salome (at the tomb of Jesus), 255
Samuel bar Abba, 110
Sanhedrin, 105–107
Saosyant, 157
Saturnalia, 44–46
Saul (biblical). *See* Paul the Apostle
scapegoat, 220, 222–23
Schliemann, Heinrich, 175
science
    and the dominance of the
        Church, 30
    in the Enlightenment, 30
    relationship with theology, 2–3,
        8
Scientific Revolution, 181
scripture(s), 5
    selection of for canon, 47
    See also Bible; Torah
senary numbers, 90, 90n98
Septuagint, 18, 92
Shavuot (Pentecost), 119, 130
Shroud of Turin, 259–63
    dating of, 262
Shroud of Turin Research Project
    (STURP), 261
Simeon (biblical), 147
Simon bar Gioras, 27
Socrates, 24
solar calendar, 112–14
Solomon, Grayzal, 19
Sosigenes (astronomer), 233
Space, Time and Resurrection
    (Torrance), 264
Star of Bethlehem, 7, 175–76
    based on Halley's Comet, 178
    Chinese explanation for, 206–
        211
    as comet, 200–206
    as the conjunction, 186–194,
        199–200
    as double occultation, 180–86

and the evidence for a March 25, 5 BCE Passover Nativity, 209–11
fiction vs. prophecy, 177–179
Matthew's account of, 149–50
as miracle of God, 178
as sequence of events, 205–206
as supernova, 194–200
Star of Bethlehem, The: An Astronomer's View (Kidger), 156

Star of Bethlehem, The: The Legacy of the Magi (Molnar), 183
Star out of Jacob, 157
Starry Night (computer program), 195
Steinmann, Andrew, 189, 190, 191, 192
Steinsaltz, Adin, 16
Stephen (saint), 63, 91
Stoic philosophy, 57, 98
Strabo of Amasia, 150
Stromata (Clement of Alexandria), 5, 74, 91
Sukkot (Tabernacles), 119, 130
Sun worship, 46, 91, 131
Sunday
  as day of rest, 115
  as day for worship, 46, 64, 116
supernovas, 194–200

T
Tabernacles (Sukkot), 130
Taker, R. V. G., 142
Talmud, 5, 6, 15, 16–18, 50, 61, 66
  Babylon, 13
  Babylonian, 49
  Babylonian (Bavli), 13, 18, 49
  banned by Christians, 101
  on the destruction of the Temple, 217
  Jerusalem (Yerushalmi), 18
  Jesus on the law, 5
  Justinian's prohibition of, 48
  negative mentions of Jesus in, 27–29
  two versions of, 18
Talmudic rabbis, 6–7, 53–55

Hillel the Elder (Rabbi), 6, 55–57, 99
Yehoshua Ben Hananiah (Rabbi), 6, 14, 58–60, 100
Telesphorus (pope saint), 132
Temple
  destruction of by Babylonians, 19, 127
  destruction of by Romans, 19, 26–27, 58, 108–9, 127, 137, 147, 209, 215, 219
  Dome of the Rock constructed on, 127
  First Temple built by Solomon, 127
  Jesus brought to, 147
  Jesus cleansing, 242–43, 279
  Jesus questioning the teachers, 243
  miracles at, 221
  plan of Temple Mount, 128
  rebuilding by Cyrus of Persia, 127, 158
  renovation by Herod, 127, 242–43
  requirement that Jews make pilgrimage to, 129–30
Temple of Hathor (Dendera), 163
Tertullian (Quintus Septimius Florens Tertullianus), 83-85
Theodosius I, 116
Theophilus (bishop of Caesarea), 132–33
Thomas Aquinas, 180
Tiberius, 166, 240
Tillich, Paul, 92
Timaeus (Plato), 25–26, 267
Torah, 16, 17. *See also* Old Testament
Torrance, Thomas, 264
Toward the Origins of Christmas (Roll), 42
Travels of Marco Polo, 153
Trexler, Richard, 168
Triumvirate, 95–96
Troy, excavation of, 173–74
Tucker, Ruth, 68

U

Umlauf, Mary Grace, 263
U.S. Naval Julian Converter, 232, 234–239
    for Passover in 29 and 30 CE, 243
    for Passover in 30 CE, 244
    testing date of election of pope Victor III, 235
    testing date of St. Ambrose's death, 238–39
    testing dates from Easter of 769, 237–238
    testing dates from the Anglo-Saxon Chronicles, 236–38
(U.S. Naval Julian Converter)
    testing dates of Cortez's assault on Tenochtitlan, 234–35

V

Victor III (pope), 235
Virgin Mary. *See* Mary the Mother of Christ

W

Walker, C. B. F., 199
Walker, Williston, 66–67, 72
Walsh, William, 88
Warren, Nathan, 45–46

Westcott, Brooke, 140
Who Wrote the Gospels? (Helms), 137
Williamson, G. A., 169
Wilson, Ian, 257
Winlock, H. E., 113
winter solstice, 91, 131
Witty, Abraham B., 55
Wolfson, Harry, 62, 74
women, special place for temple worship, 129
Wood, Michael, 176
Wordsworth, Christopher, 37
Wulfred (archbishop), 236

Y

Yehoshua Ben Hananiah (Rabbi), 7, 14, 58–60, 100
Yom Kippur (Day of Atonement), 115, 220, 222–23

Z

Zealots, 26–27
zodiac, 161, 163, 213
    symbols on coins, 185–86
Zoroastrian Theology (Dhalla), 157
Zoroastrianism, 20, 152, 156, 171
    and Judaism, 152–53
Zwicky, Fritz, 196

INDEX OF SCRIPTURAL REFERENCES

Old Testament

Genesis 1:14, 161, 197
Genesis 3:15, 177
Genesis 6:15, 275
Genesis 12:3, 177
Genesis 17:19, 177
Genesis 21:12, 177
Genesis 22:18, 177
Genesis 49:10, 177
Exodus 12:2, 121
Exodus 13:1-2, 146
Exodus 19:11, 226
Exodus 23:14, 130
Exodus 25:10-11, 274
Exodus 27:1-2, 274
Exodus 31:12-13, 210

Leviticus 16:11-34, 222
Numbers 3:11-12, 146
Numbers 18:15, 147
Numbers 24:15-19, 157
Numbers 24:17, 60, 177, 179
Deuteronomy 12:2-27, 127
Deuteronomy 16:16, 130
Joshua 3:14-17, 274
2 Samuel 7:12-13, 177
1 Kings 17:17-24, 252
2 Kings 13:21, 252
Psalm 45:6-7, 177
Isaiah 7:14, 177
Isaiah 8:1, 74
Isaiah 9:7, 177
Isaiah 47:13, 161
Jeremiah 31:15, 177
Daniel 2:44, 177
Hosea 11:1, 177
Micah 5:2, 177

New Testament

Matthew 1:1, 177
Matthew 1:1-16, 144
Matthew 1:2, 177
Matthew 1:18-19, 144, 145
Matthew 1:18-25, 144
Matthew 1:20, 139, 177
Matthew 1:20-24, 126, 138
Matthew 1:21, 145
Matthew 1:22-23, 177
Matthew 1:25, 145
Matthew 2:1, 144, 177
Matthew 2:1-12, 126

Matthew 2:2, 145
Matthew 2:3, 145
Matthew 2:5-6, 145
Matthew 2:7-12, 149
Matthew 2:13-15, 145, 200
Matthew 2:14-15, 145, 175
Matthew 2:16-18, 145, 175
Matthew 2:22-23, 145
Matthew 5:17-18, 28, 50
Matthew 12:1-12, 145
Matthew 16:21, 223
Matthew 17:23, 223
Matthew 20:18-19, 223
Matthew 23:2-3, 5, 78
Matthew 27:45-66, 254
Matthew 27:51-53, 252
Matthew 27:62-65, 224
Matthew 28:1-8, 224
Matthew 28:1-18, 253
Mark 5:35-43, 252
Mark 9:31, 225
Mark 10:34, 225
Mark 14:12, 224
Mark 16:1-19, 255
Mark 16:9, 225
Mark 16:9-20, 225, 256
Luke 1:5, 144
Luke 1:11, 145
Luke 1:12, 145
Luke 1:26-28, 144
Luke 1:26-30, 126
Luke 1:26-31, 177
Luke 1:26-38, 144
Luke 1:27, 144
Luke 1:32-33, 144 177
Luke 1:34-35, 144, 145

Luke 1:35, 144
Luke 1:46-55, 146
Luke 2:1-16, 126
Luke 2:5-7, 145
Luke 2:8-21, 146
Luke 2:11, 145
Luke 2:22-38, 146
Luke 2:25-38, 145, 146
Luke 2:32-33, 145
Luke 2:41, 211
Luke 3:1-3, 140
Luke 3:1-21, 234
Luke 3:1-23, 248
Luke 3:2, 265
Luke 3:23, 38
Luke 3:33, 177
Luke 3:34, 177
Luke 7:11-17, 253
Luke 9:22, 256
Luke 9:29-30, 261
Luke 18:33, 256
Luke 21:25, 162
Luke 22:1-38, 226
Luke 22:7-10, 226
Luke 22:7-13, 136, 226
Luke 22:15-16, 226
Luke 23:31, 280
Luke 23:50-56, 226
Luke 24:1, 226
Luke 24:1-53, 256
Luke 24:7, 257
Luke 24:9-12, 257
Luke 24:13-27, 257

John 2:13-22, 242
John 2:13-3:25, 241
John 2:20, 248
John 6:1-7, 242
John 11:38-43, 251
John 13:1, 227
John 13:1-19:42, 242
John 15:13, 82
John 19:14, 114
John 19:25-27, 140, 226
John 19:31, 227
John 19:36, 228
John 20:1, 228
John 20:1-9, 143, 227
John 20:1-31, 258
John 20:30-31, 241
John 21:22-23, 241
John 21:24-25, 13, 259
Acts 3:3-9, 69
Acts 6:1, 97
Acts 9:29, 97
Acts 9:36-41, 253
Acts 15:10-11, 65
Acts 15:19-21, 65
Romans 1:3, 177
Romans 9:5, 177
1 Corinthians 11:23-26, 229
Galatians 4:4, 177
Hebrews 1:8-12, 177
Hebrews 5:7-10, 13
Hebrews 7:14, 177

ABOUT THE AUTHOR

Robert William Weber was born in Illinois, and spent most of his life there. He majored in History-Education at Illinois State University graduating with Department Honors, and continued his graduate education at the University of Nebraska-Kearney, graduating with a Master of Arts degree in History. He has been a computer technician and secondary teacher in public schools in Arizona and Illinois. He lives in Illinois with his wife Gisela.

www.ingramcontent.com/pod-product-compliance
Lightning Source LLC
Chambersburg PA
CBHW031250230426
43670CB00005B/120